SURVIVAL
POACHING

SURVIVAL POACHING

BY

RAGNAR BENSON

Survival Poaching
by Ragnar Benson
Copyright © 1980 by Ragnar Benson

ISBN 0-87364-183-3
Printed in the United States of America

Published by Paladin Press, a division of
Paladin Enterprises, Inc., P.O. Box 1307,
Boulder, Colorado 80306, USA
(303) 443-7250

Direct inquiries and/or orders to the above address.

"A keeper is only a poacher turned outside in, and a poacher a keeper turned inside out."

Charles Kingsley
The Water Babies, 1863

CONTENTS

Foreword ix
1. Why Poach 1
2. Establishing A Territory 9
3. Entrance, Exit And Evasion 18
4. Equipment 35
5. Two Way Radios 53
6. Poisons And Explosives 67
7. Dynamite 76
8. Snares 84
9. Universal Stream Trap 97
10. Den Trap 106
11. Culvert Trap 112
12. Deadfalls 118
13. Box Traps 127
14. Dens 130
15. Deer 145
16. Butchering Deer 170
17. Nail Can Bear Trap 175
18. Beavers And Muskrats 179
19. Fish 189
20. Game Birds 209
21. Frogs, Turtles, Crayfish And Snakes 226
22. Urban Survival 237
23. The Poacher's Family 242
24. Selling Outdoor Products 247
Postlogue 256

FOREWORD

I am a successful businessman living near a fairly large city in the west.

To outsiders and most insiders, I am the epitome of honesty and respectability. These people know that I work hard at my business, that I hunt, fish and camp a lot, and that I write feature stories for outdoor, travel, hunting and fishing magazines on a regular basis.

What they don't know is that in the last twenty years I have spent less than $200.00 for meat. I have two large freezers and both are full of deer, elk, bear, salmon, sturgeon, trout, bass, ducks and geese, to mention a few. Including the vegetables from my garden and add in the money I receive from hides and furs, skulls, horns and paws, I make money rather than spend it on food each year. This in spite of the fact that I have three hungry teens to feed.

So how do I do it?

I am a poacher. For the last forty years I have poached game with impunity and ease, to the point where it is now a big game. During the course of these forty years, I have developed many quick and easy methods of collecting deer, bear, game birds, furbearers, fish, and reptiles. In poacher's jargon, this is known as "reducing to possession."

Survival Poaching is not about destroying our country's natural resources. Rather it is about techniques that allow you to keep the edible things all around you for yourself. I have also included a chapter about my philosophy of poaching, as well as one on the conservation of resources. But most important of all is the chapter on entrance, evasion, and exit. It tells how to enter a posted area, evade any authorities there, and safely exit with your catch.

In the final analysis, this book will give you the tools needed to bypass the jerk anti-hunter, environmentalist, preservationist, land-poster, and college-educated game warden, all of whom make this book so necessary.

Ragnar Benson
Boulder, Colorado
January, 1980

1

WHY POACH?

There are a number of important reasons for fairly and honestly addressing this question.

Recent negative publicity in the major media, including all of the large circulation hunting and fishing magazines, make it difficult to discuss the subject of poaching. Significant socio-economic forces are at work, however, that are contributing mightily to the necessity for poaching which should be openly explored.

Hopefully everyone who picks up this book will also read this chapter, but I am not an apple pie optimist. I realize poachers already know why they poach, although most may not be able to verbalize their feelings well. Conversely, people who don't poach may read this chapter and no others. For them, a few pages on the philosophy of poaching may have positive impact. It is my contention that those who scorn the poacher are, in many cases, the same ones who created the necessity for poaching in the first place.

My own poaching philosophy began evolving in 1947, when I and my new bride moved into a small house in a Chicago suburb. The neighborhood was tree-covered and most homes had a small yard. My wife, who grew up in the slums of Philadelphia, thought we were living on a farm. I grew up on a farm in Indiana and knew we were living in a densely populated area.

Things were tough for us that first year, and we made it principally because I had a good .22 rifle, a box of BB caps, and a few traps.

For much to my surprise, I discovered that our city—part of greater metro Chicago—had a major game population. There was a saturation population of tree squirrels, hundreds of less desirable yet entirely edible pigeons, and a surprising number of coons,

1

possums, rabbits and doves. I am confident enough game died from natural attrition each winter to feed many families like ours. The big hurdle I had to overcome was the illegality of taking and using any of this game inside city limits.

Having been raised on a farm, it never occurred to me that a law might prohibit me from catching and eating a plump, delicious squirrel, or that I might have to sneak around in the dark to check my rabbit traps. I philosophized about this situation quite a bit that winter.

According to my diary, I killed and ate sixty-three squirrels, four coons, several possums, about a dozen rabbits and too many pigeons by the following fall when we moved back to the farm.

Six years went by. We now had a family and decided to take our first honest-to-goodness, away-from-home vacation. Our few dollars got us as far as a small lake in central Michigan where we rented a cabin and went fishing.

During our second day at the lake, I was sleeping in the row boat "fishing" with a drop line in one hand. My wife and two kids had a hook and line tied to a willow cane we cut on the bank. We hadn't caught and never did catch a single fish.

About noon the local game warden came roaring up in his big power boat and demanded to see our licenses. Farmers in Indiana weren't required to buy a hunting or fishing license at that time, and I had forgotten all about the necessity of buying one in Michigan.

I told the possum sheriff that we didn't have a license, and that I just now realized we would need one because we were out of state. I claimed we weren't hurting the resources, since it was unlikely that we would catch a fish with our primitive equipment. I offered to go right to town and purchase a license.

All of this mattered not one twiddle to The Law. The fine was $40.00, payable now, and that was that.

I don't know how the bastard knew it, but $40.00 was all the cash we had in the world. For thirty minutes we talked, then argued, pleaded and then begged. But my pleas were all futile.

In those days I believed myself to be a basic, law-abiding person. The warden followed us to our cabin and I dutifully surrendered our cash. All we had left was the gas in our pickup and a few groceries in our cabin. Our vacation was over.

Time heals many wounds and often wisdom comes from adversity. It was tough to appreciate at the moment, but even in the

Cottontail Rabbit
Sylvilagus

short run I was the winner of that little contest. It was the last time I was ever arrested for a game violation but, more important, my philosophy about poaching changed dramatically.

Later on in fall, two of us went back to the same lake duck hunting, only that's not all we did. Complete with license and stamp, we looked and acted like duck hunters. We also put out a line of traps for beavers which, at the time were (1) protected in Michigan, (2) abundant in the lake, and (3) worth no less than $30.00 each.

Besides the eight beavers we caught, we shot one deer and several ducks. It was foolish to carry the deer home in our truck all that way, but we were novices in those days.

Other than the practical need for food and clothing, the first and most obvious point to these stories is that many game laws are stupid. They are out of step with conditions in the field, mother nature enforced realities, the nature of the game, and the people taking the game.

Tons of squirrels, pigeons and rabbits still die every winter in that Chicago suburb. I realized that the law would never change so, rather than go hungry, I became a poacher.

Although cities are good cases in point, it's not the only place it happens. Many western states prohibit the taking of tree squirrels—totally. Other states like Michigan, Wisconsin, Alabama, Georgia and Washington—all places I have hunted—won't allow deer hunters to harvest does. Other states like Michigan refused to allow the taking of beaver long after they were abundant to the point of being pests.

Federal law prohibits the shooting of crows, and it is practically a capital offense to keep red tail hawks away from nesting ducks. I am not talking about hurting or destroying our natural resources. That would be counter-productive to my way of life as a poacher. My reference is to legislation that purposely and maliciously prevents people from using our abundant resources.

Much of our game has filled its habitat and is dying of over-crowded conditions each winter rather than being harvested. This is a fact of life for a shocking amount of our renewable game populations, including many species of fish, frogs, small game, deer, bear, most birds and especially for hard-to-take animals such as fox and coyote.

Game laws are often promulgated by ignorant men who have a bad case of tunnel vision and little concept of what is happening

4

out in the real world. These laws are enforced, for the most part, by arrogant, inflexible, over-educated jerks who only care about the number of arrests they make each year—my experience fishing being a very good case in point.

Who among the ranks of outdoorsmen has not heard the stricken cry of the woeful preservationist?

According to these people, all our country has left is seven cougars, two whales, one woodpecker, twenty-seven bobcats, nineteen deer, eleven foxes and a partridge in a pear tree. Just don't be so rude as to ask how these figures were determined.

It is interesting to note that when one of these officials finally does go out in the bush to take a look, wonder of wonders, there is five times the game the desk-bound experts originally predicted and, even more remarkable, it is reproducing at regular intervals.

Go back and read some of the cougar scare stories, for instance, in *Outdoor Life*. Compare the numbers of animals originally estimated to live in Wyoming, New Mexico and California with "current estimates" where even the preservationists admit that there was no reason to cry extinction. But just don't ask them to open the season again once it is closed.

In 1978 the United States Fish and Wildlife Service (U.S.F.W.S.) of the Department of Interior classified the African elephant as threatened under the Endangered Species Act of 1973. Any reader who thinks that closure of federal land to hunting is impossible should take note of what happened in that case.

Acting on absolutely no expert testimony on their behalf, and despite warnings from opposition authorities, the U.S.F.W.S. closed the U.S. borders to importation of elephant trophies. In doing so they operated illegally without complying with certain requirements included in the Endangered Species Act. The U.S.F.W.S. responded to pressure from the anti-hunters. It is my contention that it is only a matter of time before all federal land in the west is closed to hunting of common species such as deer, elk and coyotes.

Outdoor Life in the January, 1979, issue carried an article about the proliferation of game due to the posting of land. The article pointed out that in many states, especially those east of the Mississippi, the resource had expanded to the point of extreme surplus, but was not being harvested because significant chunks of land were being posted and therefore unavailable for hunting and fishing.

In Idaho the Fish and Game Department has taken an active stand in behalf of the land owner who posts his property. Deer and pheasant seasons have been significantly shortened in some areas to avoid conflicts between the property owner and the sportsman, although the pheasant population itself would have benefitted from a longer season.

Large areas of Illinois, Colorado, Michigan, Ohio, Indiana and southern Wisconsin have in the last few years been virtually closed to hunting by the No Trespassing sign. Other states such as Texas, California and Oregon have been largely closed to hunting for years now. Even western Bureau of Land Management and Forest Service ground is not immune. Ranchers in Montana and Wyoming are famous for buying, leasing or just blatantly illegally posting all the access ground into major blocs of federal ground. Their control of a few key acres bans outdoorsmen from entrance into major tracts. Posting has not as yet overtaken the deep south, but I wouldn't be surprised to see that change as well in just a few short years.

Poaching is not a new or recent phenomenon. In times past many citizens felt it was an honorable calling, worthy of anyone with a "quick mind and a stout leg."

William Shakespeare is a good example. Historians agree that there is some question about good old Bill's original writing ability. Some even suggest that he may have been a plagiarist of sorts. But no one disagrees that Shakespeare made the principal part of his living by poaching the King's deer and grouse, and selling them in the meat markets of Startford-on-Avon.

That's right: Shakespeare was a damned poacher! At least in the King's eyes he was.

Robin Hood was another poacher of much renown. Robin and his merry men are remembered for their exploits in Sherwood Forest. Most people conveniently forget the reason the King was continually upset with Mr. R. Hood was because he kept collecting the King's deer. Time after time the Sheriff of Nottingham sallied forth, but not to arrest Robin for robbing from the rich and keeping thirty percent. Modern attorneys do that every day. The sheriff was upset because Robin Hood was a poacher.

Over the years the various governments of Europe have appropriated a tremendous amount of the available game habitat. This trend accelerated as populations increased. Laws were passed allowing privileged individuals to control large chunks of real estate for their own use. By the early 1800's there was little private property a common citizen could own or use, let alone hunt on.

As a result, poaching as an occupation evolved. People simply refused to stand idly by watching a resource waste in the winter.

Drastic measures were sometimes taken to discourage poaching. Castle and museum stomping tourists who have visited England may remember seeing large steel traps on display. North Americans might assume the traps were made for large bears, but there were no wild bears in England at the time. In truth the steel traps were designed to break the legs of poachers!

Perhaps it won't be too long till it gets that bad in this country. As I read their propaganda, the "Friends of the Animals" are advocating the shooting of hunters. Readers will have to be their own judge of what this literature is suggesting.

At this writing there are a number of huge forest fires burning in the west. Apparently most of the fires are raging in wilderness areas where it is illegal to use bulldozers, build roads, run trucks or even to use a chain saw to fight the fire.

According to my best information, the wilderness fires were intentionally set. Even if I have been misinformed, it is my strong contention that the citizens of the six or eight large western states where most of the Federal Wilderness Area lies will attempt to burn it off in the next few years.

Why? Because presently, millions of acres of public land have been set aside for the exclusive enjoyment of a tiny elitist minority. Remember, not one hunter in 10,000 can, as a practical matter, use a Wilderness Area. And this assumes that the bureaucrats 2000 miles away in Washington even continue to allow public hunting.

Today the game herds in the Wilderness Areas are dying. Numbers of elk and deer are falling drastically as forests mature, die from disease and insects, and fall over to rot. Browse has been shaded out or has outgrown the reach of the animals. Entire wintering grounds have been lost as a result of the fervent work of the environmentalists.

One need look no further than the Dismal Swamp controversy in Maryland to see what is in store for the hunter in the years ahead. No matter to the anti-hunter that the game population there is dying of starvation, and that its general quality has been permanently degraded. The deer can ruin their own lives and habitat, and the anti-hunter could care less, as long as no one harvests the game.

About a year ago I met two lads who poached wild burros with

7

bow and arrow in the Grand Canyon. All they kept was the burro scrotums. What would have made good dog food was left for the magpies and ravens.

Burros in the Grand Canyon are protected by one of the most asinine of all federal laws. As a result, habitat destruction is rampant. Valuable plant and animal native species are being pushed out and indirectly destroyed by the burros, but the only allowable burro control method is live removal. No matter that this method is slow and ineffective, and that it costs thousands of tax dollars for each burro removed. It is all that is allowed under the law.

These fellows were performing a valuable service and should have been rewarded, which is the entire point. Anti-hunters are not logical, rational people. But they are in the majority and will eventually try to shut down much of our hunting as we know it today.

A last important reason for poaching is as a means of survival in the event of national disaster, war or a breakdown of our traditional system.

It is not the intention of this book to discuss the likelihood of these events happening, other than to say it becomes statistically more likely with the passage of time. Skilled poachers can live through a national disaster even in fairly large cities. Yet the art of poaching is not mastered in a few months or even a few years. Starting from zero, it takes at least ten years to become a skilled poacher, so don't expect this book to turn you into a seasoned pro overnight. All it will do is sharpen your skills, and help you do a better job at what you are already doing.

Frequently throughout our country I hear the statement that "Other than the fact that it is against the law, what's wrong with what I am doing?" Certainly the statement applies to the ancient and honorable art of poaching.

Often the only recourse an outstanding outdoorsman has is to become a poacher. The transition is probably inevitable, given our national trend, for the determined hunter who *understands the game*.

2

ESTABLISHING A TERRITORY

A fox has its home range, a deer its piece of the woods and even a quail has a territory. In this sense, the poacher is no different than these animals.

A good poacher is not in business to kill off or even significantly reduce the game population. It is absolutely contrary to his best interests to destroy the game in a wanton manner. Such an approach will deny him a steady supply of game next year, and possibly all the years to come.

The concept of game as a crop is difficult for most people to appreciate. Even farmers and ranchers assume the grouse, quail, squirrels or deer that run on their land can be stockpiled. This is contrary to basic biological law, but is never-the-less a generally held concept. Study after study has shown that 85 percent of the doves, 60 percent of the quail and 40 percent of the deer, for instance, must be harvested each year or they will be lost to natural causes in the winter.

This is not a text on game management. It *is* a how-to-do-it manual that shows how someone can reduce to possession the most game in the shortest possible time. There is a broad general concept of managing one's poaching territory which should be thoroughly understood. When understood, this concept will maximize the game which can be taken.

Many hunters shoot house cats. I am no different than most in that regard, with the exception that I take the cats home and skin them as well. The skins are worth $4.00 on the raw fur market, but that's not the point. The issue here is related to why one would bother to rid the country of predatory felines. Obviously it is to protect the game population, which is exactly the point. A good poacher will learn his territory like the top of his kitchen table and then take necessary precautions to keep others (two- and four-legged predators) from infringing on it. I'll illustrate this point with an episode from my diary.

It had been dark for almost two hours. The crisp September air was starting to chill us to the point that we were thinking of packing up and heading for our jeep parked in a gravel pit about a mile away. One of my sons and I were staked out in an old abandoned orchard overlooking a large alfalfa field. A small stream cut through the far end of the field and a woods bordered half of the south side.

It was an ideal place to spot deer. Several had come out at dusk, but it was now too dark to be sure of anything. We waited on.

About 8:30 p.m. we saw a light on the lane through the woods. Bouncing and jiggling, it came on till an older model car finally emerged from the woods at the edge of the field. "These stories about a small poaching ring may be true," I whispered, "looks like they're going to try and spotlight some deer up here."

Slowly the car pulled out in the field. The driver swung the car lights back and forth, trying to pick up the glint of eyes.

Suddenly two deer jumped out of the brush and ran up through the alfalfa over a little rise in the ground. They were out of the headlights now, but the men in the car had spotted the critters as they ran off. Obviously the deer had been shined before. Even more obvious was that these poachers had worked this field before.

They gunned the car and turned on a giant spot light mounted on the driver's side of the vehicle as they crossed into the small pocket in the ground. We were now about 200 yards from their car, hidden in the orchard which was slightly above the scene of the intended crime, facing in a quartering direction across the front of the car.

Quickly my boy slipped his M-16 rifle into a notch in a tree and took a steady aim. The car stopped and I could see a rifle appear out of the passenger window. The shooter never got his chance, however.

My boy started firing in a steady cadence and by the third round had blown out the poor guy's spotlight. All was silence in the car. The would-be poachers just sat there for perhaps thirty seconds till someone had the presence of mind to turn the car headlights off.

As soon as they were out, my son switched the rifle to full auto and sent two bursts over the top of the car into the woods. The people in the car must have been terrified.

They wheeled around and raced for the field's edge and the small farm lane they had come through earlier. If we were wardens, it would have been incredibly easy to block the road with a truck and nab them. It was dumb of them to come into a place like that with no radios and nobody behind to watch. It was even more stupid to allow rumors to start about their activities and to then come back to the same place two or three times in a row.

About three-quarters of the way across the field they switched on their lights again, but it was too late. The car hit a two foot washout and stopped dead, as if it had run into a solid wall of jello. There was a tremendous cloud of dust, the engine raced and then quit. Our competition was stuck fast in the gully, scared shitless and helpless. We pulled out.

At home, we had one of my sons' wives call the farmer's wife, who was a violent anti-hunter, and anonymously tip her off. They eventually called the warden who found the car, but alas, no pinch was made. By the time he got there the rifle and several of the fellows were gone. All that was left was one of the fellows who luckily had his girlfriend with him. They claimed they were back there to park and got stuck. There was some flack from the farmer and the girl's parents, but nothing serious ever came of it.

The rival poachers suffered some cuts from the flying glass when we shot out the spotlight and some serious bruises when the car crashed, but that was all. It *did* teach them a lesson. They subsequently went out of the poaching business forever. We, on the other hand, had fulfilled our obligation to protect the game and territory we hunt in—for ourselves.

One of my best friends is the "No Trespassing" sign. I have put up literally thousands of them, and encourage farmers and landowners to do the same every opportunity I get. Anti-hunters are great ones to fall for this sham. Professional poachers won't be deterred by a No Trespassing sign, but they do tend to keep the rank and file hunter off the ground. This reserves the game for the person who knows how to work the country which, if I am around, is me.

A lot of good game country is owned and controlled by absentee landlords. It is easily possible to find out who the owner is by checking at the county Soil Conservation Service office, the county assessor or a local realtor. I often do this when I suspect that someone from afar owns the property and I want to tie it up for my own use. It is also possible to determine who farms the land, if it is farmed, by checking at the local feed mill or farm store. Due to the fact that I occasionally dabble in real estate, my discreet inquiries have never been questioned.

Knowing who controls the ground is an immense advantage. At one time I found that a half section of good squirrel woods was owned by a saw mill company many miles away. I promptly cut a small track into the half section where I could hide my jeep. Next I put up No Trespassing signs every 150 feet along the property edge. By so doing, I was able to use the land as a safe base of operations for years and years.

Be on the lookout for landowners who have their property leased or rented to second party farmers. Often one won't know what the other is doing. It is possible to post the property, operate on it and control the game with one continually thinking it is the other's doing. This is especially true in the case of large, busy commercial farmers and owners who may live in town rather than on their acreage.

Not only must a good poacher keep others off his country, he must know what the game is doing on it. I make frequent trips through my territory. There are always mushrooms to pick, berries to collect or an old abandoned apple tree to harvest, so the cruising I do is not simply a hike.

Protecting one's territory must be done on the basis of knowledge of its terrain. I can't stress that too strongly.

Again the S.C.S.—Soil Conservation Service—at the court house can help. They have aerial photos of the land as well as information on how these photos can be purchased.

Another source of information in the west is the Forest Service and the Bureau of Land Management. They have good maps that in many cases show ownership if the ownership is in large blocks. Some states have private map companies. Look in stationery and sporting goods stores for these.

One source of excellent information that is often overlooked is the state land grant college. Call the dean of the College of Mines, Agriculture or Engineering and talk to the secretary. Be persistent. Most universities have some sort of map facility. It often takes some sleuth work to uncover these.

Local chambers of commerce, the corps of engineers and state park associations all have maps available that can be of immense value. Ask and thou shalt receive.

I like to hunt on military bases. Maps of these areas are around but often unavailable to civilians. Securing one can be the handiest thing since sliced bread, so making the effort to get copies is time well spent. Pilots' sectional charts, available at most airports, are a start, but the really good army maps are best secured from GI's stationed on that base.

Try visiting some local bars where one can strike up a conversation with enlisted men. Often they will help for the price of a few beers.

As an aside I feel it is very important that poachers never drink on the job. I am as strict about this as I am about slamming car doors. Should we want to take a cooler of wine out in a boat and enjoy the day, that's one thing. But don't ask me to check fish traps or set some charges when drinking, because the activities don't mix. Similarly I never plan a hunt in a bar or, for that matter, with people I meet in bars.

Knowing the territory also implies knowing the potential of that territory. I am always analyzing my country, dropping some parts of it and adding others that can better provide the game I need. A good poacher is always evaluating his country and looking for new, more productive territory.

Knowing one's country also is important in terms of getting to the game before the competition does. There is a fine line here which is difficult to articulate, but it is a concept that must be thoroughly understood by the expert poacher.

The muskrat season in Iowa is a good example. In times past it opened about the 15th of November and closed about the 10th of Janaury. The pelts were prime by the first of November and stayed prime till about the 15th of March. They were, in fact, better *after* the season closed than before or during the season, but I was reluctant to trap after the season. Usually the competition for rats was fairly keen and a good allowable harvest had been made by the first of February. If man hadn't made the harvest, nature did, as the bitter winter cold reduced the food supplies and thinned the colonies.

For this reason I liked to start early, and take the best rats before regular season arrived. Then the pickings would be slim for the guy who came after me. Often other trappers would conclude that there were few rats in the marsh and move their traps elsewhere. Or I might move their traps for them.

The art was knowing when to begin. Start too early and the pelts weren't prime; start too late and there might not be enough time to take in the harvest.

The same problem confronts the deer hunter, squirrel shooter, fish trapper and anyone who is taking the harvest from the woods and fields. There is no simple answer to the problem. The only solution is to spend time in the field, to study the game and to know one's own abilities and techniques.

In some cases it is important to get out and educate the game so that the amateur can't get them. I do this with deer, coyotes and beaver. By starting the season early I make the game cautious enough so that it is virtually impossible for the casual hunter to take, come the regular season. For many years, for instance, we used to drive the deer out of an old abandoned orchard in southern Michigan and pepper them with bird shot as they went. Nobody ever got a shot at these critters till our trained team of drivers moved in and made the harvest later on.

When trapping it is important to remember that fur buyers can tell when small game is taken by the condition of the pelt. Even if the fur is prime or almost prime, it may not look like others taken in the same area during the legal season. Wardens often inspect fur barns so it is best to be cautious.

I always sell my fur to a large house that handles a lot of pelts. If a discrepancy seems possible, I have my brother send them in for me. He lives much farther south than I do and fur from his area looks like early caught northern goods. In return I often send in his late caught stuff which looks good for my area. It's a balancing act that one must master to stay out of trouble.

I am continually concerned about falling into somebody else's trap. Probably this is true because so many amateur poachers have fallen into traps wardens and sheriffs have set for me.

Knowing one's territory can preclude that. If there are new car tracks in an alfalfa field, it is reasonable to assume that someone has been jacklighting it. A muddy path in a swamp suggests visitors, and a broken path through the woods tips me off that others may have worked the area first. Amateur poachers leave piles of feathers, guts, tracks and all sorts of signs.

It is, then, imperative that you watch for visitors and exercise extreme caution. The ideal situation requires that you get there first. That failing, it then becomes increasingly important to determine in what capacity previous visitors have come and what appropriate measures can be taken.

14

In all my years of operation, about the only evidence of somebody else getting in ahead of me has been my finding a couple of fish traps, some evidence of squirrel hunters, some signs of jack lighting for deer and a few instances when someone opened the fishing season early. At times I have been with hunters who very suspiciously kept an extra duck or quail but in general nothing much more serious than this. Perhaps I am deluding myself, but I strongly suspect that there are very few good professional poachers operating today. Most poaching is a haphazard hit and miss proposition with little planning or thought.

If there is a pattern, it is among trappers who will invariably try to set a trap or two out early. I run into these with enough regularity to feel that this is a common mode of operation. One seldom sees sophisticated den traps, fish pens, blasting, shining fish or frogs, or duck pens. As I have said, serious poaching is nearly a lost art.

When I do spot someone on my territory, I try as I did with the deer spotters to conjure up a sufficient surprise to persuade them to leave for good. At times we have located the offender's vehicle and shot out the tires or even rolled the rig down a hill into a rival's pond.

Never, under any circumstances, personally face the offender. It is always best, I have found, to remain anonymous. Use your imagination and let someone else do the work.

Most folks are very jittery about No Trespassing signs. It has always been interesting for me to note the respect that people have for them in spite of the fact that most state trespass laws are so weak they are a joke.

The individual poacher should either check with an attorney or go to the library and read the code regarding trespass before he does trespass. When researching code books, remember to check the update section inserted in a pocket at the back of each book. It is impossible to summarize the law for the entire 50 states. In general, though, trespass is not a code violation until the trespasser refuses to leave the property.

I have never been caught in the bush, but were I to run onto a farmer/landowner, I would quickly tell him I was lost and ask directions for the quickest way to leave the property. Should there be an obvious problem such as an owner coming up on me when I had game or when I had just crossed a fence over the top of a No Trespassing sign (which actually happened one time) I would turn my back on the guy and quickly melt into the woods.

In the case of my crossing the fence, a farmer spotted me at dawn as I was walking across a 300 yard plowed field toward a river bottom. The drop car was long gone, but I was in plain view in the middle of the open field. The guy stood at the fence hollering that the land was posted and that I was under arrest. I walked rapidly to the field's edge and hopped into the woods. It was about 500 yards along the creek to the side road bridge. As soon as I was in cover, I ran to the bridge and crossed under the road to the other side. The farmer roared up to the bridge and, as far as I know, is still there bellowing to the empty river bottom about my being on his property. What made this even more interesting was that I jumped and shot a rabbit while running through the woods to the bridge!

At times it is appropriate to disguise and coordinate one's activities with existing seasons. The best example is my long standing use of double barrel rifles to shoot deer during rabbit and quail season. No one has ever suspected that the gun I carry is actually a rifle and not a shotgun. My problem then becomes one of getting the deer home, and not one of being out in the country. Traditionally I am on good terms with the wardens and land owners, but only in that I am always where I should be, and never with more than the allowable limit of game.

When I was living on a farm in Illinois, we were plagued by poachers who were spotlighting coons along the river near one of our larger fields. I pretty much knew who they were, and decided to put a stop to their nonsense. Late one night I spotted the fellow's truck towing a boat towards the river. I called my uncle who threw a canoe in his rig and was at our place within thirty minutes. In the meantime, I assembled a pack containing a large flashlight, three pounds of stove wire and six pounds of dynamite.

My aunt dropped us off and away we went down the river. Suddenly, up roared two state trucks and about six wardens. We kept out of sight while they unloaded their boat. Obviously they were out to catch the same poachers we were. We paddled on downstream like the devil was on our tail till we saw a light ahead of us. It was the competitor clumsily trying to shine up some coon eyes to shoot at, oblivious to the drama unfolding around him.

Quickly we put in to shore. To me it seemed like a shaky deal, but uncle was cool as could be. "Let's spring the trap we had for the poacher on the wardens," he said. And so we did.

Uncle nailed a mouse trap onto a tree about three feet above the water level. I quickly paddled across to the other side and securely fastened one end of the stove wire to a tree. We fastened the other end of the wire to the vertical mouse trap cross bar, setting up a cross river trip wire. When pulled, the wire would spring the trap.

Next I put an electric cap in four of our sticks of dynamite and attached about 30 feet of drop wire to the lead ends of the cap. I tied the dynamite into a bundle and slung the whole charge up in a tree about 12 feet above the river.

Uncle took one of the flashlight D cells and taped it into the dynamite drop line. Carefully he then taped one end of the drop wire to the mouse trap cross-bar, and the other to the trap body, where it would be hit by the cross bar when the trap sprung.

Having accomplished all of this, we set off down the river as fast as we could. About a mile downstream we came to an old mill race where we took a left into the woods. From the mill race we dragged the canoe about 200 yards into an old bayou which we paddled across for another 700 yards. We beached the canoe on dry ground and walked a small finger of land through the swamp to a corn field.

Just as we reached the corn field there was a sharp flash of brilliant white in the river bottom and a heavy rolling thump as the dynamite went off.

Next day the whole county was full of talk about the three wardens who were half deafened and scared out of their wits by a poacher back on Rock River. Seems the hapless coon shiner was caught by the other wardens. Although they never convicted the coon shiner of planting the dynamite, the wardens were sure they were set up by this "arch poacher."

I still remember the poor soul's name. Perhaps he lives to this day, so I won't mention it. Unfortunately I don't know the identities of the three wardens who probably often say "what" when anyone tries to talk to them.

17

3

ENTRANCE, EXIT AND EVASION

The ability to move in and out of a chosen piece of country is, to a great extent, an art. Truly successful poachers are like smoke. They move silently and invisibly wherever and whenever they please.

The skills necessary to operate in this manner do not come easily and are often acquired only after years and years of practice. It will help to read specific methods presented in this chapter, but until the entire concept of evasion becomes so ingrained that it is second nature, the average poacher will continue to find himself in constant peril.

I at one time walked almost a mile to avoid crossing a 200 yard snow field. After hiking all that way around to the other side, it occurred to me that in this remote area it didn't matter if my tracks showed in the snow. But I couldn't bring myself to the point of giving away my position even though in this case nobody cared. That's an example of natural caution that will keep a poacher out of trouble.

Having become a master at the art of movement, the poacher can operate with impunity and ease to the continued exasperation of those who regularly suspect they have been hit, but never know for sure.

I woke at 3:30 a.m., got out of my warm bed and walked over to the window. It was as black as the inside of a priest's pocket. The wind was blowing gently and fog as thick as axle grease covered everything.

Numbly I dialed my boys' house.

"Looks like a good day," I told the sleepy voice. "Can you be here in about 40 minutes?"

"Sure," was the now alert reply. "You have something in mind?"

"Come by and we'll talk," I replied.

Our house began to stir as some kind of invisible plan became operational. My wife scurried around putting together a lunch. It was early September—still green but very grey. I picked out some light OD coveralls to wear along with a short light green poncho and a broad brimmed canvas camouflage hat.

By this time the boys had assembled.

"What do you think?" I asked. "Maybe it's a good day to hit Nelson's and Fogert's ponds and the old gravel pit," I said. "There are lots of people around the country but nobody is going to be out much today, especially early."

"We could make a day of it," one of the boys replied. "Hit the ponds early and then walk the Des Moines (River). Maybe fill up the freezer with fish for the winter. Pickup could be at the bridge where 30 crosses the river."

And so we put a fishing trip together. We packed our camouflage gear to match the day. I put 15 pounds of 60 percent dynamite in my pack, along with a spear and collapsible pole. The boys took a second spear, the caps and fuze and a couple of burlap bags for the fish. We took one gun, a .22 Ruger Standard Auto with silencer.

About thirty minutes before daylight my wife dropped us in a little grove of trees about 500 yards from the first pond. She left immediately with instructions to pick us up shortly after dark that night near the Highway 30 bridge approximately 5 miles south of our present location.

The first pond was an irrigation storage impoundment filled by large deep wells. At that time of year the pumps ran continually. We could hear the motors whir the minute the car left.

It was extremely important to hit that pond first. Because of the constant mechanical activity the area was under almost continual surveillance. Second and more important, the owner's home overlooked the pond not 150 feet away. It was vital to get in and out before full daylight and the fog started to lift.

I capped three full stick charges as we walked in. By the time I was finished, our point man had cleared the area, given the all clear signal and we moved in.

A noisy flow of water obscured our hearing. Good to muffle the blast but bad for security. One of the boys moved up the path toward the house to watch. The other rigged the spears.

We could see ten or a dozen large stocker trout feeding on the surface. Because of the constantly flowing water, the trout in this particular pond were huge and well kept.

I picked what appeared to be the three deepest holes and arranged the charges with the longest fuze on the end of the pond we intended to start with.

Point gave the all clear and we started lighting charges. All three landed in about the right spot but sank much deeper than I had supposed the pond to be. On a really deep shot, the fuze can at times be drowned.

Dynamite properly placed under water goes off with a muffled "whoomf." There is a sharp silver flash and the water boils in an upward cone for twenty to thirty seconds. Contrary to popular belief, a proper charge is relatively quiet.

Charge one went on schedule, then a short pause. Two and three exploded almost simultaneously.

Hurriedly we ran down to the bank to collect the surfacing trout. Fish under these circumstances will turn and float to the surface for the next four to five minutes. Small minnow sized ones will often be killed, but the bigger fish will quickly revive and swim away. It is important to spear the big fish as they surface.

Both of us waded out to our waists and within minutes had about two dozen twenty inch trout. Foggy, soggy daylight was now full on us, so we quickly pulled out and headed for the next pond.

Houses surrounded us for a time, but it was still very early and foggy. Soon we cleared civilization and arrived at our next destination—a fairly remote farm pond.

Trampled grass on shore and an old leaky boat suggested that the pond had been fished recently. Probably often.

Since this water was much shallower, I rigged three half stick charges and we shot the second pond. Tens of thousands of three inch bluegills rolled to the surface but nary an eatable specimen appeared.

"Typical midwest pond," snorted one of the boys, "all the fish are stunted from being so crowded." We left quickly for our next target.

It was a full hour till we got to the old quarry. Houses surrounded it at a distance, but we were able to get in unseen along a fence line and then through some old strip piles.

The pond was large and deep at one end but we shot it with three sticks anyway. This time we got some twenty pounds of carp, but we left them for the coons. It was already a chore to carry the trout and no one wanted to add to the burden by hauling along carp.

We reached the Des Moines about eleven and broke off for lunch and a rest.

About 2:00 we started down the river, working most of the deeper holes. Fishing wasn't tremendous, but we did manage to get several nice small mouth bass. But trouble was brewing.

About a mile from the bridge, I rigged a full stick charge and slid it into a back eddy. Instead of going down, however, the current carried the charge in next to the bank where it lodged against a large limb in a nest of twisted sticks and branches.

The charge went off with a substantial noise, blowing wood and water thirty feet in the air. Unfortunately, the noise alerted a fellow who was sitting in his parked car with a girl about fifty yards away at the end of a grassy lane. It must have been the landowner's son. He ran over, took one look at the smoking, roiled water and ran back to his car. He never did see us.

As soon as they left, we cleared, but in twenty minutes there were three more rigs down at the river and perhaps eight people.

Now we were in a corn field back about 300 yards from the river. It was safe enough but we couldn't make for the road or the bridge through all the people.

Finally as dark approached, we moved out of the corn field. A quick check confirmed the fact that the warden's truck was on the highway not half a mile from our pickup point.

"Our pickup will never stop," one of the boys said. "She won't even come back past him a second time." All our pickup people are well instructed. They know that if there is trouble, we are best left to walk it out.

It was a long bleak hike but that's how we got home. Twelve miles through the rainy evening till we reached safety about 11:00 in the evening. Generally a second pickup point is agreed on. One where we can meet a car several hours and miles away from the original spot, but in this case we quite foolishly had made no such arrangements.

Was it worth the work? I thought so. We had eluded a well-organized search force and had collected about 100 pounds of nice trout and bass. Not a bad day, we all agreed.

Although many details are missing from this true account, it does illustrate the necessity of using good entrance, evasion and

21

exit strategies. We were a well-trained, disciplined crew, well aware of the various elements of movement that allowed us so much success.

These elements and strategies may be broken down as follows:

Transportation

In this day and age, most poachers get to their territory by car or truck. When I was much younger and lived on a farm, we would often walk a mile or two into a good squirrel woods, or to a duck pond. But in today's urban society this is almost always impossible, unless of course the reader does live in a rural environment. A close variation involves riding to the country one wishes to hunt or fish and walking home. A good system but again, unfortunately, often impossible.

Traveling by car or truck to and from a game area requires the use of a nondescript, common-looking vehicle. A few years back, a young fellow we know of tried to use his Datsun 240Z car to poach. In two weeks, everyone in the county knew the car. The hapless fellow couldn't make a move without someone recognizing him.

Eventually we found the car parked in an old abandoned barn and let the air our of all the tires. Our Johnny-on-the-spot warden nabbed the guy late in the afternoon, ridding us of one more competitor.

Good poachers never use motorcycles or open jeeps. The former are too noisy in the woods and both are open and revealing. Any idiot can look at a jeep or bike and decide if the rider is going hunting or fishing. Bringing game out is, of course, out of the question with either one.

I personally like a clean, late model intermediate sized car to poach with. A pickup truck is fine in a farming community, but I seldom haul game out in one. I have found it best to lock the deer, or whatever, in the trunk completely wrapped in an air tight, blood-proof plastic bag.

Some years back I did make an exception to my rule concerning jeeps and purchased one to poach with. I ordered a brownish O.D. colored rig with black steel top that was very similar in color to those used by the Rural Electric Authority. The utility didn't have a jeep, but no one seemed to realize that. Every place I went, people assumed I was from the power company.

Never under any circumstances ride with poached game unless all hunting clothes, guns, spears and other paraphernalia are left behind for later pickup. Carrying game *and* two or three hunters, no matter how they are attired, is asking for trouble. On a significant pickup, involving several deer, bear, elk or moose, it is best to have a well dressed woman do the driving. Have a second rig get the hunters.

Slamming car doors on either drop or pickup is a mortal sin. I carefully explain that doors are not to be opened or closed loudly, and become very irate if someone doesn't comply. It is infinitely more difficult to tell what is happening, or if the car or truck in question has even slowed if the doors can't be heard. A listener 300 feet away becomes immediately suspicious, however, if a car door slams.

Always make the drop in an obscured place where the poachers can quickly move into cover. Have all the gear ready in easily carried packages that can, until the moment arrives to hit the ground, be kept out of sight on the floor of the vehicles.

Try not to drop or pickup in the same place more than once or twice a year.

Coming and going, wear something that does not look outdoorsy. I carry a camouflage jacket in my pack and wear an old sport jacket or something similar in the car.

The pickup car should be unobtrusively distinctive if the pickup is done at night. We use a small flashlight laid on the dash of the car. Drivers should be instructed to travel the roads at an average speed, slowing quickly to make the grab. If there is game, it should be loaded in an obscure location out of view from the road, buildings or open fields.

If at all possible, I like to carry game home without using a vehicle. At one time I packed a nice white tail three miles through mountains rather than use a pickup on a commonly traveled road.

A drop should never be made where other vehicles are parked or if there are other cars or trucks on the road. Allow enough time to make the drop and get away. This means the hunters are in cover and the car is over a hill or two before anyone can come by. The best way to do this is to keep a sharp lookout front and back when driving in. Slow quickly. Roll all the windows down and everyone listen for traffic. Then, if the coast is clear move out.

Unless it seems possible to walk in, we set up an alternate pickup point *at least* two miles from the original location. Drivers are warned to be very cautious and to leave the country completely if there is any sign of trouble. Should we miss the second pickup point, we stash our gear and walk to a town where we call and report our position, and make arrangements to be picked up. Two-way radios are an immense help when coordinating pickups.

Pickup times are always set so that the car never waits. We wait for the car. If the car arrives and we aren't there, the driver moves on immediately without stopping or acting suspicious. Often we get something right at dark or are slowed by the need to carry heavy game. If radio contact can't be established, we send one man on alone to coordinate the pickup which may be somewhere else entirely.

Camouflage

Good poachers learn how to dress inconspicuously. Lots of different clothes are required, but it's part of the price one must pay for moving through the country with impunity.

An easy place to start is with white in snow. Some hunters already know that given just a few blades of grass for cover, they can become practically invisible wearing white in snow. Precious few, never the less, seem to take advantage of this first basic lesson in camouflage.

We often use white J.C. Penney coveralls. As incredible as it may sound, few people are suspicious of white if there is no other evidence of outdoor activity. Probably they think the wearer is a milkman, painter or even a mechanic. Don't, however, try to fool lawmen with this disguise. Seen in a car or truck out in the country it will arouse suspicion.

In late spring and early fall, I often use light green or medium grey coveralls. They blend surprisingly well. Again these standard colors do not alarm people who see them in a car and generally raise few suspicions.

Other times of the year I wear standard camouflage pants and jacket, but there are problems with these. In most cases the camouflage outfits that are available are not specifically tailored to the area one may be hunting. It is tempting to overlook this lack of compatibility but I feel it is foolish to do so.

Better to carefully evaluate the camo outfits available and then pick one that can be modified to match the color of the bush it will be used in. In the past I have always been able to do this by bleaching a dark outfit lighter or by purchasing a lighter outfit and dyeing it either yellow or green.

Perhaps it isn't necessary to mention this to the seasoned outdoorsman reading this book, but always wear wool if available. If wool is impossible, then choose soft cotton or perhaps a cotton blend. Successful hunters never, never wear scratchy loud canvas or nylon. Incidentally, nylon shines in the woods, especially on rainy days.

Time spent evaluating hunting outfits is time well spent. If you are like most, your hunting clothes will appear dark and contrasting to the bush around. Hands and face will shine like mirrors. A little work will improve the situation dramatically.

When To Hunt

Under normal circumstances, most game wardens will work Saturday and Sunday, and take Monday off. Farmers work any day of the week the weather is fit, but generally limit their visits to the fields to planting in the spring and harvesting in the fall. Rural residents, who work in town, almost without exception work weekdays 8:00 a.m. to 5:00 p.m.

For these reasons I like to plan most of my activities on Monday, Tuesday or Wednesday, or during inclement weather. This implies a thorough knowledge of agricultural practices in our area of operations. I can not stress the latter too strongly. For instance, if corn is the principal crop, one should know when the ground is likely to be plowed, when it may be worked and planted, how much cover the growth will provide by a certain date, when it will be harvested and so on.

There is nothing so embarrassing as having to lie in a fence row waiting for a corn picker to pass, or a wheat combine to move on, or running into a whole field of pickle pickers when one is out trying to move through the country.

It is impossible, in this book, to list even the major crops and seasons a poacher is liable to encounter. There are just too many and the seasons too diverse. My advice to anyone wanting to become a master poacher is to:

    1. Identify the major crops grown in one's area of operations.

    2. Determine when the ground is likely to be plowed, worked, when it will be planted, what the crop looks like as it matures, and when it will be harvested.

    3. Be aware of what cover a crop will provide, what game will be attracted and the likelihood of people doing hand work on it.

    4. Learn what special jobs might bring people out to the woodlots and fields, such as spreading manure, feeding cattle, moving irrigation pipe, etc.

5. Be cautious in forest areas, around logging pulp operations or mining activities. In these cases it might be wise to operate on weekends or when the weather is very bad during week days.

Many of my activities revolve around ponds, marshes and sloughs. Some are popular fishing areas during the summer. Be extremely cautious about entering these areas right at dusk till about an hour later. Until I learned, I almost ran into silent fishermen on several occasions. They apparently came in the twilight and stayed fishing until it was pitch dark.

Security Principles

The following rules must be inviolate. Neglect to observe them and you will eventually get nailed. It's as simple as that.

First of all, never hunt alone, unless one is on very familiar, relatively safe territory. This could be a remote woods, property owned by you or some member of the family, or perhaps the season is open and your only problem is trespass. Never hunt alone.

Otherwise, I feel three is the perfect number. Four people are too many and with two, much security is lost. Put one man fifty to 100 yards ahead on point and move silently through the bush. Of the two remaining, at least one would be constantly surveying the horizon with a pair of binoculars.

Never talk above a whisper. Human voices under some conditions carry for such a distance it is frightening. Hopefully, two-way radios will be available. Whisper when talking on these as well. Stay in touch visually, by radio, or at night by sound with everyone continually. In this regard it is important that everyone know the intended line of march. There should be no question about where to end up and what route to take getting there.

If someone does see or hear something suspicious, let the others know immediately. Better to have a dozen false alarms than to be negligent when the chips are down. If an alarm is confirmed, immediately melt into whatever cover is available but keep in visual contact with each other *and* the intruder, if possible. Determine if you have been seen. If so, look for signs of coordination with others and, based on a knowledge of the terrain, make plans to leave the area completely.

Always stay cool. A good example of incredible cool is the white tail deer. They manage to take advantage of every shred of cover to walk away from danger. Good poachers are serious students of white tail deer and learn from their example.

Should the peril be great, split up and meet again at some pre-arranged spot. And never leave a novice in the woods alone. They will end up in the warden's truck blabbing their guts out.

Many times I have been completely surrounded and seemingly enmeshed hopelessly in an elaborate trap laid especially for me by wardens and landowners. By moving into cover immediately, using every tree, fence row, hill and field of grass, I have *always* managed to evade my pursuers.

Run, if possible, when out of sight. By so doing, one can swap country and be quickly out an area where others suppose you still are. Good poachers have a strong, fast stride in the woods, have better stamina than their competition and can run like a deer.

At times it is best to find a heavy thicket and hole up rather than running. I have done this on numerous occasions and had the opportunity to listen to the conversation of the pursuers. This takes a lot of hair, especially if there are dogs around, but it's the most common and successful method of evasion for white tails.

Most of the time a good poacher will spot danger long before his position becomes known. It is then best to hole up and wait for the people to pass, or perhaps consider moving around and past to another less guarded area.

If the point man does run smack into someone, he must in a loud voice proclaim the fact that he is lost while out walking or target practicing. The noise would warn those coming up in the area.

Point should never carry heavy equipment such as fish traps, spears, or traps. He should never carry game under any circumstances.

Never skyline yourself. Always use and stay in whatever cover is available.

Never, if at all possible, travel the same road or trail twice in one day and never travel the trail if it is possible to move silently 10 yards to either side of it.

Don't linger where several trails meet, in fire cuts, open fields or the like.

When coming up on a road, be especially quiet and check the area before exposing yourself. Listen for cars or trucks, and for two way radio transmissions, which carry a long way in the woods.

A crew that can do all of this well requires training and practice. Get out in the bush often, but more important, don't ever bring in outsiders. These people tend to be klutzes, and unless you have known them for years, could be in the employ of the wardens.

Tracking

Comments about leaving tracks for others to find are deceptively simple.

First and foremost, if at all possible, don't. Stay out of mud, walk in the grass, on rock or across logs. Pick places where the ground is hard.

When entering an area where tracks are impossible to cover, such as in snow, or a marsh, walk in the brush or high grass rather than established paths. This won't fool the pros, but 95 percent of the rest of the world won't be able to figure out what happened.

It if is impossible not to leave tracks across an area, obliterate the approaches by walking in circles and then cross the area walking backwards. Do this crossing roads, fields or coming up paths.

Be cautious of tracks and trails. A little effort obscuring and confusing will pay big dividends. I have even lost wardens in eight inches of new snow by being careful how I moved through an area.

A few years back an acquaintance had to endure some unpleasantries because of the unique design of his custom boots. He left a clear track in the mud near a deer kill. The sheriff photographed the track and on a hunch matched it to my friend's boots. Since that time I have always been very careful to buy common boots from Penney's or K-Mart that I know thousands of other people wear.

At times when I was younger and running a trap line, I would walk for miles in a stream. Seasoned trackers can often determine that someone has moved through an area in this manner, but it does throw a novice farmer or college-trained warden off the track. In real life it is very difficult to walk a stream any distance at all without making a mark in soft mud or sand of some kind.

Movement At Night

A good poaching team will work as well or better in the dark than they do in broad daylight.

I learned to be comfortable in the woods at night while possum and coon hunting when I was very young. Now cruising the country after dark is second nature to me. I tend to forget that for some people it is a very traumatic experience. Since many drops and pickups will be made in the dark, an aspiring poacher will, for this reason alone, have to learn to acclimate himself to the dark.

Working well at night is a function of practice and of getting over one's unreasonable fears of blackness. I have no quick cure or instant advice, other than the necessity of understanding that most night fears are unreasonable. Thankfully wardens and landowners have the same fears, so often it is a trade off.

It has been suggested that knowing the country well is the answer for good night movement. Certainly a knowledge of the terrain helps, but we have explored an awful lot of new country at night so we could figure out how to move over it during the day.

At first it is better to stay bunched up a bit more, use two way radios less, walk slower and use more audible signals.

Our signal is a bobwhite quail call during the day, and a horned owl hoot at night. A close friend used to make a noise like a cricket and another simply snapped his fingers. All worked well, but be sure any audible signal is used sparingly and without any accompanying talking, coughing or foot stomping.

Be doubly cautious about using roads or paths at night. People who don't get out much in the woods at night *only* use common paths. If they are out looking for something, this is the only place they will look.

I often carry a light at night but its use is almost always related to some sort of special hunt. The light is therefore appropriately shaded or hooded for use shining frogs, coons or fish. I never use it while traveling over the country. When coming in after dark from a rabbit hunt, for instance, I *always* travel without the help of any artificial light source.

Dogs

Even a very average pooch can be a lot of trouble for a poacher. They will invariably hear or smell you first and sound the alarm. Fortunately not one dog owner in 1000 pays any attention to his hounds, so most of the time we just let them bark. This is especially true of farm dogs and those owned by rural residents.

Occasionally we have run into guard-type dogs or trained nose dogs used by wardens at check stations. This has happened most often in the south. There are several ways to handle these situations.

A few years back we were hunting crows on a very private arboretum in the deep south. Three of us parked our rig about a mile away in the back of a public rest area and walked to the large fenced estate. It was broad daylight but we had good camouflage outfits and there were lots of trees, bushes and tall grass.

The crows were nesting in a triple row of pines planted along the west of the place as a windbreak. It was about 40 feet to the tops of the trees and the line extended for perhaps a mile or more.

After crossing the fence we entered the trees and walked along completely obscured to within 300 feet of the main house. Nothing much happened till I shot the first nesting crow with a Ruger 10-22 rifle. The gun had a very good commercial British silencer on it so the report was barely audible. Two big Dobermans heard it, however, and came bounding over to investigate, ears laid back, acting like leopards. One of my friends without further ado shot both of them stone cold dead with his silenced .25-.20. He got them within five yards of each other right between the eyes.

Handling the situation in this manner has a great deal of finality and class if one likes bold, positive action, but does have its drawbacks. Needless to say, it's hard on the dogs. But more important, the dogs' owner will probably find the wasted critters unless great care is taken to dispose of them. This will alarm him greatly and provide certain evidence that someone was there. Unfortunately, it is often the only way to handle unattended, trained watchdogs while in the field. Another way to control dogs is with tear gas in aerosol cans, or a squirt gun filled with ammonia.

Wise watchdog handlers don't allow their animals to run at large unattended. I have occasionally been tracked by super sniffer-type hounds held on a leash by members of the local posse. One time I rode a boat out of the combat zone. Another time I put enough distance between me and the slow moving posse to make my pickup point and ride to safety.

After that escapade I went to the nursery and got a can of dried deer blood sold to keep the pesky critters out of gardens. I mixed the blood meal with fine ground pepper and put this in small two ounce plastic containers.

Alas I never did get to try the mixture, but a friend eventually made good use of it. He got caught in a check station with several dozen rabbits under his back seat and a warden's dog sniffing around. The guy had the presence of mind to dump the mixture in the gravel by the car. According to his telling, the dog sniffed around in the blood pepper mixture for several minutes, sneezed twice and then lay down by the warden's truck.

When talking with a warden, it is important to remember that the first thing they look for is blood on one's hands or clothing. Be careful—be clean. Wash up in a creek or pond after dressing any kill.

Another important fact of life regarding wardens is that they will seldom, if ever, leave the road and their rig alone unless in hot pursuit of something or someone. If I spot an officer in the woods I always assume he has lots of help and that I had better hotfoot it out of there, lest I become involved in a surprise party set up for my benefit.

Some of the old Kentucky squirrel hunters I knew when I was a kid claimed that they occasionally threw a round or two over the warden's head if they caught him in the woods. They said it kept wardens on the road, but of course I wouldn't even suggest something like that. Others merely hinted that they might take similar action which also tends to keep the possum sheriffs bunched up and out of harm's way on the road.

Noise

There are several aspects to noise and success as a poacher which have already been covered.

These include:

1. Never slamming car doors;
2. Never talking out loud on radios or to each other in the woods;
3. Using private, barely audible signals to communicate.

All of these noise problems are related to people and not animals. A noise problem that is a kind of 50-50 don't-scare-the-game-attract-the-people situation involves moving through the woods without snapping brush. There are no real words of wisdom that I can impart in this area except don't. Don't step on dry sticks, don't snap off dry limbs, don't thump your feet on the ground and don't kick stones down the hills. It's all a matter of practice. If you cannot now move through the country silently at a reasonable speed, you will have to learn. More because of the game being scared off than because of what people may hear, although the latter is important.

How to accomplish this seemingly impossible task? Again there is no quick cure, only a few general suggestions:

1. Start by moving absolutely silently, taking as much time as is required to get the job done perfectly. After a few weeks, begin to push yourself faster and faster, remembering always that silence is golden.
2. Walk somewhat toe in. A flat-footed hunter can't feel the ground as well while he walks, will tend to thump

when placing his feet, and will snag more sticks and brush.

3. Wear thin soled boots, or go barefoot in rubber boots if possible. One can avoid stepping on crackly brush better by being able to feel what's on the ground before it crunches.

Be sure to use plain toed boots rather than moc toes that are more prone to catch brush.

4. Even in summer my grandfather used to wear all wool hunting clothes. Judging by the canvas-nylon array of hunting clothes commercially available today, the lesson of how to dress to move through the bush silently seems lost on this entire generation of hunters.

If not wool, then wear cotton, but don't plan to be silent in the brush and then wear pants or jacket that scratches every time a stick drags across it.

Next time you are around a group of grizzled old hunters and trappers, take a look at the clothes they wear. It's always rough wool, as opposed to the warm, dry modern nylon-canvas togs the dudes wear, but which make so much noise they are worthless.

5. Perhaps it is redundant to mention this, but plan to hunt on days when the woods are quiet. These times occur after rain or snow, when a gentle wind blows, or during mid day when the sounds of day, such as planes, tractors and trucks, cover noise of movement.

I become so conditioned to moving through the bush with absolute silence that at times it is difficult for me to shoot, the noise is such an affront to my efforts.

Many accomplished poachers use one or more silencers, but in many cases this isn't the entire answer. Ownership of an unlicensed silencer is a serious federal offense. Carrying one must be done with extreme caution. If anyone who knows the score sees a hunter use one, he will immediately be tipped off to what is happening.

In the past, we have taken along a silenced .22 pistol and a larger bore silenced rifle. Shotguns cannot be successfully silenced.

The point man should not carry a silencer. If possible, the guns that are equipped to take silencers are carried with the units disassembled, hidden in pockets or boots. Large bore, high power rifles can only be silenced to the extent that it is difficult to tell where the round is coming from, the rule of thumb being that if the round travels faster than 1190 feet per second, it can not be truly silenced.

The astute poacher can often use his unsilenced shotgun or rifle without undue danger. I have shot an incredible number of deer, fox, ducks and geese, coyotes, rabbits and other game that was practically in someone's back yard. There are several tricks that make this possible.

Most important is to shoot only once. Unless the shot is very near and very loud, it usually won't arouse suspicion. Also, the noise won't give away the shooter's location. Shoot more than once and the noise becomes directional. The landowner will surely come running then to see what is going on.

Some time back I shot a very nice six point white tail buck in the front shoulder forward of the ham. The round went through a corner of the ham into the brisket. It was a short fifteen yard shot, but alas, done with a .257 Roberts through heavy brush.

The deer ran about 200 yards and collapsed. It now lay not 100 yards from a farmstead in a brush fence row.

I tracked it through to where it was lying, only to have it get up and hobble another twenty yards closer to the farm house. Dark was about an hour away, so I decided to play a waiting game, maneuvering around to get another shot.

After another thirty minutes there was still no indication that the farmer knew I or the deer was there.

I crept out of the fence row, around the deer and finally managed to chase it back towards the woods. It ran over a small hill and collapsed again in a swale, but I still couldn't get close enough to finish it with my knife.

Dark was now almost here. I had a two mile hike home with a 175 pound deer, so I decided to risk one more shot and get the job over with. Carefully I pulled up and touched a round off at the critter's neck. For some reason I missed. Quickly I snapped off another round. The deer rolled over dead, and the farm house door slammed shut.

Frantically I pulled the deer for the woods. A truck engine started and before I could reach cover, was roaring out into the field. Reluctantly I abandoned the deer and took cover in the woods. A very fortunate farmer pulled up to the deer, glanced around once or twice, and loaded the trophy-sized animal into his truck.

My error of firing twice in the quiet evening air caused me to lose a very nice animal as well as tip off the land owner about what was going on. It was, in general, a disgusting event that still upsets me.

The lessons, nevertheless, are good ones.

Always shoot with a tree, hill or barn barrier between you and suspicious ears.

Take advantage of a plane passing overhead, or a strong wind to blow the noise away from habitation.

Use a gun big enough to get the job done, but stay away from the ear-splitting magnums.

But most of all, fire only once. A good poacher doesn't need more than one round unless there is more than one animal. Then it's best to wait an hour or more before taking the second one.

Getting Rid Of Evidence

The goal of the good poacher is to never, under any circumstances, let anyone know for sure that he or she was ever there. To do this, one must become a master at slipping in , making the harvest and slipping out, without leaving a pile of grouse feathers, deer guts, muskrat carcasses or any other game leavings.

We scatter deer guts in heavy thickets, bury the head, and carry, not drag, the rest to the pickup vehicle.

Fish guts are scattered back away from the water.

Small game carcasses, such as mink, coon or coyote are placed in a burlap bag and sunk in a river.

All of these specific details are probably not important. What is important is the concept of not leaving the unused pieces lying around where people can see them. Do whatever seems best at the time, but do something.

Once upon a time there was a farmer who for some reason was making life miserable for us. To show our admiration we collected up eleven fresh deer hides and had one of the boys sneak in and hang them in his barn along with a number the farmer had collected privately. One of our wives anonymously tipped off the warden and the old buzzard was fined almost $2000.00. That was back in the days when dollars were big, round and hard. A good lesson to keep in mind when disposing of bones, hides or other deer parts.

4
EQUIPMENT

Good equipment is essential to the serious poacher. However, one does not generally walk into a hardware store and buy the necessary tools off the shelf.

This chapter deals with the equipment I mention using in other portions of this book. The items covered are general in nature and part of the basic bag of tricks a poacher might ordinarily possess. Other, more specialized items are detailed in the appropriate chapters dealing with the game they will be used on or, in some cases, an entire section will be devoted to a specific type of gear.

In preparing a chapter of this nature, it is very tempting to list names and addresses of the people who make and sell the items you and I need. In some cases I have, but usually the reader will only find broad hints regarding the exact whereabouts of the hardware described. After giving the problem a great deal of thought, I have decided that to specifically name manufacturers, mail order houses and others who carry poaching gear would be hazardous for the dealer/manufacturer, and counterproductive for people like ourselves who need these items. Mere mention by name in a book of this nature would orchestrate such a barrage of wrath that no dealer could survive, so bear with me and try to read between the lines.

In some cases and in some states, simply owning some of the items mentioned is illegal. Each individual will have to thoroughly research his state law and then weigh the risks and decide whether they justify using the items I have described.

The best example I can think of is possession of silencers. Very strict, severe federal laws limit their ownership to the point that I have never personally owned one. Many of the people I hunt and fish with do, however, and I have often seen them in operation. After almost forty years in this business, I find I can get along without one quite nicely, but that is a personal decision I can't make for anyone else.

At any rate, the following is a list of hardware that is often very helpful.

Spears

A good spear is a first line piece of equipment, useful for everything from collecting fish after a pond or stream has been hit (dynamited) to collecting frogs, turtles and, at times, even beaver and muskrats. For a number of years I made my own spears. Now there are commercial units on the market which do very nicely without resorting to the blacksmith shop.

Effective spear heads should weigh around a pound each and be fitted with a sturdy, collapsible handle. I like a spear that is at least 5 inches wide with either 4 or 5 tines. The tines should be nicely barbed and be fairly heavy but not over 1/4 inch in diameter. Some people get along well with three tined spears and that is fine. The limiting factor usually is the length of the tines and not the number. Best, in my book, are the units that have tines no less than 5 inches long, that will completely impale the target.

Several domestic models are available with needle thin tines, and cheap, light shanks that are advertised as bullfrog spears. Every time I have tried to collect frogs with one I have ended up with broken barbs, bent shanks and even missing tines. Tougher fish floating in a water environment are impossible with these little light toys.

I like the LEW's spear made by a Japanese firm, though other makes are probably available that are just as good. There are a number of different kinds of LEW's spears available, ranging from small frog models up to large units that would probably handle a sturgeon. Alas, no two dealers seem to handle the same two models, so some persistence hunting around for the correct spear may be necessary. At present, at least four major fishing tackle distributors list the LEW's in their catalogs, so there should be no major bar to finding a dealer who has one or can order one.

Another brand to look for is the SHURKATCH. Thousands of little country hardware stores carry SHURKATCH frog spears but finding the heavier, more adequate fish model is sometimes a chore. At least one can safely assume that a dealer who has the tiny frog model could get the better fish type without too much trouble.

Proper accurate use of a spear isn't particularly difficult, but few people seem to have mastered the process.

When we were kids, my youngest brother (now deceased) could throw a conventional fish spear with incredible accuracy. He used to wade up the middle of a frog pond and plunk everything within 20 feet of him. Other than a couple of deck hands I met in Cuba, he was the only one I ever knew who was that skilled with a spear.

Throwing a spear is showy, but completely unnecessary. As I have told dozens of neophyte spearmen, you don't throw the damn thing, you jab with it. The proper way to handle a spear is to reach out to within 4 to 6 inches of the prey and then execute a sharp jabbing maneuver. At times the gap distance, spear to prey, may be up to a foot or more, but never, never let go of the spear.

Small fish floating to the surface are some of the hardest targets to impale. Nothing behind them holds them, so the spear jab must be very quick. If not, the victim will merely be pushed away through the water. In the case of dynamited fish, they may revive and return to the bottom.

Spear points should be kept needle sharp and shiny clean. Good spear heads are made of malleable steel that rusts easily. Clean them with steel wool before each use, and dress the points up with a file or stone. I carry a stone and pliers with my spear so that touch-up repairs can be made in the field.

Carrying an assembled spear is poor business. I cut my pole into three pieces and used three 6 inch pieces of 3/4 inch rigid copper pipe for couplings. Works well, is easy to assemble, and the whole thing can be carried under my jacket or in a pack.

Silencers

In 1935 the U.S. Congress made the unlicensed ownership of silencers a federal offense. Many states followed Uncle Sam's lead under the guise of crime control.

For perhaps twenty years the entire area of silencer technology remained in a kind of mystic limbo. There was little private interest in silencers. Few people used them and whatever publicity did occur amounted to at least 99 percent bullshit.

With the U.S. involvement in Vietnam, interest in silencers picked up and new technology blossomed. As a result, there are now a number of excellent texts on silencers that contain information that was essentially undiscovered fifteen years ago.

Since this book is about hunting, the technical information pertaining to silencers is not complete. A serious poacher who wants to get into the silencer business is well advised to buy a book specifically about the subject area. Many fine silencer titles are available from PALADIN PRESS, Box 1307, Boulder, Colorado 80306.

My first contact with silencers occurred years ago when I hunted squirrels with some folks from southern Kentucky. Almost every one of them had a heavy barreled rifle modified to accept a silencer. They crept through the woods like Indians and really stacked them up. Later I had another friend who made a silenced rifle for a .32 S&W pistol cartridge.

In those days it was possible to send seven dollars to Parker-Hale in England and have them send one of their commercial model silencers through in the mail. The custom declaration said the units were "sound modifiers," which let them pass our border guards with little or no problem.

Other sources of silencers were from the original Hiram Maxim models sold before Congress acted in 1934.

Mechanically a silencer works much the same as a muffler on a car does. It seals off the gases from the burning powder and allows them to escape gradually, thereby reducing the noise. However, the similarity is a weak one and there are many inherent problems to contend with when silencing a firearm.

First and foremost, the unit has to be properly designed. In other words, it must contain the correct components of sufficient capacity to get the job done. There are a number of unique space-age silencer concepts floating around, spin-offs from Vietnam, that employ weird alloys, valves, neoprene gaskets, difficult machine parts and exotic sound deadening material. All of these, as far as I can tell, are compact, more efficient applications of the basic design Hiram Maxim came up with before the turn of the century.

Fortunately for the poacher, Hiram Maxim's design is not an unduly difficult one to duplicate in the home workshop.

The first decision a poacher must make when he decides to acquire a silencer is which gun and what caliber.

Military silencers of sorts exist for the standard M-16 (.223 caliber) and the old M-14 (.308 caliber). They are not truly silenced weapons, however, because all that is contained is the noise from the muzzle blast. Bullets traveling faster than the speed of sound (1190 feet per second) will crack as they pass stationary objects, emitting a kind of mini-sonic boom. There is no way to mitigate this effect other than by dropping the velocity of the rounds below the magical 1190 feet per second mark.

I saw graphic proof of this a few years back while at Fort Benning, Georgia. An officer friend borrowed an experimental M-14 equipped with a silencer. We spent the day playing around with the thing. The most interesting experiment we conducted standing on a set of railroad tracks, shooting the rifle horizontally down the road past a number of telegraph poles. It was possible to hear the round crack as it passed every pole till it was out about 800 yards. When fired straight up, the rifle gave off a kind of healthy pneumatic thump. With no obstacles to pass, it was very quiet indeed.

Rounds fired from a weapon of this type are difficult to place since the noise they make is relative to the objects they pass in flight. Fine for military application but worthless for the poacher. I don't care if the critter knows the quarter from which he is being fired upon. I only fire once anyway. What I do care about is having a bunch of people hear the shot and know someone must be out there pulling the trigger.

Complex silencers have been developed that use standard issue, high velocity ammunition. Actually they are two silencers in one. The first chamber bleeds off enough gas right ahead of the chamber to drop the velocity of the bullet to less than 1190 ft/sec. The second, fastened to the end of the barrel, soaks up the muzzle blast in a conventional fashion.

For poaching purposes I feel it is best to stick with the subsonic rounds, or those that can be handloaded to subsonic levels. Information that follows is all related to this more conventional, easier area of silencer technology.

Twenty-two rim fire rounds can be nicely silenced if they are the standard, or target velocity. Hi-speed ammo stored in a deep freeze for a month or two can also be made to work, but my recommendation is not to buy hi-speed .22's in the first place. Of all the possible calibers one might silence, the .22 rim fire is about the most practical.

Other good rounds to silence include:

      .32 auto
      .32 S&W short and long
      .32 Colt short and long
      .32 new police
      .38 S&W

.38 Colt short and long
.380 auto
.38-.40
.44 S&W
.44'.40
.45 Colt
.45 auto

A silenced .22 rim fire is fine for shooting frogs or coons out of a tree, for use on a trap line, for crows from a blind, or even for protection from dogs, but for taking deer, fox, coyote or other larger game it is next to worthless. Obviously the above calibers are all pistol rounds, so it is apparent that not all the answers are in yet.

One solution to the problem is to handload. By using a very heavy bullet and a reduced load of slow burning powder, a standard rifle and cartridge can be matched that will silence nicely. Several suggestions are the:

.30 caliber carbine
.30-.30
.300 Savage
.303 British
.308
.25-.20
.32-.20

Heavy bullets fired at minus 1190 ft/sec using any one of these cartridges will have plenty of energy to do the job on big animals at short distances. Problems sometimes arise when novice shooters try to use the slow bullets with their big looping trajectories. A little practice surmounts this obstacle nicely.

Back in the era from 1900 to 1930 there apparently were a number of Winchester 92's in .25-.20 caliber that came from the factory threaded for commercial silencers. I have never seen one of the silencers but, to this day, I still manage to run across the rifles from time to time. Thirty years ago a friend bought one and mounted a homemade silencer on it. This proved to be a very nice set-up indeed. Later he sold the 92 and made up a new single shot .25-.20 with silencer that was even nicer. As a result I am extremely partial to a silenced .25-.20 and might even break my prohibition against owning one if a good unit like my friend's came along.

He used 117 gr. 257 Roberts bullets and a few grains of very slow powder. (I think six grains of BL-C.) The gun had plenty of whallop for deer and was so quiet it was frightening. By far and away the loudest noise occurred when working the action or at short ranges as the bullet thumped into the target.

Silencers can be deceptive in this regard. It is easy to lose respect for a firearm that doesn't make noise. Be forewarned. Don't treat a silenced firearm carelessly.

Other options exist to stepping down rifle cartridges.

Service Armament Co. in Ridgefield, New Jersey, among others, imports a number of lever action rifles in pistol calibers. They are available in .38 special, .45 ACP and .44-.40. All could be nicely fitted for silencers.

Submachine gun look-alikes with legal length barrels and semi-automatic actions are another possibility. Auto-Ordnance makes a legal Thompson .45 ACP and there are a number of others that shoot either 9 mm or .45 ACP. Most 9 mm ammo is supersonic, so handloading would be necessary.

Some people are turned on by the thought of owning a sub-machinegun-type weapon. I personally wouldn't carry one poaching under any circumstances and doubt if other good outdoorsmen would. Casual observers who see a gun of that type are immediately fearful and suspicious. It isn't worth the risk to wave a red flag in the face of the citizenry.

Automatic pistols, with few exceptions, can be silenced, but it is virtually impossible to "hang a can" on a revolver and have it work. Revolvers are too loose between the cylinder and the barrel.

Some automatic pistols, and for that matter rifles, are difficult to adapt to a silencer because the barrel is obstructed. Silencers must be firmly and accurately mounted which usually means threads. On some guns the sight or magazine is in the way and there isn't enough room to thread the barrel. It—the barrel—can be bored out and threaded back on the inside, but that process is complex compared to the relatively simple procedure of threading the outside.

Threading a rifle or pistol barrel is best done by a machine shop. The job should be accurate and true since silencer alignment is extremely critical.

The hillbillies who used the silencers I observed as a kid used friction-fit collar affairs that screwed into the silencer, slipping over the end of the rifle or pistol barrel to hold the silencer on. The little adaptor was very practical since one did not have to carry around a rifle with a threaded barrel (a dead giveaway to the law).

41

On the other hand, aligning the silencer was a chore. I remember laughing my ass off several times when they'd fire their guns after bumping the silencers out of alignment. The things blew to Kingdom Come.

Like anything good, silencers are a mixed blessing. One .22 pistol with a decent can on it can provide sport, security and an abundance of game. A heavy rifle with silencer can similarly bring home lots of bacon without advertising the fact to the neighbors. However, they can be difficult to build and maintain, and are of course seriously illegal.

Binoculars

Unless we are hunting in extremely heavy timber, I always insist that someone bring along a decent pair of binoculars. It isn't necessary for each member of the party to have a set, but the point man always should.

During the day binoculars are essential to clear the area around the field of operation. Point should continually check the path ahead, fields before they are crossed, high surrounding hills, lakes, marshes, and even watch for suspicious vehicles on distant roads. At night they may very well be the margin which keeps one's ass out of a sling.

Poachers buying glasses for their activities should consider purchasing only those models that meet the most demanding requirements. In other words, don't look at anything except night glasses.

This rules out the tiny, easy-to-carry compact binoculars, zoom binoculars and cheaper promotional glasses sold in the discount stores.

I have used Bausch & Lomb, Zeiss and Bushnell glasses and liked them in about that order. Certainly there are other makes of night glasses on the market, but at least these three are a place to start and/or a standard of comparison.

When buying binoculars, look for seven power models with 50 mm objective lenses. I know of no night glasses with 21 mm or 35 mm objective lenses. Another cue is power. Night glasses *all* come in seven power.

Unless one wants to merely sail into the nearest sporting goods store and pick out one of the brands listed above in a 7 x 50, the best plan is to go at night and compare. I have spent hours standing in sporting goods store parking lots looking at distant roof tops evaluating glasses. But it was time well spent.

Guns

I was sitting next to an old three strand barb wire fence in a scraggly, light pine thicket eating a sandwich when I spied a white tail doe working her way uphill across a draw to my right.

The shot was a long one, but I had a good rest so decided to give it a try. I put the cross hairs right at the hairline on her back at the front leg lump and touched off a round. There was time to bring the scope back on point and watch, the shot was so long.

When hit, the deer fell on her nose. The round neatly clipped both front legs off at the knee, the bullet having fallen more than two feet in flight. I polished her off with a round through the heart. The shot was longer than I had thought, but my trusty rifle managed to deliver the goods again.

During the regular hunting season, for big game, I prefer a .338 Winchester Magnum rifle with six power wide angle scope. The gun, in my estimation, has the rare ability to shoot accurately into the wind across canyons, or in heavy brush where the average shot is not over fifty yards. As far as I know, there is no other cartridge that will do all that.

In addition, the gun is a fantastic meat getter. I never have to shoot more than once, even on moose or elk, which in my book counts ten points to start with. The rounds don't ruin meat like the smaller, high velocity ones do, so I often use the gun on smaller coyotes, antelopes or peccaries.

Getting the most out of a .338 can only be done by hand loading. I feel the ideal bullet weight in that caliber is 225 grains. No factory ammo is available with 225 grain bullets, plus I drop the velocity about 200 feet per second on my home built rounds. By so doing, I get a cartridge with modest recoil which is no noisier than a .270 or .30-06.

Before or after season, when I must use a big rifle, I use an old Remington 600 bolt action with a four power wide angle scope in .308 caliber. We have stripped the rib off, put a recoil pad and sling on it, and it's a going little concern. The rifle is small, light and doesn't make an undue amount of noise with heavy bullets. Alas, they have been out of production for many years now, so don't expect to run to your nearest dealer and pick up a new one.

Another rifle that is a favorite of mine is the .257 Roberts. Again, because it is quiet, but also because they are so accurate.

Savage model 340's and Remington 788's in .308 Winchester Magnum and .30-.30 caliber are good rifles for silencing. Both are

43

cheap bolt actions that lend themselves well to this application.

Lever action rifles in .25-.20 or some of the common pistol cartridges were discussed in the section on silencers. The only limitation with these guns is the fact that the poacher is going to have to be a cool, steady shot, or the limited power will foil him.

Shotguns are not silenceable, yet some are very quiet. A .20 gauge, low base shell, for instance, fired in a reasonably heavy pump gun, will have such a gentle thump that it may not arouse suspicion. Consider an Ithaca model 37 for this work as well. The 37 is very durable if the elements are a consideration.

Double rifles or shotguns fitted with ball ammo liners are another possibility. Poachers who would like to acquire a double rifle can do so easily without great expense by either purchasing commercially made pistol or rifle cartridge liners, or having custom sleeves made for their double barrel shotgun. Several gunsmiths who advertise in *Shotgun News* offer to modify Savage 311 shotguns for about two hundred dollars. Rifle or pistol rounds fired in a shotgun action are somewhat quieter but less accurate than the gun they were originally designed for. At short ranges, however, the accuracy difference is immaterial.

Harry Owens, Box 5337, Hacienda Heights, CA 91745, has special inserts for any break open .12, .16, .20 or .410 shotgun. Calibers available include .22 LR, .22 WMR, .22 Hornet, .38 Special, .357 mag., .41, .44, .45 LC, .45 ACP, .45-.70 and .30-.30. The .30-.30 is an excellent meat getter when fired out of a shotgun action.

One terrible cold, blowy day we went pheasant hunting in northern Illinois near the Wisconsin line. Nobody was out. It got to five below and the snow was moving so fast that our tracks were covered in five minutes.

We hunted most of the day without success till we happened on a small brushy woodlot of perhaps four acres way back in the middle of a section. The first time through we noticed sign of hundreds of birds, but couldn't get any of them up. Feathers and other pheasant pieces were scattered around all over the place. It was evident that the foxes had found the birds before we did.

Rather than continue to tramp, I went to the downwind side of the woods on stand, and my two companions made a slow noisy drive through the brush. That did it. Pheasants by the dozens came sailing out of the cover, headed one and two at a time for all the little brush heaps and woodlots we had already hit.

Using my Browning two-shot automatic I was, in about ten minutes, able to down twenty-six pheasants. All but two were cocks. This true account is illustrative of the reasons I feel the now out of production Browning two-shot auto is the finest poaching shotgun ever made.

The principal this Browning works on is to hold one shell in the chamber and one shell in reserve in the bottom of the gun. When fired, the reserve shell is automatically snapped into the barrel as the spent shell is ejected. All the shooter has to do is push anqther loaded round into the empty reserve, a maneuver which can be accomplished with one hand without looking at the gun. Should both rounds be fired, the shell that is inserted in the reserve will automatically be carried up into the barrel ready to be fired. Everything is automatic.

The design never caught on because most people didn't understand them. For my money, however, the two shot auto is much faster and better than any pump or auto, even if the latter has an extended magazine.

As an aside, six and eight shot extended magazines are available for most pump and auto shotguns. See the ads in *Shotgun News* if this is a needed item.

There are a multitude of .22 rifles on the market that make good poaching guns. So many, in fact, that it's mostly a matter of personal preference as to which one is chosen.

Two to consider if one has not are the Marlin 39 A carbine and the Armalite AR-7.

The Marlin is a little short, heavy gun that lends itself well to being silenced. (The barrel can be taken off and threaded easily.) It is also a very accurate gun.

An AR-7 is ideal because of its size and the fact that it can be folded up for transport in a pack, or under a jacket. I have used one to shoot a good number of grouse in Canada where a pistol is a problem.

Personal prejudice enters in, but I have never found a satisfactory revolver. The only selling point a revolver has is its ability to hold the cartridges till emptied by the owner. Other than this, they are noisy, bulky, expensive and unreliable. The few revolvers I have owned were always breaking.

Silenced or unsilenced, I like the Ruger Standard auto or one of the Hi-Standards with removable barrel in a .22.

Single shot Thompson Contenders make good center fire pistols. They are available in a multitude of calibers.

The best poaching center fire pistol I ever saw was a Browning Hi Power with shoulder stock and an inside threaded barrel with silencer and foregrip. It was a very good, reliable gun with great potential as a meat getter. However, it was extremely expensive to build, was very illegal to own and took ammo that had to be custom loaded.

All of our rifles and shotguns have shorter barrels, slings and recoil pads. Even the .22's are equipped, if possible, so they can be easily carried and set down silently.

No pistol is ever carried outside of its flap holster. In most cases these must be custom made, but are worth the price in protection to the gun and as security from prying eyes. Some folks don't even recognize flap holsters as being a container for a gun.

Literally hundreds of good scopes are available in the general sporting goods market. I like wide angle, steel models and usually go for six power rather than four. A scope lasts me about two seasons of rugged use before I have to send it back for repair. Rather than bridle under this constraint, we simply purchased a reserve scope to rotate onto the gun while the broken sight is away at the factory.

Lights

We use three types of lights to shine game. Twelve volt, hand held spots that are usually carried in a vehicle, gas lanterns and portable battery operated flash lights. I don't like permanently mounted spot lights that hang conspicuously on a vehicle for every warden and sheriff in the county to see.

Several enterprising companies market hand-held spot lights. They are known as Pennsylvania Buck Lights, Q-Beams or Aircraft Lights. All run from a power cord that plugs into the cigarette lighter socket of a vehicle. Ownership of one light is plenty as they can be switched from car to truck to tractor or boat with ease.

Rating is done by candle power. No less than 200,000 candle power should be purchased. Newer, quarter million candle power units are definitely the light of preference if available.

Cost of a good unit is around $20.00. A cheaper, $12.00 outfit we purchased last winter fell apart after a week or so of use, leading me to believe that price may be a reasonable criterion to use in evaluating spot lights.

Acquiring a hand held spot in the 200,000 candle power range can be a chore. They just aren't available some places in the U.S.

Try automotive supply houses, pilots' shops at airports, or larger wholesale hardware outlets in the bigger cities. Thousands are sold each year. It just takes some persistence to locate the dealers who have them.

Coleman makes the best gasoline lantern that I know of. Most people have been around a pump-up lantern at some time in their life so there isn't much to say about using them. Shielding the light with a coffee can does seem to be a lost technique, though. Gas lights are dandy for spearing fish, providing light in a boat at night, for shining birds and many other activities. Their big problem is that they shine out indiscriminately, blinding the user, giving away his position without concentrating the beam for constructive use.

But cutting out the top of a regular three pound coffee can and slipping it over the top of the lantern, the poacher can make a dandy shade reflector. Remove about three inches on one side, give or take a little, and the lantern becomes a safe, controllable tool, valuable for many activities.

As far as I am concerned, the only type of flashlight worth carrying in the woods is a FULTON with rheostat beam or some other similar brand. I use the seven cell model with Alkaline D cells and a PR 20 bulb. Features that set this light apart from all others are the ability to go from a dim glow to a super bright spot by turning the rheostat, and an adjustable leather sling.

Again this flashlight is very difficult to find. Some hardware stores have them, but I have never seen one in a sporting goods shop. Pester the major sporting goods and hardware wholesalers or, that failing, write Buckeye Sports Supply, 2655 Harrison Avenue, S.W., Canton, Ohio 44707 and ask them.

Knives

Obviously a poacher needs a good knife. What constitutes a good knife is the subject of heated debate and not something I want to get into here. There are enough knives on the market to keep anyone happy, no matter what their desires. But I will offer a couple of suggestions.

Consider first the standard military survival belt knife. They are made out of good steel, and have a one-piece handle shank and blade. The grip is lacquered leather, quiet and easy to hold. There is a saw blade on top of the knife, which is handy for splitting the chest cavity on large game. The blade is hefty enough to beat through the pelvis bone of a moose or it can be driven like a nail and twisted without damage. The leather scabbard has a safety tie and a pocket in which to carry the touchup stone. On the army surplus market these knives sell for about $15.00, a price that I feel is incredibly cheap for what one gets.

I have gutted over fifty deer with one of these jewels.

Exploding Bullets

There are, at this writing, at least two firms that are manufacturing and marketing exploding bullets. Because of their extreme sensitivity, these bullets will detonate on impact with an empty aluminum beer can.

I can think of no practical poaching application for ammunition of this type.

Another recently developed bullet contains a liquid mercury core. The sectional density, and thus penetration, of these bullets is fantastic, but the mercury is a poison that will eventually kill the critter if the original shock of being shot does not. The mercury could also kill the poacher if he ate it.

Available Light Sources

In addition to silencers, another area of poacher technology got a tremendous boost from Vietnam. This is the field of fiber optic night vision devices.

Poachers should, at the very least, be knowledgeable about "available light scopes," as they are called, since they will definitely be encountering them in the hands of wardens in years to come.

Fiber optics combines space age chemistry and electronics to produce a night vision device that gathers available light and magnifies it 50,000 times. The image is seen directly through a one to six power scope or binocular and although greenish, is really quite good.

They work best on moonlit nights. But if one looks directly at a light source as intense as the moon, he may well burn the unit out. They will not work in the complete absence of light— underground, for instance.

At present, the scopes and binoculars cost about $2500.00 and up. They require batteries to operate and are constantly in need of service.

Cheaper units—$500.00 to $800.00—can be made in home work shops using surplus parts, but these are even more temperamental.

There is no doubt that there will be significant technological advances in the next ten years that will substantially reduce the cost of these devices. They are part of an entire area of communications technology that is on the verge of becoming what computers and calculators were yesterday.

In the meantime, those who want to buy a military fiber optic scope or binoculars can get them from:

Impossible Electronics Techniques, Inc.
Box 69
Wayne, PA 19087

or

Single Point
Box 5337
Orange, CA 92667

Those who want to build an available light device from surplus can get complete step by step instructions from:

Fantastic Research
Box 96568
Cleveland, OH 44101

I use a home-made available light spotting scope to hunt everything from deer to ducks. It is especially useful for calling coyotes and fox at night. I believe that one could go to the bank and borrow the money for one of these devices and make it back collecting animals and selling their hides. It works that well.

Problems with my unit relate to its constant need of maintenance and the fact that it is a spotting scope and not a gun sight. We have the unit strapped to a little .308 but it is still pretty inaccurate shooting.

BB Caps

A surprising number of hunters don't know about .22 BB caps. I use them extensively for animals in the one to three pound range at distances up to six yards. Carefully placed shots at these ranges will always make clean kills, but their real advantage is an almost complete lack of report.

In 1957 my dad and one brother lived near me for a time in a suburb of a large city in the mid-south. We all resided in an older tree-covered section of town where the lots were large and often surrounded by ornamental shrubs. All of this herbage created a tremendous environment for red and grey squirrels, rabbits, possums and coons, which had no enemies except the weather. They all existed in tremendous numbers.

One Sunday toward the middle of July I pulled in my drive and scared three big squirrels up a buckeye tree in our yard. It was a stinking hot mid-day, with no one around, so I dashed in the house and got my .22 rifle and a handful of BB caps.

By carefully screening my movements, I worked around to the tree which stood alone in the middle of the yard. In addition to the three squirrels I originally chased, there were four more already in the tree. One by one I started plunking them. The loudest noise was the bullet hitting. Five minutes later all seven were on the ground, reduced to possession, as they say in the trade.

After cleaning them I called Dad and brother to brag a little. "Why don't you," said I very magnanimously, "come over tonite and have some squirrel stew?" Everybody did, and it was then that I sprang the biggie on them about the squirrels coming from the back yard.

Not to be outdone, my brother shot nine squirrels in his own yard by the following Friday. Dad had a little tougher situation with a smaller yard and less cover, so he set out a few traps. Gradually they began to produce a nice flow of game.

During the next few months an intense rivalry developed, the three of us each trying to outdo the other.

I don't remember the exact number for Dad and Brother, but by Christmas I personally had collected 84 squirrels. This in my own yard in the middle of a large city. I won the contest, but as I remember the other two were also very competitive. Along wtih the squirrels Dad got a few coons and possums. All of this tremendous pile of game—about 250 squirrels plus other critters— came from a city area of not over two square miles.

Every one of the squirrels I got were with .22 cal. BB caps. The wonderful little ammunition that allows one to shoot in town without bothering with a silencer.

BB caps were first invented in 1845. They were the first cartridge ever used in firearms. Manufacturing specs through the years have varied, but generally they have 21 grain bullets in a rim fire case that is about two-thirds as long as a short. Some have powder and some rely on the primer for the only propellant.

Most .22 bolt action and single shot rifles will fire this ammo single shot. They can be dropped singly into some autos and lever actions, but they are so small it is sometimes a chore. Muzzle velocity is about 750 ft./sec., and accuracy is very good.

Thirty years ago Winchester and Remington stopped making

BB caps and one had to get them from Alcan or the two or three Canadian ammo manufacturers who still manufactured them. Lately, BB caps, or a variation of BB caps, are again available from Winchester and from CCi. They are called CB caps because the bullet is the same weight as a .22 short and the case body is also very similar to a short. The powder charge, however, is much reduced from that of a standard short.

Performance-wise, the CB is every bit as good as the harder-to-find imported BB cap and has the added plus of being functional in clip and tube magazines that will handle shorts.

Keep asking for them and eventually your sporting goods store will start carrying them. BB or CB caps are essential for the well-equipped poacher.

Hearing Aid

Believe it or not, an old hearing aid can make an effective poaching device. I have never used one because they are, in general, a bloody nuisance, but I have seen them work.

A friend used one over a period of quite a few years to hear deer in the woods, squirrels climbing trees, wardens approaching, ducks coming in to a call, and to spot bullfrogs. The latter was an incredible activity. We used to sit on the road at night in a car and he would stuff the thing in his ear and listen for the deep bass harrump of the frog. We located a number of productive little ponds using this method.

Should the reader ever run across an old hearing aid, it might be fun to experiment with a bit. Just turn it down before you shoot!

Improvised Guns

Home made guns have a place in this chapter, but the reader would probably agree that there is a fallacy with spending too much time discussing them.

Just about anyone worth his salt can make a better gun than I will describe in their modestly well-equipped home workshop. The item that can't be made easily at home is the ammunition.

Rather than worrying about improvised guns, I suggest spending more time on traps and snares. But for the record, here are two quick, easy firearms that anyone can make in a home workshop in four hours or less. They are crude but they will work.

Go to a junk yard or parking lot and secure a car radio antenna. On the way home, purchase a four inch door slide bolt . . . and pick up a few scraps of one inch square wood stock, some rubber bands and some electrical tape.

Select the section of antenna that will most closely allow a .22 cartridge to slide into it. Cut off about 6 inches of the antenna and 2 inches of the next size larger. Cut the 1 inch wood stock into two 6 inch pieces and make a "T" out of them with a 2 inch wood screw.

Tape the 6 inch section of antenna to the top of the T securely, leaving about 3 inches protruding over the front. Similarly, fasten the 2 inch section over the back of the barrel (6 inch) section, overlapping the barrel about 1 inch. This piece becomes the breech.

File out about two-thirds of the tip of the bolt on the door slide bolt so that it could crush the rim of a .22. This is the firing mechanism. Fasten the slide bolt immediately behind the barrel on the T block.

Loop rubber bands from the front of the T block to the slide bolt handle. Place a .22 in the barrel. Push the bolt handle up with the index finger and it will slam forward, detonating the round.

The device can be dressed up a bit for appearances.

A very serviceable .12 gauge shotgun can be made as follows: Purchase 2 feet of 3/4 inch pipe and another 1 foot section of one inch galvanized pipe. Also needed are 3 feet of 2x6 pine board, a 6 inch piece of 2x4 and a lot of electrical tape.

Mount the 6 inch piece on the 3 foot section of 2x6 about 1 foot from the end on the narrow edge of the board. This piece serves as a breech block. A nail is driven into the breech block, and cut off about 3/8 inch from the board. This is the firing pin.

Mount the 1 inch section of pipe on the board, using the electrical tape. Call this the breech slide.

Put a .12 gauge shell in the 2 foot 3/4 inch pipe and slide the pipe back into the 1 inch pipe. When pulled sharply back the 3/4 inch pipe will carry the shot shell back into the nail which will detonate the primer and fire the gun.

In real life this is a pretty good gun. It can be equipped with a safety and foregrip to help control the weapon, making a very accurate, rugged firearm.

Guerrilla fighters all over the world have used these for years.

Automatic Weapons

Full auto weapons are a lot of fun, but as far as I can determine, have no practical application for the poacher.

They are inaccurate, noisy, and use lots of ammo. People who hear or see them are immediately frightened and alerted.

5

TWO WAY RADIOS

Slowly and carefully, I pulled the antenna on my walkie-talkie. It was a beautiful clear fall day. The sun beat down on the small fern patch where I was laying, and it was tempting to forget the whole thing, roll over and snooze.

"Red Raspberry," I called, "this is the Purple Turnip—come back."

"Purple Turnip, this is Model T," cracked the radio. "Raspberry is with me here by the car, what's your 10-20?"

"In on top of the high knoll just west of Monroe," I replied. "Two duded up bird hunters are coming off the county road up the brush draw that runs south."

"O.K., Turnip," he broke in, "I know the place."

"Well," I continued, "if you guys get your lazy asses on over to the McGraw place and come up through that little draw where all the big oaks are, we may be able to poach some of the old man's turkeys."

"Those bird hunters are going to move 'em out of the thicket and I'm perfect to keep them from going over the top."

"Roger, Turnip, we are on our way."

Probably forty minutes elapsed till the next call.

"Turnip, we hid the car and are in place now. How does it look?"

"Great," I responded, "the dudes are lower than I like but they're still a thousand yards from you guys. Any signs of the turkeys?"

"Yeah, we might have 'em coming. Can you swing down the hill farther and move 'em a little?"

I worked through a sumac tangle and into a little draw where I lost sight of things for a few minutes. The three or four gunshots I heard were probably ours, but I wasn't sure.

"Model T or Red Raspberry?" I called, "any sign of our game?"

"Yep, didn't you hear us shoot, we got at least two. Two it is, we got two turkeys."

Sounds like a great way to go, doesn't it? Use hand-held, portable radios to coordinate activities and keep track of the opposition. It would be, too, except the previous account is pure unadulterated bullshit. The incident never occurred that way, and never will if I'm involved. One does not use handles, broadcast positions, make long transmissions, admit what they are doing, or even talk in anything but a whisper when using walkie-talkies. In addition, it is foolish to expect as much reliability from radios as I attributed to them in the previous fictional account.

Portable two-way radios have great potentials as poaching tools. Unfortunately, two way radios are erratic, unpredictable and difficult to use. They break down often, are expensive to maintain, and unreliable to the point that I feel I am lucky to get thirty percent of the potential out of the damn things.

There is no mechanical-electrical device in existence that elicits a stronger love-hate emotion from me than do portable two-way radios. I have used them now for fourteen years including nine different brands, and my response is still the same. An expert poacher often has to use them, but what a pain in the ass!

There are two distinct aspects to successful use of radios to secure game. They are gathering the necessary equipment, and then training oneself and his crew to use it.

Let's take a look at equipment first.

When referring to a portable two-way radio, one probably has a hand-held unit in mind that most laymen would identify as a walkie-talkie.

There are a few mobile units—those designed to operate in a car or truck—that can be adapted to portable use.

Midland, Realistic and Radio Shack, for instance, make a case and battery holder that will house one of their standard car/truck CB transceivers. The unit has a wide carrying strap, is heavy and cumbersome and uses lots of batteries.

On the plus side, it has great range and better-than-average reliability. I don't presently use this type of radio because of the purchase cost and the weight, but may go to them in the future as they become even more reliable and smaller.

Much preferred, at least till these mobile rigs are perfected, are the small hand-held units about the size of a quart milk container.

Of these there are several basic types. Most reliable of the bunch are the "ham" units used by amateur radio operators. They are well constructed, reliable and, by reason of the bands they operate on, have small, easily protected antennas.

Range is very good and since all are either one or two watts, the power consumption is low. All will transmit and receive in normal operation from ten to twelve hours before recharging, over a five to ten mile range.

On the face of it, these radios would seem to be the most ideal choice. But from the poacher's standpoint, they are the worst possible unit for outdoor work.

"Red Raspberry," crackles the ham radio, "this is Model T, what is your position?"

What happens? Since these radios are commonly on two, six or ten meter bands and have tremendous range, every ham in the country is going to drop in on the conversation. People who have nothing better to do in life than talk on their radio may try to chat. But even more important, unless you have a ham operator's license, broadcasting on one of these frequencies is illegal.

Now I am not given to sitting around and worrying about such matters, but in this case perhaps a moment of reflection is in order.

Without a rudimentary knowledge of these radios and their operation, and without a call letter designation that every ham gives out every time he utters a word, it is going to be immediately obvious that you don't belong. Like any other narrow interest group, ham radio operators are peculiar. One of their peculiarities is a disdain for the illegal non-conformist masquerading as one of them. Use radios very much any place at all, even the deep mountains of Montana, and there will be a veritable army of irate amateurs trying to get a fix on your position so they can be the first to report you to the Federal Communications Commission.

Radio repeaters are another related headache. Electronic miracles that they are, repeaters are black boxes that sit on high buildings, towers and mountain tops. They pick up weak signals from below and send them to God-only-knows where. My little call to a buddy on a deer drive north of Altoona might be broadcast all over Pennsylvania, New Hampshire, upper New York State and Maryland.

Obviously I have learned to live with the sheriff, the farmer and the warden, but thrown in the FCC and a million anxious underlings, and I say let's look at something else.

55

Other lesser problems also preclude use of ham frequency portable radios. They are expensive—about $250 per unit—and difficult to have serviced. Large cities do have big expensive repair shops, but even using these can arouse suspicion since most hams do their own service work.

AM or FM business radios are the next logical step. They are incredibly small, very rugged, have good range and low power consumption. They are also a bit expensive. Price on these starts at around $200.00 and goes up to just about anything you want to pay. A pair, in other words, will cost about $400.00, but generally two radios are not enough to hunt with.

All walkie-talkies need service. Business band AM or FM transceivers are no exception, and this is probably the principal reason I don't use them. The original purchase price may be tolerable and they won't break down as fast as CB's, but when they do, the repair tab is a lot higher and good servicemen far fewer.

No test is required to operate business band radios, but there is a rather extensive form to fill out. One must have a business related reason for using the units and always broadcast the assigned call code before and after each transmission.

A few years back I used a set of GE business portables with reasonably good success. But I eventually sold them and bought standard CB's. We were the only ones on our assigned frequency so nobody walked on us, but every time we opened our mouths I felt anyone listening knew exactly what we were doing.

It is our custom to use a peculiar jargon when out with our radios, not at all related to the handle call code situation CBer's use. Nevertheless an astute listener might decide something is going on, especially if they were suspicious to start with.

Checking to find out who in a given area is licensed on a predetermined frequency is easy, so neglecting to give the call code doesn't help much. About the only way I would use business AM/FM radios again would be to purchase them for a business far removed from my common area of operation.

Back home it becomes extremely important to find a serviceman who will work on the FM business radios. Even better is to find someone who will change their frequencies and not ask too many questions. After this the only problem remaining is to be double damn sure the frequency the radios is on is not somebody's assigned business frequency, and that if a legitimate license holder does start complaining, that you turn your radios off and not use them again in that area, ever. It won't do to change crystals (frequency) because those who want to listen will do so on a scanner—a device that covers all frequencies in a given band.

Sources for ham and business radios are not unduly difficult to find, although it is a bit optimistic to walk into a radio shop and expect to buy needed walkie-talkies off the shelf. Look in the yellow pages under Radio Communication Equipment and Supplies. Almost any city of 50,000 or more will have several listings. Wholesale catalogs are available through dealers who advertise in *Ham Radio Magazine* or in *Radio-Electronics*. Once a decision is made on equipment, it is wise to check these two sources for prices.

Surplus military walkie-talkies are the last category of radios that I have used. Other than some obsolete back pack types, the average poacher is likely to have his choice of an AN/PRC-6 or an AN/PRC-6T, or some variation of these.

The latter is the preferred unit since it is transistorized and will accept standard commercial batteries. Surplus electronic shops are good places to look for these units or refer to the ads in *Soldier of Fortune* magazine and the *Shotgun News*.

Price for the 6T is about $100 to $150, depending on the extent of reconditioning and guarantee. Straight 6 radios cost about $35.00 each, but unless you are a radio technician, worth about that much if the other guy will agree to keep them.

Military radios are wonderfully rugged and reliable but the big hurdle again is service. They will break down and unless some preliminary homework is done regarding parts and repair, the units will shortly be inoperative and worthless.

AN/PRC-6T radios, depending on the crystal chosen, operate on an assigned military frequency. This sounds dangerous, but my experience indicates otherwise. The military has a tremendous number of frequencies, so the likelihood of talking on them is not nearly as great as it first seems. When operating surplus equipment I find it wise to listen for chatter first before going on the air. Should there be traffic, switch crystals immediately. Be similarly alert when using the radios in the field. Don't try to share with the military; they are poor sports about such things.

This leaves us with the least of many evils, the hand-held portable Citizen Band radio. They are the radios I now use and, all things considered, probably the poacher's best choice in communication equipment.

In the past, portable CB's came in all kinds and grades, from a two-for-$12.95 kids' toy to overdone 40-channel monstrosities selling for upwards of $200.00. Industry sources estimate that over three million of the better CB walkie-talkies have been sold in the United States.

In my estimation, no one has yet made a truly workable, reliable CB portable. You may want to ask them why anyone would want to fool with radios that can cause so much grief.

The answer is simple. A good professional poacher can't be without two way communications, and the citizen band option is the best there is despite its shortcomings. It's the art of the possible all over again, more things being possible with CB than with any other rig.

Because the Citizen Band industry is in a state of disorder, acquiring radios is no longer easy. I believe we will eventually see the advent of sophisticated new packages that can be used to turn car/truck mobiles into portables. Perhaps this is all for the best, since the mobile conversions that I have used are much more rugged and reliable than traditional walkie-talkies. It may be time to phase out the hand-held portable for something better.

So until the time when mobile/portable conversion packages are readily available again, the poacher will have to locate some of the few remaining new units still on dealers' shelves or scrounge around and buy in the used market.

Portable transceivers are rated by power starting at 1/10 of a watt on up to five watts, the legal maximum. Wattage is a unit of measure used to describe one aspect of a CB's circuit, but has little to do with the overall quality of the radio itself.

Two watt portables can have a stronger signal, better reception and more durability than five watt models. What matters is the total circuit and most of the time that's difficult to evaluate.

As a general rule I feel that five watt models having a battery level meter, six channel capacity, with a facility to plug in an outside battery charger are superior, but this is only a very general rule. I would never purchase any radio outside the top third of the price range.

There is a form inside the box of every new CB. It provides a means of registering the radio and securing a set of call letters to be used when operating the unit. Those who don't fill out the form are treated about the same as those who do. You won't be assigned a number if you fail to complete the paperwork, and if you intend to use call letters for your work, you are reading the wrong book.

58

Millions of people make billions of transmissions each day without call letters. When you make yours no one will notice. Government estimates indicate that there are now over 25 million CB radios in the U.S. That's one for every nine people and at times I swear they are all on the air at the same time.

In part this is a blessing. With all that chatter, it's impossible for authorities to monitor all that goes on. A poacher's transmission is beautifully lost in a wall of nameless, faceless, incoherent verbal garbage. At times it is so bad that important conversations are lost. But with a good CB it's fairly easy for a poacher to switch channels and go on with the business at hand.

During the last year we used our radios in the mountains of Montana, Utah and Idaho. On the mountain tops we received transmissions from as far away as Georgia and Mexico. Down in the deep valleys we had the airwaves to ourselves.

CB radio, by nature of its design, has a generally restricted range. We count on a three mile range from portable to portable. To a car or truck radio, the range is better, but the poacher still doesn't have to assume he is talking to the whole world every time he cracks the mike. This, I feel, is a major advantage of a CB radio.

The last time I bought radios I got a total of five units. Most of the time there are three of us out together, but occasionally we have a fourth. The extra radio is a back-up since one radio always seems to be in the shop.

Past records indicate that I spend about twenty percent of the radio's original purchase price each year for replacement antennas, speakers, transistors, transformers, rechargeable batteries and switches. CB portables seem to need almost constant maintenance, but at least good CB repairmen can be found just about anyplace. Tiny midwestern villages of 6000 often have someone who can work on them. Service people are everyplace, and in big cities one can even find factory authorized stations.

In the final analysis this is why I use CB's—service is available and my transmissions are anonymous.

Buying A CB Portable

Start with the criteria previously mentioned. Five watts, battery meter, internal charger and either three or six channel capacity, in the top third of the price range.

Some units have a one or two watt power saver switch. The user can set the radio on five watts and push a signal through a lot of green brush, over the top of a million other CBers and reach a partner who may have the squelch on his radio misadjusted as a result of busting through a thicket. After the initial contact is made, the radio is switched back to low power to talk. I believe this feature is desirable.

Usually channel selectors on portables are marked ABCD, etcetera. One set of channel crystals comes with the radio. Others must be purchased at a cost of $4.00 to $6.00 per radio.

Crystals for handhelds are now available for channels 1 through 40. Channels above 19 are not used as often, but that is not a consideration. I install two crystal sets (each radio has a transmit and receive crystal) on channels below 19 and two above in each radio.

Avoid heavily used frequencies such as 9, 11 or 19. In some areas, special use channels come into being. If you don't know, ask a CBer what places to avoid. Wise poachers don't end up on the same frequency as the local volunteer fire department.

Install the crystals in illogical order. Later, when discussing use in the field, it will become obvious that "dropping from C to A" for instance, on the channel selector can well mean going from channel 4 to 33. Don't install the crystals in ascending or descending order.

At an average of $20.00 per set for crystals, times four to six sets, the radios now cost considerably more than the original purchase price, but there is more.

Should one be able to win the confidence of a good serviceman, it is possible to drop one channel of the radio's frequency completely out of the 11 meter band into the top of the 10 meter range. If feasible, I strongly urge that this be done. Range and reception are much better and most CB monitors won't cover 10 meters. Used sparingly and with discrimination, that channel can be an ace in the hole when the going gets rough. The last time I had this done it cost $7.50 per unit. Well worth three times the price.

Batteries in my radios usually go dead about 4:00 in the afternoon after a hard day's use. It helps a bit to transmit on two watts whenever possible, but one is still faced with an expensive battery proposition if the units are used enough to justify themselves in the first place.

Nicad rechargeables are the only practical solution.

Most walkie-talkies use eight AA penlite cells. Common lead-zinc batteries last about two hours. Alkaloid types last one day and

Nicad rechargeables go up to about 500 chargings and will hold on about as long as alkaloid cells between chargings. Nicads cost $2.00 to $3.00 each. Ten are required and they are not permanent. I have had some cells last two years and others only four weeks. Perhaps every two weeks or so during their heavy use period, I have a radio that will quit transmitting and only receive. When this happens, I fire it down to the shop where the batteries are tested and the defective cells replaced. On the bright side, I deduct the repairs from my income tax as a cost of doing business. I am an outdoor photographer and use the radios to do my work, so Uncle Sam picks up the tab.

Chargers for the battery packs vary tremendously in price. Some start around $6.00 and others cost close to $40.00. Ask before buying and be sure of the price and compatability.

I use a heavy duty, homemade case for my radio. The case is stitched up out of double buckskin and has a hip length strap sewed down the entire side of the case. There is a piece of rug pad in the bottom to cushion the unit when it is dropped. The flap protects the speaker and controls from rain, mud and snow. Some cases that come with radios are worthless.

Standard telescoping steel antennas give the best transmission /reception performance. However, they break off with maddening frequency so I generally give up and replace them with a "rubber duckie" flexible neoprene antenna. Rubber duckies cut transmission ability about forty percent and occasionally come loose off the radio, so take your pick. Cost for one of these is about $10.00.

Use Of CB's In The Field

Contrast the following true story with the one heading the chapter. It illustrates the system we use on the air when poaching.

Tranmission	What Is Happening
	The group of four poachers move out. They are going to drive a thirty acre woods behind a small country church while service is in progress. The drop has been made, positions assigned, and the men move off to their stations. Only three hunters have radios.
"300 radio check"	The drive leader is establishing radio contact with the two standers before they are out of sight.

"257 check" "308 check"	Rather than names, the group uses rifle calibers to identify themselves. Transmissions are very brief and done in a whisper.
"Drop to D"	Perhaps because of other traffic, someone has called for a change to another channel. Volume on the walkie-talkies must be kept extremely low or the game will be spooked. Receiving a message becomes an art requiring almost a sixth sense to know when someone is trying to get through.
"300 check" "257 check" "308 check"	Miracle of miracles, we have all switched channels and reestablished contact. A sign of an experienced well-trained crew who have worked together often before.
"257 in position" (pause) "257 radio check" "257—300 come back" (pause) "257 check"	The guy with the .257 Roberts is in position. He is ready to start the drive but can't raise anybody else.
"300—257 check"	Radio operators must continually play with the squelch control. 300 is finally receiving 257 and acknowledges.
"257 in place"	Everyone on the hunt knows that 257 and the man without a radio are in their predetermined location. The drive can start.
"300—308 let's go" "308"	The hunt starts with two men driving and two men about a mile from the church woodlot where they know the deer will cross. Distance is their ally. They don't want to shoot behind the church.
"308—300" (pause) "308—300" (pause) "308—300"	308 wants to tell 300 where he is but can't get through.

"300—308" "308 go"	300 decides to call 308n and gets through because of 308's previous efforts at tuning his radio.
"I'm about fifty yards in overlooking Sandalfoot."	Sandalfoot is a town about fifteen miles away. The town he is overlooking is Kruger but everyone in the hunting party knows that. People with long ears who might be listening in on the conversation think action is 15 miles from where it really is.
"Anything?" "No cars"	Never mention the game. Cars are the deer. A truck might be an elk if there are any around and a bike a coyote. Use common terms.

15 minutes later . . .

"300—308. I am through"	
"300—308. There are two cars headed your way doing well.	300 has jumped a buck and a doe at the east edge of the woodlot at the end of the drive. He hopes that driver 308 has heard him.
"300—who can see the cars?" "308—looks like you better ask them for directions"	308 acknowledges but doesn't know yet that there is a buck and a doe; only that two deer are headed his way. The deer have decided to stay in the woods rather than go ahead of the drivers to the stander. 308 is likely to get a shot.
"257" "Can't help you 257, stay in touch"	257 has heard the transmissions and knows that for the moment he is out of the picture. One of the drivers talks back very briefly.

Perhaps a thirty minute silence ensues as the drivers jockey around to get a shot at the deer. Church is out and the slamming doors keep the deer from going west out of the woods, but make the hunters very nervous.

"308—300 look"	300 misses that call, but the standers on the hill know the deer are moving back toward the first drivers who originally jumped them.

"300 the car is o.k. but not running. See if you can swing west and watch."	The first drive who originally drove the deer over to the second driver dropped a huge buck whitetail as the deer tried to clear the woods but were caught between the two hunters who had reversed the drive and cornered the quarry.
	The hunter who didn't shoot swings in behind the church to watch for company. Obviously the worshippers have heard the shot, but one round is hard to locate.
	The shooter confirms the kill and pulls the animal into a small thicket and dusts the trail. He then moves off a hundred or so yards, watching his back trail and the edge of the woods.
	As he backs off, the successful poacher hears a noise behind him. There is a small, low, brush clearing. Slowly he takes a position behind a large tree and waits.
	After about thirty seconds a large doe moves a few feet at the far edge of the clearing.
	Slowly the hunter raises his rifle and puts the crosshairs of his scope on a small opening ahead of the deer. Supported by the tree, the hunter waits.
"257—300. Check"	The deer hears the radio noise and lunges ahead. As soon as there is hair in the scope, the hunter touches off a round.
	A second deer drops, shot through the ribs on an angle. The bullet exits the brisket.
	Quickly the hunter stops the deer from thrashing and cuts its throat.
	Two deer are down now and the hunters have to assume someone is going to report them.
"300—308. Please stop in next time you're by and help me with these cars."	The transmission is made but never goes out. The batteries are dead on 300's radio. Futilely the shooter tries to raise his buddy.

"308—300. What is your 10-20?"	308 has raised the standers but still doesn't know what is happening.
"308—257. Can we help?"	He swings past the church and sees that no one seems to be paying much attention to the shooting. Slowly and silently the second driver moves away from the church through the woods, watching intently.
"308—257. Hold on"	Walking east from the little church, 308 meets 300 who explains what happened.
"257 come to the fence. Drop to B"	The two remaining radio men make plans to get together and also change channels again. One man watches while the other guts the deer. Together they drag them into a thick draw at the wood's edge. By then the standers have joined the main group.

Radio silence is maintained for at least an hour and it begins to get dark.

	Two of the hunters take one functional radio and walk to the road about 3/4 of a mile away. They find an old farm road and determine that it is safe to bring in a car.
"22—radio check"	Shortly after dark the pick-up person—a well-dressed woman in a clean, late-model car—calls on her mobile rig. She tries from three or four miles out on a pre-arranged channel. After a bit she raises the two waiting near the road.
"257—22. We need help loading a car. Be on the north road near our last spot."	The pick-up person knows the hunters are waiting on the road near where she left them off, and probably have something. A small flashlight glows in the window of the car. Only a few cars are on the small gravel farm road now, but the marker is an added precaution. As the pickup car approaches, the two men on the road wave it off on to the lane and into the trees. One man rides along, the other with the radio watches at the road.

Both deer are laid in plastic in the trunk. A hunter with clean hands—no blood—takes off his jacket and cap and exchanges them for a clean, neat sport jacket in the car.

On an "All Clear" signal from the road, the car leaves.

As soon as the car has dropped off the deer, the woman returns with another vehicle for the remaining hunters.

Recapping the above account, a good radio hunting team will **NEVER:**

1. Make long transmissions.
2. Stay on the same frequency for any length of time.
3. Let it be at all obvious what is happening.
4. Make a series of transmissions one after the other.
5. Use names.
6. Identify places recognizable to anyone but the hunters unless to obviously mislead listeners.
7. Get panicky if the radios fail.
8. Turn up the volume past a whisper.
9. Come on the air after a shot unless it is absolutely necessary.
10. Say anything about changing channels or be specific about which channels one is going to. Always use the ABC type designation.

Good radio work hunting comes from good practice and can't replace a good basic knowledge of the outdoors. Two way radios are a damn fine piece of auxiliary equipment for the poacher but also one of the most difficult to use properly.

6
POISONS AND EXPLOSIVES

My purpose in presenting this chapter is to suggest some poacher's uses for a few common chemical compounds.

I am fully aware of the fact that an entire book could be written on the subjects of poisons and explosives. I have found through the years that most of the more exotic mixtures are of little use no matter if one is a saboteur, anarchist, sadist, democrat or just a poor poacher trying to get by in a hostile and crazy world.

For this reason the items mentioned here are relatively few and not particularly obscure. On the other hand, they are not difficult to obtain and, given a modest amount of common sense, not unduly difficult to use.

Before starting in, two stories come to mind. One is true. The other may be apocryphal—the reader will have to decide.

It seems that in a small southern commuity there was a fellow with an outstanding reputation as a fisherman. Every day that he went out fishing, he came back with his limit of bass, sunfish, perch or whatever species he tried for.

The fellow was a tight-mouthed sun-of-a-gun so no one knew what he used for bait or where he even fished. Since the fellow's success was so outstanding, the Fish & Game Department decided that it was important to document his methods for posterity. They sent in one of their best undercover agents who spent months working on the poor old gent trying to persuade him to arrange a joint fishing trip.

Finally after an interminable amount of coaxing, the secret agent finally got an invitation to go fishing. The next day they drove to a secluded lake, climbed in an old boat and rowed out to a good spot, whereupon the old duffer took a stick of dynamite out of his pack, lit it up and threw it over board.

It exploded and the fish started floating to the surface.

The agent looked on for a brief moment, then sucking in a breath he whipped out his badge. "You know," he lectured, "that it's illegal to fish with dynamite and now as a representative of the law I am going to have to arrest you," he said.

The fisherman sat there quietly. Finally he took out another stick of dynamite and lit it. No sooner was it going well than he handed it to the warden.

"Well," the wise old gent said, "are you going to just sit there and talk all day, or are you going to fish?"

The other account is of a fellow I knew as a young man, who dabbled a bit in explosives.

One day he rowed his boat out on a small pond. In it he had several sticks of dynamite and a jug of corn whiskey. The fellow sat out on the pond for probably an hour drinking the corn and enjoying the beautiful spring day.

Finally he decided to fish, and capped up two charges. He lit the first and threw it overboard, but didn't let loose of the second in time. The blast took his arm off at the elbow. It was a good and valuable lesson which I never forgot.

None of the chemicals I describe here are completely safe. So if you are a klutz, *don't fool with them*!

Quick Lime

Most poachers have heard of lime. They know that lime is the white powdery material that gardeners put in their soil to make it sweet and that farmers have to put on their fields to balance the nutrient level.

While it's nice to start with some basic information, the facts relating to lime are jumbled by use of colloquial terms and must be clarified. Technically speaking, lime is CaO. This is an oxide of calcium. Calcium is a metal, but it is never found in its pure form in nature and is very unstable, even in the CaO state.

Calcium carbonate—$CaCO_3$—is found abundantly in nature. Limestone rock, shells and marl are all made up of $CaCO_3$. When a gardener or farmer orders a load of "lime" they are actually ordering a load of ground up $CaCO_3$. The common term 'lime" is inaccurate but it is the one people use.

Common limestone—$CaCO_3$—is heated to produce what chemists refer to as lime—CaO. CaO is also known as quick lime, unslacked lime or burnt lime. It is this lime that poachers are interested in, but one more lesson in chemistry is important before coming back to CaO.

Masons and other people who work with cements, plaster and mortar use a product they call slacked lime. To add to the confusion, they often drop the "slacked" part and just say they are using lime. This is another product again, made by combining CaO with water. The result is $Ca(OH)_4$ or calcium hydroxide.

Limestone and slacked lime are very easy to acquire. They can be purchased in building supply outlets, farm stores, garden shops and even at places like K-Mart and Penney's during the spring planting season.

Unslacked lime is difficult but not impossible to buy most places in the U.S. At least one store seems to carry it in most larger cities unless local laws make this impossible. In Chicago, for instance, the Mob used CaO in the past to dispose of bodies. As a result the city regulates CaO sale. Other than Chicago, I have always been able to locate a source of quick lime by getting on the phone and calling around. The material is used to clean out outdoor toilets. I tell the clerk that's what I want it for and ask if there are any restrictions on sales.

Another reason lime (CaO) is not carried in every corner hardware store is that it is difficult to store. When mixed with water, it expands about three times in volume and gives off a great deal of heat. The bags it is kept in must be heavy, sound affairs not given to tearing or spilling. CaO will cause horrible caustic burns if spilled on wet flesh and not cleaned immediately.

For poachers CaO has two uses, one of which is very important. If explosives were ever unavailable, for instance, CaO could be used for some demolition applications.

The method is as follows. It should be thoroughly understood and then carefully and meticulously complied with.

Collect a number of one gallon glass jugs. These must be glass and similar to those used for vinegar, wine or apple cider with a small neck and secure cap. Clean the jugs thoroughly and then dry them out till they are absolutely bone dry. No moisture can remain in the jug.

You must have about five pounds of clean dry pea gravel for each jug. Five pounds is about two #6 peacans full. Dry this gravel over a low fire, and then pour it lukewarm into the gallon jugs. There should be a good healthy inch of gravel in the bottom of the jug. At first it is advisable to test the gravel to see if it is heavy enough to sink the jug. Cork the glass up tightly and float it in a barrel or tub. There must be enough gravel in the jug to sink it without hesitation.

Having done all this, dry the jug again and carefully pour in one #6 can of CaO in each of the prepared jugs. Replace the cap, making sure that the jug is sealed air tight. The explosive jug can now be safely stored till it is time to go fishing.

I usually take two or three of the jugs with me in the boat. They will arouse no suspicion until used.

To prepare a jug for use, uncork it and hold its mouth just below the surface of the water. Allow about a quart of water to pour in. Cap the jug quickly and let it sink to the bottom.

Properly done, the jug will go off with a very nice blast in about one minute. The concussion will kill fish just about on a par with a one stick dynamite charge. Quickly collect the fish as they float to the top with a spear or net.

I don't believe it is advisable to use these lime bombs in less than 5 feet of water. At least I have never tried it in shallow water.

By being very careful, I have been able to shoot several large areas in rivers with lime jugs. It is tricky to set the charge standing on the bank, but it can be done.

Deep gravel pits are ideal targets. Often I have trouble making dynamite go off in water more than forty feet deep, but the lime jugs always work. The only problem, as most skilled outdoorsmen know, is that there aren't very many fish at those depths much of the year. Still, it's interesting to see the flash and, after a moment or two, watch the water boil.

Shrewd readers will agree that there could be a number of applications for the lime jug technology. I really don't know precisely why the jug bombs explode so violently. Is it simply the glass jug coming apart under heavy CO_2 gas pressure, or does the heat crack the glass and chemical react violently with the water?

I have never tried to explode a lime jug on land because it would send glass shards flying everywhere. Perhaps an experiment on land would be revealing, if it could be arranged safely.

Another use of CaO is to deteriorate and destroy bones, feet and other game refuse.

Dig a hole in the ground about three times the size of the refuse. The hole should be located in an area free of surface water but not in a place that is arid and dry without any ground moisture at all. Put the refuse in the hole, cover it with about an inch of CaO and cover with dirt. Complete breakdown of the material takes thirty to forty-five days.

I have always been able to locate and purchase all the lime I needed. However, if it ever become impossible to find CaO, I believe the material could be made at home by roasting common agricultural grade ground limestone $CaCO_3$. In years to come, this may be very important to know.

Bird Lime

Liming, or catching birds with a sticky substance, is a very old and effective technique. Liming has been done in England for hundreds of years to trap large numbers of pests, and to catch robins and blackbirds for food.

In this country, liming has a limited but useful application. It is of no use, for instance, on larger birds like quail, pheasants or even pigeons, but it will rid an area of sparrows very nicely. Other application for small birds, bats and reptiles are obvious.

The ancient recipe for bird lime is to boil down the bark of holly to make a thin but very, very sticky paste. I have never tried this recipe, principally because I have never had a good supply of holly bark.

A better, easier way is to buy a gallon of linseed oil and boil it slowly for at least 8 hours till it gets very sticky. Coat this stuff on a limb, wire or ledge and it will hold little birds like flypaper. Depending on how much dirt is in the air and how many birds step in the stuff, it will last from three days to about two months.

Bird lime does not work well during the winter.

Iron And Meal

I have occasionally had problems with sparrows or pigeons in the barn and robins in the orchard or berry patch.

By far and away the best material to take care of this is a mixture of one part corn meal, one part flour and 1/4 part fine steel filings. I get the filings from a local machine shop where I pick it up and sort it out with the help of a 150 pound-pull magnet.

By keeping trays of the stuff out where the birds can get it, they keep themselves under control. The poison is not fast acting or dramatic. Don't expect it to work the day the cherries get ripe.

On the other hand there won't be dead birds scattered around the neighborhood that can be collected up and sent to a lab. If they are identified as having been killed by strychnine or some other poison, it can cause you all kinds of trouble.

Potassium Chlorate Powder

The secret of potassium chlorate powder is an important one that the reader should remember. This powder is interchangeable with black powder on a basis of about one to one or slightly less, and is every bit as good as black powder when properly used.

In the past there have been two separate occasions when I didn't have needed gunpowder, but was able to make enough potassium chlorate powder to get by with. These were both when I was overseas, but I have had ample opportunity to experiment with it in this country.

The powder is made by taking equal volumes of $KClO_3$ (potassium chlorate) and sugar and melting them together. Common table sugar can, of course, be purchased in any super market. Potassium chlorate is bought off the shelf at the drug store.

Place the sugar in a heavy iron pan as if to make fudge and add a few drops of water. Heat this mixture slowly till the sugar completely melts and heat the mixture slowly to a temperature of about $250°$ F.

Take the sugar from the fire and stir vigorously till the temperature of the melted sugar drops to about $150°$ F, or the point where it is just possible to put one's finger in the mixture without undue pain.

Stir in the finely divided $KClO_3$ slowly and evenly. If there is a hint of spark, wait till the whole thing cools down a bit more before continuing to add the potassium chlorate.

When the blending has been completed, turn the mixture out on a smooth hard surface to cool and dry. I like to use a piece of old plywood for this purpose.

After the powder has cooled, it should be off white in color and fairly hard. When rolled or crushed, it should break up in small pieces. If the stuff has the consistency of cake frosting, or fudge, the sugar was not melted sufficiently. If it is very rock like, the sugar may have been heated too much.

The reader is well advised to experiment with a small batch the first time out.

Grinding the powder is not dangerous as far as I can tell. I have never been able to make the stuff go off from a blow.

I screen the powder in an old double steel door screen. As with black powder, the grain size determines the burn rate. The smaller grains become shotgun and pistol powder, the large grains .45-.70 powder. A second, very fine screening can be made, producing a powder suitable for use in .22 rim fire cartridges.

These .22's work fine but are much more powerful than factory ammo. I want my .22's to be slower and quieter and therefore don't have much use for sugar powder reloads.

In muzzle loaders, the sugar powder replaces black on a one to one basis, or try one part black powder to three parts sugar powder.

Chlorate powder does have its drawbacks. It isn't effective in high power, high velocity guns. Also it can be hard to detonate. I tried some experiments with sugar powder pipe bombs and got poor results. The sugar powder doesn't burn fast enough under modest compression to produce a bomb. As an aside, some of the powder can be dissolved in water and used to soak heavy cotton string. The result is a reasonably good fuse.

Should the reader ever use potassium chlorate powder in a gun, it should immediately be cleaned. Sugar powder will start corroding gun metal in a matter of hours.

Ammonia Iodine Primer

Another stopgap item, only desirable if regular manufactured primers are unavailable. The explosive is tricky to handle, and I recommend making only small batches of it with extreme caution.

The explosive part of the primer is made by soaking iodine crystals in ammonia. Both are available from the corner drug store, but I wouldn't buy them simultaneously or even at the same place.

For starters take about two ounces of iodine crystals and cover them with approximately three ounces of pure ammonia. All this should be done in a wide mouth glass jar that can be sealed, but that is easy to take the materials in and out of. I try to screen or sort the crystals before starting. In some cases they will need to be crushed. The best size is about half the size of a pea, but a number of smaller crystals can be held together with Elmer's glue to achieve this size.

After about three days take one of the smaller crystals out and allow it to dry on an absorbent towel in a well ventilated warm room. Don't try to hurry the drying process. After the crystal has dried, put on a pair of cotton gloves and carefully throw the crystal at a clean, hard cement floor. If it goes off with a fairly sharp report, the material is ready. If not, pour off the liquid and put new ammonia over the iodine crystals.

It is important at this point to continue to test and experiment. Perhaps a third washing with ammonia will be necessary.

After the crystals have reached the stage where they explode satisfactorily, they can be placed in small tinfoil cups for use as primers in a muzzle loading firearm. TV dinners have heavier tinfoil. I have had good success punching out this material for primer cups.

I always leave the iodine in the ammonia till the day before I intend to use it. This method seems slightly safer.

Although I have never tried it, I believe a fairly good improvised explosive package could be made by using a rat trap for a striker, ammonia iodine for a primer and potassium chlorate for the main explosive.

Ammonium Nitrate

This material is used in large quantities as a commercial explosive. It is very common and maybe familiar to some folks who read this book.

Ammonium nitrate explosives work well just about anyplace a case or more of dynamite would normally have been used. Small charges are not practical but, conversely, large charges are very practical. I at one time helped set off 1100 pounds of ammonium nitrate all in one shot. It was in 200 pound sets about 30 feet apart. We would have set additional charges but we ran out of daylight and didn't want to leave it wired over night.

When fired the explosion felt like a giant sledgehammer hitting the ground even though we were fully half a mile from the shot. Dirt, trees and debris flew at least 300 feet in the air, but houses within half a mile did not suffer any damage. No foundations were cracked and no windows broken.

From a poaching standpoint the principal use of ammonium nitrate is to blow ponds. As was mentioned, it isn't a good small explosive and blowing out ponds is the only major use of explosives I have ever encountered poaching.

On two occasions I have used ammonium nitrate to shoot extensive ponds without the owner of the ground knowing it was done. Both were in the midwest. One was on a farm owned by a fellow who inherited it and lived in a distant city. The other was in an old bayou where the ownership was disputed or unknown.

Both areas had at one time been open water. But after hundreds of years of stagnation, the trees, brush and vegetation had choked the water out. To revitalize the stagnant ponds, we blew open an area about 80 feet wide by about 160 feet long and 8 feet deep. In two years there was a fine population of bass, muskrats, ducks and frogs on the previously barren grounds.

My first experience with ammonium nitrate was bad. I couldn't get it to go off. After a while I learned the secret and now have no problems with it. Be sure to follow these instructions closely.

There are two kinds of ammonium nitrate. One is coated with calcium for farming use and the other is specifically designed as an explosive. I buy the uncoated explosive type if I can do so without arousing suspicion. Otherwise I use the standard ag grade.

Ammonium nitrate comes in plastic 50 pound bags. I build a wood trough to hold the amount of ammonium nitrate I need for each set. Open the bags carefully on the top and dump them into the trough. Over the top of this, pour standard kerosene. Enough to make a nice soupy slurry. I use about five gallons of kerosene for 300 pounds of nitrate and make a big batch. Mix the slurry with a hoe.

If the ammonia is the coated type, the mixture will have to be agitated for at least twenty minutes and be allowed to sit before firing for at least two hours.

Dig the shot holes down as deep as is practical. Either to bedrock or down till the water runs in and further digging is impossible. Always pick a dry August to do this sort of business. A hole 6 feet deep will make a nice 8 foot deep pond 30 feet across using 200 pounds of ammonia.

Shovel the fertilizer oil slurry back into the bags and quickly place them in the hole. The oil will deteriorate some plastic so work quickly.

I fire each set with ten sticks of 60 percent dynamite. The cap sticks should be carefully placed in a good thick plastic bag and placed solidly on top of the ammonia. The set should be covered with at least a foot of good solid fill. If more than one set is made, the shot must be fired electrically.

Oil ruins conventional powder. The blaster must be very careful to keep the dynamite out of the oil. On the other hand, ammonium nitrate only detonates from intense heat, so the cap charge has to be well-placed.

The ammonium nitrate shot itself is more of a big shove than a sharp jolt. The effect is beautiful. There is no spoil bank to clean, no heavy equipment to mar the land, and in many places no one will even know what happened.

7
DYNAMITE

For the intelligent, cautious poacher, dynamite can make the significant difference in ability to collect game. This chapter will *not* transform a poacher into a skilled demolitions expert. It does not contain sufficient information to allow the average reader to handle even 80 percent of the potential situations where use of powder would be productive.

After reading this chapter, a person could very easily go out and either blow himself to hell or create such a nuisance that he will be locked up indefinitely. The material we are talking about is foreign to most people, dangerous and feared by the uninformed.

This chapter will in a general way teach the uninitiated how to acquire dynamite and how to safely use it. There is something of a trick to purchasing and using dynamite that must be mastered before one can proceed. That is what this chapter is all about.

For twenty years I worked part time as a contract powder monkey. I also sold dynamite at retail. My total supply of all but one kind of powder was stored in a pump house on the farm not fifty feet from my bedroom window. Statistically and in actual practice, my dynamite store was far safer than a similar volume of gasoline. All dynamite will burn like paraffin if set afire. Some will not go off even if shot with a rifle or otherwise impacted. It will not freeze or melt as a general rule, and is far tougher to explode than propane gas or coal dust, for instance.

Dynamite *does* evoke an irrational fear among law enforcement people. If a warden or farmer suspects powder is being set to catch game, they will expend alot more effort to apprehend the user than is normally the case. A poacher caught using dynamite will face some very severe penalties.

Through the years I have developed a set of simple questions that one can ask himself to determine if he should use dynamite. If honestly considered by the individual, these questions virtually guarantee safety. There is no room for rationalization with the procedure.

The questions are:
1. Do I have above average intelligence?
2. Can I carefully follow a regimented procedure?
3. Am I methodically attentive to detail?
4. Can I remain calm in a crisis?

If there is even one "no" answer, skip this chapter or just read it for entertainment.

The first step to using dynamite is to acquire it. For those who have never worked with explosives, this may seem like an insurmountable task, but in real life it isn't all that difficult. Dynamite is used in most basic industries. Mining, forestry, construction, road building, farming and even manufacturing rely to some extent on the use of it.

For this reason, dynamite is always on hand and available. I have yet to find a large city that didn't have a dealer. Until relatively recently, it was handled by a surprising number of rural hardware stores and small powder vendors scattered throughout the U.S. I have always been able to find powder by either looking in the yellow pages under explosives or by contacting a heavy equipment operator who sold it to me or told me who sold it to him.

The trick is not finding who has the powder but convincing the vendor that you are competent to safely handle the materials they sell. There is no prescribed, easy formula for doing that. Every explosive dealer I have ever dealt with has been extremely squirrelly about selling to me till they were convinced I knew what I was doing. Understandably, they did not want to be the dealer that sold powder to some nut who got in trouble with it.

A federal form must be filled out by an explosive purchaser. It is not unduly difficult or particularly subjective, but it would be the better part of wisdom to examine the form before walking into the dealer.

Section 9 includes categories for intended use. This is the section that the dealer always uses to quiz the intended purchaser. I usually list agriculture as being my intended use, but must always be ready with specifics.

Most of my powder actually does end up removing stumps, smashing rocks or blasting ponds, so my statements are not inaccurate or untruthful. Their conception of what is meant by "shooting ponds" and my definition are obviously not always the same! Other uses for dynamite include making ditches, splitting stumps, taking out cement walls and footings, and other light construction chores.

If the user is more familiar and comfortable with construction use of powder, that can be listed. Just be ready with specific information as to how you intend to blast out the hardpan for the footings, where that wall will be shot to break it, or what steel beam is being removed and how.

There is, of course, no category for poaching, but it has always been my feeling that agricultural uses of dynamite have to include outdoor activities. I believe that to list agriculture as the intended use is the most honest, and not a violation of the disclosure laws.

Dynamite is purchased by the pound. In times past it was possible to buy eight or ten sticks, a few caps and some fuse. In this day of red tape and bureaucracy, the minimum allowable purchase is a case of 50 pounds.

The cases are made out of heavy cardboard, generally of a slip cover design. Inside, the cartridges are stacked neatly in a heavy plastic sack. Each case of dynamite has an identifying code that is recorded on the transaction record form.

As a general rule, the dynamite used in agriculture and construction comes in half pound cartridges. At times, three pound chunks are available, or loose powder that can be repacked, but I never buy dynamite in that form. I also don't recommend its purchase by others. The only loose explosive I buy is ammonium nitrate, a special purpose material covered in the previous chapter. Its only relationship to dynamite is that the latter is used to set ammonium nitrate off.

One firm—DuPont—no longer makes dynamite. They have an explosive product that, I believe, is called Trovex. It does not freeze, will not go off from a rifle shot and is generally very stable. So stable that it won't go off below $0°$ C, and is tough at temperatures substantially above freezing. The material does leak out of the cartridges badly, so it is sticky to handle.

True dynamite is graded by percent of strength as compared to pure nitroglycerine of the same weight. I have seen 20 percent dynamite on up to 85 percent.

The 20 percent type did not, as far as I know, have any practical purpose. It is not generally available anyway, so should not be seriously considered by the poacher.

People using ammonium nitrate are the chief consumers of 85 percent dynamite. It is very fast and very hot, two qualities needed to make ammonia explode.

Dynamite can either be nitro based or ammonia based. The ammonia based product is only rated at about 40 percent, but is commonly used in agricultural applications. Forty percent is slower burning, and will throw a rock or stump out of the ground rather than shatter it. I don't like it as well as the equally common 60 percent dynamite for outdoor work, but often it's all there is available.

Sixty percent dynamite is used to shatter rocks, break up cement, blast out ponds and break up a hardpan. It is also just the ticket for fish, dens, beaver dams and noise making. All 60 percent powder, as far as I know, is nitro based. It is a bit more unstable than 40 percent but not much. Forty percent dynamite won't go off when shot with a gun, for instance.

The only powder I won't use is ditching powder. This material is made to propagate, or go off, from the concussion of a near shot. Usually the charges are spaced about three feet apart in a swamp or partially filled ditch and one is fired. It, in turn, sets off all the other dynamite up and down the row, blowing out a nice line. Standard, non-ditching powder is much more stable and will only go off if it is actually touching a stick that blew.

One other type of dynamite is occasionally encountered. That is permissible explosives, or powder certified for use in mines. Fumes from standard nitro powder cause an acceleration in heat rate. Permissible powder does not create smoke with this problem. I don't use permissible powder because of the added expense, but would if nothing else was available.

Standard 60 percent dynamite is, as of this writing, about $40.00 per case. In 1968 it was $12.50 per case and there wasn't nearly as much paperwork involved in buying it.

One more bit of advice. Don't buy any dynamite that is oozing liquid. It may be unstable, and is therefore unpredictably dangerous.

Making dynamite go off under controlled circumstances requires blasting caps. If anything is dangerous about dynamiting, it is these caps. They will explode from heat, fire or rough handling. I carry my fuse caps a few at a time rolled in tissue paper inside a 35 mm plastic film container. Larger electrical caps are carried in a wide mouth plastic pill bottle.

Always carry the caps separately from the dynamite.

There are two kinds of caps—electrical and fuse. Fused caps are attached to a fuse that is fired with a match. Electric caps are detonated from a battery, generator or wall outlet.

People using matches and fuse should proceed as follows. First cut the fuse to the desired length. Fuse burns about 15 inches per minute, but never cut it less than 12 inches long. As a precaution, trim about half an inch off one end of the fuse to be sure the exposed end is new and fresh. Be sure this trim is made straight and crisp without bending or crimping the fuse. Several companies make a special non-sparking tool for trimming fuses which is very desirable. I would not handle dynamite without one of these special trimming tools.

Push the freshly cut fuse into the cap, firmly, without twisting and without a great deal of pressure. Crimp the cap onto the fuse with a pliers or dynamite tool. Crimp it hard at the skirted end of the cap.

Split the other end of the fuse back about 3/4 of an inch to facilitate lighting it. The split end should be pinched together until the user is ready to light it. Then separate the ends and light the exposed powder. A well lit fuse does not spew black smoke or burn with an open flame. It expels fire and a thin stream of smoke.

Practice lighting a small piece of fuse before capping. Watch it burn through to the end, and generally become familiar with the process.

Next, put a cap on a fresh piece of fuse and fire it. Be prepared to spend whatever time it takes to learn how to correctly cut and cap fuse. Also, time various lengths of fuse to get an idea how much time expires from lighting to explosion.

Caps now sell for $.75 each. Fuse is $8.00 per 100 feet. Spend twenty bucks learning how to crimp caps and light fuse. It's a good investment and not unlike setting off firecrackers.

Dynamite, as mentioned, comes in half pound cartridges. The cartridges are rolled out of heavy waxed paper. They are dark brown, usually printed with the word 'Dynamite," the maker, and the strength. I recommend that the user take a short hardwood stick and pry open one end of a cartridge to see exactly what this explosive is.

One stick in each set is used as the detonating cartridge. Other cartridges used in the same set must be placed so they make firm contact with the cap stick. If possible, they should be tied together with the cap stick securely in the center of the bundle.

There are various opinions as to how best to put the cap in the cartridge. My method is to punch a shallow diagonal hole into the cartridge about a third of the way down from the top of the cartridge. Extend the punch hole deep enough to take the entire cap, but don't run the hole out the other side of the cartridge.

Securely tie a piece of baling cord around the cartridge at the cap. This cord should hold the cap and fuse in the cartridge securely. Be sure not to kink or bend the fuse.

Electrical caps are inserted in the cartridge in exactly the same way. Some people tie off the cap by wrapping the lead wires round the cartridge, but I always use a piece of twine. It is important that no stress be placed on the wire leading to the cap. I have found that using a twine tie is the best way of preventing that.

After the charge is primed and ready, the wire leads will be securely attached to the two drop wires, which lead to the power source. The drop wires should be at least number 18 wire, no less than 200 feet long. Charges over four sticks should be fired from 300 feet, but the average poacher will seldom use any charge that heavy. All wires should be corrosion-free and well-insulated. All equipment used in blasting must be clean, neat and in new condition.

The lead wires on the cap are left in their holder till connected to the drop wires. But first bind the two leads together on the power source end of the drop wire as a safety precaution, and leave them together till the charge is actually shot. Be sure the wire is not near a power line, electric fence or other power source. CB radio transmissions, for example, will detonate electric caps.

I fire my electrical detonators from a large flashlight battery or truck battery. One advantage of electrical caps is that they facilitate firing multiple charges. The wiring for these charges is complex and often one small battery is not enough to do the job. I only use single shots when poaching, and recommend that the reader do the same.

I seriously suggest that the novice powder monkey take the time to first detonate some one or half stick charges. Half sticks are made by rubber banding a baggie over the fresh end of a stick cut in two. Use a very sharp knife for the surgery. The problem with practice rounds is their noise. When properly set in ponds or dens, dynamite makes a very subdued thump when it explodes. It is as if someone hit the ground with a giant sledge hammer. A deafening roar is a sure sign of an overcharged set.

My suggestion is to bring a shovel and bury the practice charges under ground two to three feet before they are fired. It won't be so surprising to the neighbors that way.

Some people feel it is not necessary, but I always put any charge I intend to shoot under water in a plastic bag. Use a thin baggie, and tie the top shut with a piece of light string.

Setting powder is quite an art, involving a structural knowledge of the area being shot, the ground around it, and the power of the powder.

Misfires

Every person using explosives must be prepared to handle a misfire.

Over the years I have shot literally tons of explosives but have had only three misfires. Failure to fire comes from poor preparation. Set up the cap sticks properly, place them in the charge correctly, use clean, dependable equipment, and failures will be rare indeed.

The charges generally used for outdoor activities are small and therefore not a horrible problem if they don't go off. The simplest example is the ignition failure of a single stick of dynamite thrown in a pond. In all likelihood, the powder sank too deep too fast and the fuse was drowned out.

A single stick of dynamite lying at the bottom of an eighteen foot pond does not constitute much of a hazard, and I would forget about it. Within a day the cartridge will be so soaked that nothing will make it go off.

If an above ground charge does not go off, it is mandatory that the users pull back and wait at least twenty-four hours. After that time has elapsed, carefully dig out the set till a stick of the dynamite can be seen. Push another freshly capped charge in next to the exposed cartridge and attempt to fire the entire set by use of this second freshly capped stick.

About the worst problem of this sort occurs when part of the charge goes off without detonating other remaining cartridges. If unexploded sticks of dynamite are seen around a fresh shot, stay away from the set for twenty-four hours. Then approach very carefully and, with as little disturbance as possible, collect the sticks into a central place where they can be fired with a freshly capped stick.

Most dynamite can be neutralized with thin oil. Damaged sticks can be soaked in oil or sprayed with oil and rendered harmless. Leaking, wet, squashed or broken sticks should be disposed of in this manner. If there is no imminent danger, I take them out in an open area and slit open the bad stick with a carpenter's knife. Scatter the contents out on the ground and let the elements degrade the material. Don't mow or otherwise use the disposal area for a few weeks.

I have had one miss in a deep pond, and two failures to get ammonium nitrate to detonate. I abandoned the water shot and recharged and detonated the ammonium nitrate shot without complications. As I said before, careful preparation can prevent 99 percent of all misfires.

8
SNARES

Snares can be used to collect just about any type of game. We collected many a muskrat with them as kids. Larger, more sturdy snares work half-well for beaver. If there are bobcat or lynx around, snares are about the best trap going for these cats.

About the easiest animal to take with a snare is the rabbit. Deer are probably in second place and, after that, it's a tossup between bass, trout, suckers, coyotes and fox. If there are bear in your territory, there is only one easier method of taking them, which is covered in a following chapter.

Hunters and outdoorsmen need to rediscover snares. They are convenient, light and can be made out of a variety of junk found lying around the house. When set, they are very difficult to discover. Many wardens and landowners have never even seen one.

The problem that keeps most people from using snares is that they are a bit difficult to learn to operate correctly and successfully. It's tempting to give up early and try something else rather than roughing it on through and learning the techniques. This is true even with fish snares which are a little more interesting and immediate than those used for mammals.

The easiest snare to make and use is a fish snare. The same snare works for rabbits and muskrats, and a multiple version is dynamite for birds.

To make it easier the first time, I suggest using identical materials to those in my description. Later on when it is obvious what the end results are to be, the reader may want to rummage around in his junk pile for snare makings.

Start with a 20 inch piece of 18-2 wire. This is standard appliance wire sold in all hardware stores for five cents a foot or less. Split the wires so that there are now two 18 inch long pieces each with their soft rubber insulation still on the wire.

Cut the insulation back about 2 inches on one end of one wire, exposing the 50 or so hair-thin strands of copper. Carefully separate the wire bundle from the insulation and, using pliers, pull the wire out of the insulation. Be sure that all of the wires are grasped evenly by the pliers, or they will ravel and tangle when pulled, making it impossible to separate the strands later on.

The snare builder will find that the enclosed bundle of wires is slightly twisted. Before attempting to divide them further, the wires must be untwisted in the least destructive manner possible.

Separate the wires into two fairly even groups and carefully work the wires apart. It may be necessary to tangle and ruin one half of the wire to save the other half.

Ten to 12 hair thin strands of copper wire should remain from the last split. Twist these up slightly to hold them together, and cut the ends off evenly. Wind the wires together into a lasso, with a loop on one end to tie the snare to a longer line or anchor wire.

This one 20 inch snare is expandable, small enough to catch smallmouths, carp and suckers yet large enough for most salmon. For really small fish in the 4 to 6 inch range, the wire will have to be divided again down to about 6 strands.

The smaller snares have no lock on them. They keep their tension by cutting into the game slightly because of the ductile nature of copper. With fish, the snare is snubbed onto the critter. On rabbits and muskrats, a springy bush may do the job. This is o.k. for small game or for situations with fish, snakes or alligators where the poacher is right there to hold on, but for larger game the snare must lock.

This is true even when spring pulls or balance sticks are used. An understanding of spring poles is important when setting snares, but first one must know how to build larger snares that have a lock as an integral part of their construction.

I build locking snares in three sizes. A small one made out of 1/16-inch airplane cable is used for coyotes, beaver and fox-sized animals. The cable should be about 3 feet long and the loop, when set, approximately the size of a small pie pan. It is sometimes difficult to hide extra cable, so I try to make the snare as close as possibly in length to what I will actually use. Hiding or disguising snares is quite important for smaller game.

The second size is the common deer model. Occasionally I have

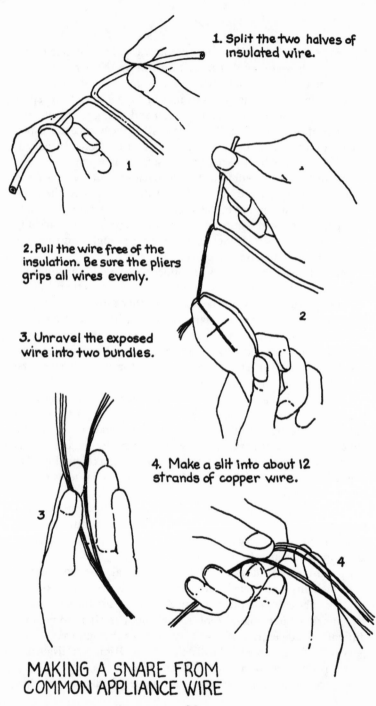

1. Split the two halves of insulated wire.

2. Pull the wire free of the insulation. Be sure the pliers grips all wires evenly.

3. Unravel the exposed wire into two bundles.

4. Make a slit into about 12 strands of copper wire.

MAKING A SNARE FROM COMMON APPLIANCE WIRE

86

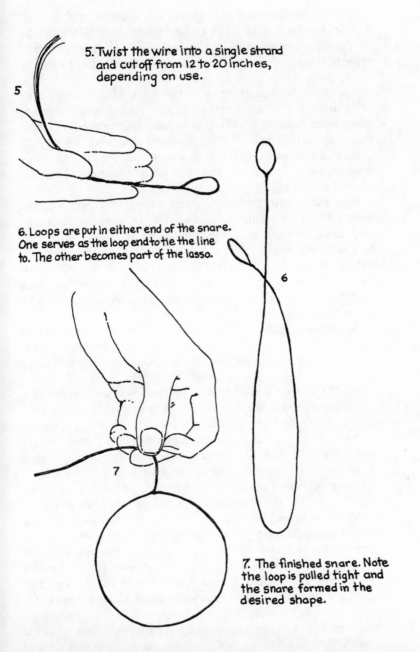

5. Twist the wire into a single strand and cut off from 12 to 20 inches, depending on use.

6. Loops are put in either end of the snare. One serves as the loop end to tie the line to. The other becomes part of the lasso.

7. The finished snare. Note the loop is pulled tight and the snare formed in the desired shape.

87

used them for moose with success. The snare is made out of 3/32-inch cable and should be about 7 feet in length. Loop size for deer is the size of a bushel basket, so it takes a fairly long piece of cable to get the job done and still have something to tie to a drag or spring pole.

I don't use the third size snare a whole lot, but like to have two or three around in case I decide to make a set for bear. In spring, when bears come well to bait, or in fall with burnt honey, these snares are surprisingly effective. They are made out of 5/32 inch cable and are either very short—just to include the loop itself—or long enough to set a loop 14 to 16 inches in diameter and then tie around a drag log.

Bear snares cost less than $3.00 each to make, compared to at least $100.00 for regular steel jaw traps. In addition, steel bear traps are dangerous, subject to much easier detection than snares, and so damn heavy I really wonder if they ever were used as extensively as one is led to believe. I can put three bear snares in a pack and they take up less room than my lunch. Try putting three Number 5 bear traps in a pack sometime. There won't even be room for a lunch.

Assuming the cable is cut to the proper length, the next step is to put a loop on one end. On the smaller snares, I double the cable back and crush a nut on the line. For bear-sized snares, I use a small cable clamp.

Cable locks are very simple "L" shaped pieces of metal with a hole drilled in each leg. The hole must be slightly larger than the wire so it will slip under tension, but not so large that the cable can be backed out. Look at the diagram and then experiment a little. I use a 1/4 inch hole with 1/16 inch cable, 5/32 inch with 3/32 inch cable and a quarter inch hole for my bear snares.

Loop one end of the cable through the top of the L backwards, then fasten it to the other leg with a crushed nut or cable clamp.

My uncle helped me snare my first bear when I was 15. The old toothless critter had started raiding our cream cans, and my grandfather was livid. We separated the milk each day and then stacked the cans of cream on the north side of the milking parlor where they were picked up by the route boy every other day. For several weeks the bear had been sneaking in at night, tipping the cans over and wantonly wasting the old man's primary source of income. This was apparently a cagey old bear. Often he would knock the lid off a can and put his paw in the cream without

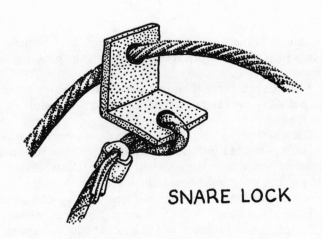

SNARE LOCK

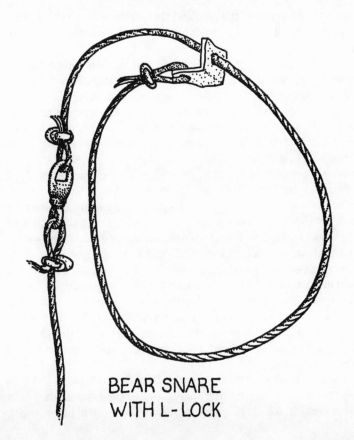

**BEAR SNARE
WITH L-LOCK**

89

drinking or otherwise disturbing the contents. Grandpa had to dump such cream himself then, which didn't help his disposition either.

When the bear came, the dogs barked and carried on. We tried to get out with a light and gun, but it always took off before we could get there.

The first thing uncle and I did was to build a three sided pen for the cans out of ten inch logs. We put a good stout top on it and wired the whole thing together with #9 wire. Bears are incredibly strong. The logs probably wouldn't have kept the critter out, but they did steer him to the open end where we rigged a snare.

There was a scroungy old hackberry growing by the barn. We took one limb and bent it down to make a temporary spring pole. The snare itself was securely fastened to a 5 foot maple log that weighed at least 75 pounds. By rigging a line from the tree limb to a nail in the entrance to the pen, and then to the snare, we were able to rig a breakaway spring pole that looked like it would do the job nicely.

As it worked out, the bear pushed into the pen and pulled the snare tight around its neck. This, in turn, pulled the wire off the nail and allowed the tree limb to snap up. The limb pulled on the snare, snubbing it around the bear's neck. In response the bear fought the snare and pulled the temporary line off the limb. Now all that held the bear was the drag, but the snare was so tight he no longer could pull free.

Mr. Bruin took off running, dragging the log behind, the dogs howling at its heels. Probably forty minutes later we followed.

As surprising as it may seem, the bear made it for about half a mile before the log hung up on some small aspens and he choked up, out of breath. We found it without much additional ceremony, and that was the end of the cream can robber.

Sometimes when making snares, it is advisable to put a small stop in the loop to keep the animals from choking to death. I don't care if rabbits, muskrats or coyotes are dead when I get there, and bear won't generally strangle themselves, but for deer it is essential. I crimp in a small nut on the line about 12 inches from the end. Deer can't pull their head back through, and they won't kill themselves either.

I always anchor a bear snare to the drag log with a swivel. Swivels aren't necessary on the littler snares, but on the big ones they help prevent excessive tangling. Even with a swivel, it will be necessary

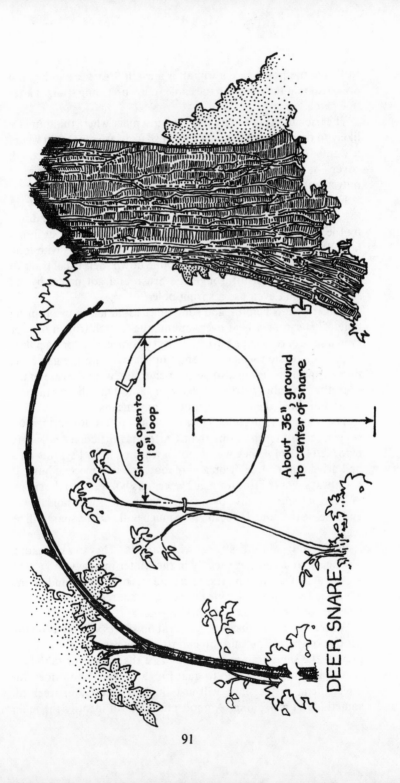

Snare open to 18" loop

About 36", ground to center of snare

DEER SNARE

91

to throw the bear snare away after a catch. Bears are so big and powerful that they kink up the cable so it won't hang straight after one catch.

The trick to using a snare is to set it in a place where the animal is likely to try and push through the brush in an attempt to get where it wants to go. Animals are used to doing this—pushing through cover—so using a snare fits into their common pattern of movement.

I caught five coyotes at a deer kill one time by setting snares in the three trails leading to the dead buck. It had been pulled down by the coyotes on a small finger of ground extending out into a lake. I tied the snares to some small brush in the trails with long pieces of grass. When the coyotes came down their usual trails to eat, they had to push through the brush and got nailed by my snares. I didn't even use a spring pole.

Generally it is helpful, and sometimes essential, to use a spring pole. This can be a bent over sapling, the branch from a tree, or even a sack of rocks hung over a limb. The object of a spring pole is to provide tension which will snub up the wire on the game. At times a spring pole will also be an anchor, but as in the case of the bear, this isn't always true. With larger game it may be impractical to try and hold them in one spot by any means.

There are more ingenious ideas kicking around for spring pole trigger release mechanisms than Carter has little liver pills. My favorite is a simple peg with a notch whittled in it. I set this on a nail driven into a tree or on a wire loop tied to a piece of bush. It has always worked fine for me. The critters will get into the snare, pull the peg slightly, dislodging it from the nail or wire hold down, and release the pole. It doesn't take much pull and the snare will be set.

Begin your snaring efforts with rabbits. They make readily distinguishable trails, especially in the winter in heavy snow, and are not at all fearful of snares. There are lots of them around, so my advice is to set a few simple copper wire snares for bunnies and work from there.

Where there are bobcat or lynx, rabbit snares will occasionally get one of these. The cats come in to eat the rabbits, and will fall prey to the same trap in the same place that is set for rabbits.

A snare is an ideal trap to guard a game trail. Snow does not affect them, so the snare will just sit there week after week till something comes along. A good poacher will identify the main

SNARE SET WITH SPRING
POLE TRIP AND DRAG

A=Nail in tree; B=trip peg whittled from limb; C=spring pole with temporary trip wire fastened to snare; D=snare loop; E=grass strands hold snare; F=slack loop in snare; G=drag.

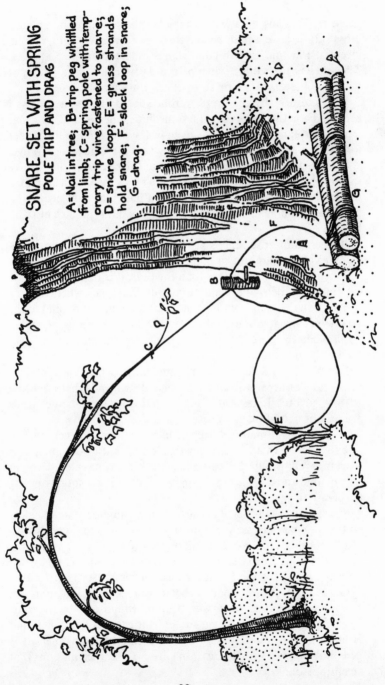

93

game trails in his area. These may be places where the animals cross ridges, have a path beaten through a fence, cross to a creek, etcetera. Put four or five good snares out to guard these places. Then during the winter, when pelts are prime, it's just a matter of walking by every week or so to check the snares.

Foxes, especially the greys, can be snared. The best success I ever had on the latter was in some brush heaps and in cedar marshes. Again, I placed the sets in well worn game trails, under logs and in tangled bulldozer heaps where these guys like to live.

Snares are effective on dens. Most of the red foxes that I have taken in snares were in front of dens. If I know there is an animal in the den, I set the snare and then pile a bunch of light brush and weeds on the hole. The fox pushes his way out right into my wire line.

Badgers and groundhogs are two other animals that are relatively easy to snare out of dens.

When setting snares other than for bear, it is imperative to use existing trails, dens or other natural runs. Bait sets—where the bait is placed in the woods with the hope of drawing the animal to the set—won't usually work. The animals are just too wary. A big natural bait like a dead cow, horse or deer will attract animals, but then only down existing trails.

During the middle of winter, game birds will often flock in a brush hole or aspen thicket. They beat down trails that are often used by coyotes, foxes and bobcats looking for a meal. Such trails are another good place to set a snare.

Some survival manuals suggest using leather shoelaces or fish line for snares. In an emergency this is o.k., but I can't imagine it working well. Maybe by waiting patiently near the snare, it might be possible to catch a rabbit or two, but this all sounds pretty desperate to me.

Snares are easy to set. They are so cheap anybody can own lots of them. Nevertheless, the point is not to cover the woods with snare loops, but to make a few good sets that will go on producing year after year. Keep the concept of snare locations in mind when cruising. Look for the few ideal locations and use them.

Once caught, most small furbearers are killed by a snare set using locking loops. They won't jump around and be obvious. Spring poles can even be rigged to pull the game out of sight if that is important. Should a snare be discovered and/or stolen, it is generally no problem. Snares don't arouse near the emotions that steel traps do.

Moose
Alces

Additional information on snares is included in the various chapters dealing with specific game. I strongly urge the aspiring poacher to master this art.

A few years back I camped for about thirty days in Alaska. We fished in a small stream that ran through a marshy flat spot of about twenty acres. Moose sign was very thick. Apparently they came in from the surrounding hills on a regular schedule to eat the watery grass and bask in the sun.

We decided to try and get one for camp meat.

I picked up some old cable at a garage about sixty miles away, and made two snares. They were about the size and weight of the ones I customarily used for deer back home. I had never snared a moose before, but reasoned that one would be hard to hold in a solid set, and perhaps impossible to snag because of their massive head and horns.

By carefully studying the ground around the marsh, I found a place where the moose regularly walked across a large log. The barrier constricted their movement and they seemed to put their hooves down in the same spot every time.

I put two snares over two deep imprints in the ground within 2 feet of the log. The loops were constructed to be only slightly larger than the tracks. Instead of spring poles, I simply tied the snares to some 6 inch aspen poles that were about 4 feet long. They served as drags.

The morning after I made the set I snagged a moose. In the process I—or the moose, depending on one's perception—almost destroyed what looked like a significant portion of the park. The destruction was incredible.

Grass was flattened, trees knocked down, brush crumpled and the stream turned to mud. We found our catch on the far end of the clearing about 100 yards in the woods, hung up in a small aspen grove, in an absolute rage over his predicament.

Deer, if one is not careful, will bang themselves up so badly in a snare that they are inedible. For a time I thought this might be true with our moose, but he wasn't bad. We fed a small part of one hind quarter to the dog and ate the rest ourselves.

It was an interesting episode. One we could not have experienced without a knowledge of snares.

9
THE UNIVERSAL STREAM TRAP

The trap described in this chapter is a maverick. It might be a snare or, then again, maybe it's a deadfall. Perhaps it shouldn't even be in a book on poaching skills since it is a difficult contraption to hide.

No matter what its classification, the stream trap does meet two criteria related to poaching which qualify it for inclusion in this book. It can be built with an axe and a few pounds of wire without relying on any other manufactured materials, and it can reduce a lot of game to possession with a minimum amount of effort, even under adverse circumstances.

The chief selling feature of the stream trap is its unerring ability to collect everything that moves up and down a channel of water. The design is apparently a very old Indian concept that uses some uncanny animal psychology to draw the game to its doom. One trap handles everything from small rats and mink up to large beaver and otter.

Fluctuations in water level do not affect the stream trap. One of these little jewels sits between two lakes about seventy miles from my present home. The lakes are part of a hydro-power impoundment. Some days the water level fluctuates two feet, and in some months it may vary six feet in total. No other trap I know of would work under those conditions without a lot of tinkering. My stream trap just sits there working like a champ day after day. About all I have to do is re-hitch the weight pole from time to time, if the water is really rising or falling.

Many locations between tidal flats, on dam-controlled rivers or between lakes, are natural pathways for water animals. Small game traffic on some is intense. But the problem has always been how to get the animals into a trap. Beaver don't come to the same bait otters do. In addition, a beaver trap will cut a muskrat in half, and ruin a mink pelt. There just isn't a single set that works in a place like a channel crossing where, because of the animal traffic, it is only logical to try and set a trap.

To a certain extent, ice does not affect the operation of these traps. Because of their unique design, the trap area is the last place to freeze. But, in spite of being frozen in, they will continue to work until it becomes seriously cold. In the southern states the trap will work twelve months of the year, if the owner wants it to.

Finding a good location for the trap is absolutely crucial. It has been my experience that it often takes two to three years to identify the right spot. No harm is done by building a trap in a mediocre location, but they are so darn much work to put in that I don't want to make the effort unless I know it will produce.

A good location should have at least most of the following attributes.

The stream should be a connecting route between bodies of water that is frequented by an obviously large population of aquatic animals. Look for sign of beaver in either end of the lake. If a channel in a marsh is considered, look for a large population of muskrats.

Don't put the trap on a small upstream tributary of a nondescript creek. Put it where the animals travel regularly: in a bayou, just off a main river in a side stream, or in a main channel through a swamp. The trap must be constructed in a place where the water moves but is not flowing. Fast moving water will soon wash it out. Banks on either side should be fairly steep so that the creek channel is definitely defined and will not meander out of the area where the trap is located.

Water depth is crucial. I like about four feet of water evenly across the entire channel at the trap site. If the water is shallower on one side, but the set is otherwise ideal, that is o.k. The floating log and trip pole are always installed over the deep hole. If there is only one deep hole, there can only be one catching apparatus. This halves the effectiveness or doubles the work, depending on one's perspective, but in a particularly good location, this is acceptable.

A stream trap can be successfully built in a gravelly, rocky river bed, but it's a lot easier to build one in a mud bed. I try to find a grassy meadow where the soil has been deposited for hundreds of years and start work there.

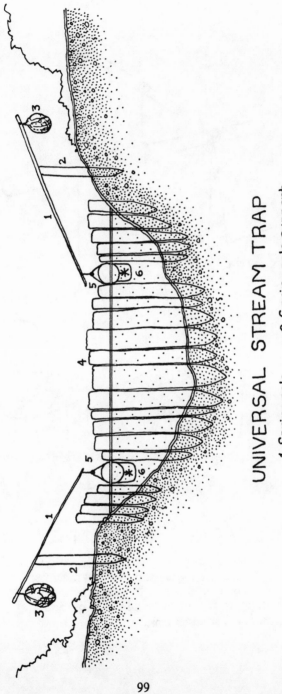

UNIVERSAL STREAM TRAP

1. Spring pole
3. Sack of rock
5. Loop stick
2. Spring pole support
4. Trap pen
6. Wire loop and trigger

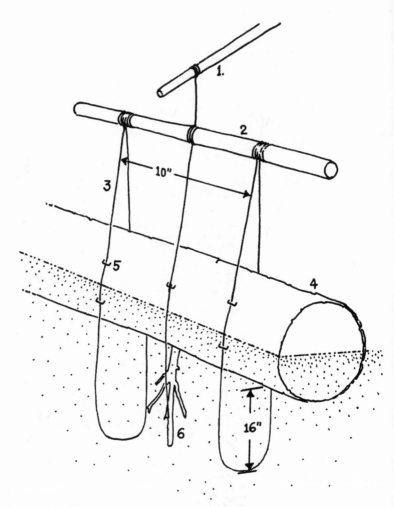

FLOATING LOG ASSEMBLY

1. Spring pole   2. Loop stick
3. Two wire loops made with #12 wire
4. Log, 5 ft. long   5. Fence staples,
drive in half-way, to serve as guides
6. Trigger mechanism

It takes a good hard day for two people to build a stream trap. I have put quite a few of them in with an axe, maul, hammer, wire cutter and pocket knife. If one is available, a chain saw is also very helpful. All that is needed for materials is a handful of wire staples, five pounds of #12 or 14 wire, 3 pounds of #16 wire and a gunny sack.

Always plan to build the trap during the summer. It takes a few months for the animals to get used to it. The poles have to age, etcetera, but most of all, building the trap requires getting in the water. Not a fun job during late fall or winter.

The first and most time consuming job is to build the trap pen. This requires a large number of straight posts, sharpened at one end and long enough to extend up out of the water at least three feet at its highest when the trap is in use. If the creek is deep—5 feet or more—the poles will have to be quite long.

Drive the poles into the river bed, side by side, using the maul. If the creek is deep, it will be necessary to build a walk out on the existing piers to stand on while doing the pile driving. Rocks in the river bed will throw the poles off and leave gaps. These gaps in the pen must be closed off with boards or a second layer of poles.

Leave a 10 inch gap in the pen over the deepest hole. Hopefully, the site selected will have steep banks and be uniformly deep so that two openings can be made, each a foot or so from either bank. Animals like to swim near the bank rather than up the middle of the creek, so the trap will be more natural if the openings are on the sides. Nevertheless, the opening(s) must always be over the deepest part of the creek.

A suitable pen can be built out of steel farm posts, stock wire and boards. It takes less time, and the steel posts drive better in rocky river beds, but the expense of doing it this way is prohibitive.

If boards are used, extend them up above the water the usual three feet. The rest of the closure can be made of stock and chicken wire. Just be sure to leave no opening larger than two inches square.

Spring floods can ruin these traps. The wire kind seem to take a worse beating than the pole type. Each summer I plan a day or two for repairs, although it usually doesn't take that long.

After the pen is completed, carefully cut and peel a six foot log that will just float in the pen openings. If there are rough edges or branches sticking out, slice them off with an axe. These logs must float freely in the pen opening and move up and down as the water level does.

Cut one good stout balance pole for each opening and construct a pivot support on the bank for the poles. Wire the front end of the balance pole to the loop stick.

There are 3 wires on the loop stick. Two of them are the trap loop wires, made out of the #12 or 14 wire. Construct these about 10 inches apart and half-drive the two fencing staples into the log on each side to guide the wire. The wire loops should extend down and below the log about 14 to 16 inches. Be sure the balance pole pivot is high enough to accommodate this much movement. It is important to use either #12 or 14 wire for these loops. Lighter wire will damage the pelts of smaller critters and larger wire is cumbersome and will slow the trap. Wire for the trigger is always as light as possible. Use only a heavy enough grade to hold the balance pole and no more.

Without a doubt, the most difficult mechanical part of the stream trap is the trigger mechanism. Build it correctly and the trap should get something every night. A clubby, insensitive trigger, however, will miss many of the small animals like muskrats and mink.

Two suggested trigger designs are diagrammed for the reader. An ingenius poacher will probably think of others, but these two are proven and a good place to start.

The heart of the trigger is a limb from a tree to which the trip wire is fastened. This limb must be sound and hard with a number of branches about the thickness of a heavy pencil radiating from it. All smaller twigs, leaves and bark should be removed from the limb, and the radiating members trimmed back so the branch just fills the opening under the floating log to a depth of about one foot. It is important that the limb be fairly full of branches, but if there are too many, the animal's view will be obstructed and it will dive beneath the trigger and the wire catching loops.

To hold the trigger in place, I use either a cross-stick braced against a pen side, or a stick braced up to the main log. When the trap is tripped, this stick will often be lost, but that is no problem.

The big problem is replacing the trip limb. These break or are lost with maddening frequency. Some trappers try to use expanded wire, 2 inch wood stock or some other commercial material for a trigger. I believe a branch is much better. Water animals are used to pushing limbs aside as they swim and will move into a limb trigger much more readily.

I am continually on the lookout for spare limb-triggers for my

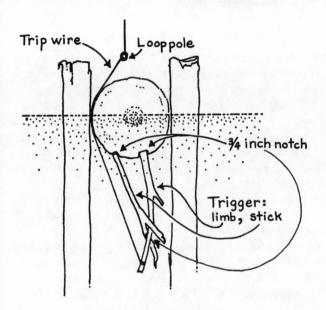

Trip wire

Loop pole

¾ inch notch

Trigger:
limb, stick

A Type Trigger

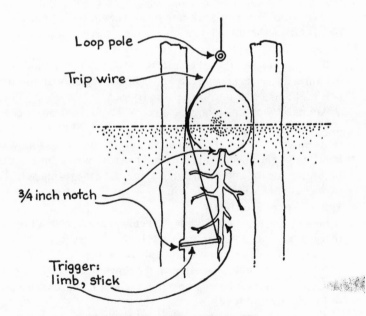

Loop pole

Trip wire

¾ inch notch

Trigger:
limb, stick

TWO POSSIBLE
TRIGGER MECHANISMS

stream trap. Sycamore makes an ideal trigger as does walnut and maple. In the west and some sections of the south, a pine branch is all that is available. Pine is o.k., but must be replaced often.

Practice setting the trap in the summer. At first, they are an absolute bitch to trigger without getting thoroughly wet. With practice, one can learn to do it quickly. I cut a small 3/4 inch notch in the bottom of the log and in the pen side wall for the trigger pieces if I am using a cross-stick trigger. For the 'A' type trigger, I cut two notches in the log.

Be sure the pole trip wire—the one to the trigger—is rigged long enough so the trip limb won't hang up on the staple guides and keep the pole from lifting.

Counter weight for the pole is provided by putting rocks in a gunny sack and tying this to the other end of the spring pole. Be sure the weight is heavy enough to close the trap smartly.

The best way to actually set the trap is to assemble the trigger pieces and lay them on the floating log. Then walk out to the trap with waders. Hold the balance pole with one hand and put the trigger limb in its notch in the log. If using an A type trigger, quickly place the cross stick into its notches in the log and trigger limb, and release enough tension to keep it there. The procedure is the same for the cross-stick trigger as well.

Be sure to master the art of setting the trap in the summer when it's warm and nice. During the winter I nail a log or board onto the pen wall and stand on it to set the trigger.

Animals swimming along the creek will come to the barrier and dive under the log to get through the opening. The stream trap relies and plays upon the animal's natural tendency to follow the log through the opening in his path. They will swim right along the bottom of the log and hit the trigger, releasing the spring pole. The two wire loops will trap the critter against the bottom of the log, killing it almost instantly.

Damming up the creek with the pen will create a small current that will keep ice away from the set. Even after ice forms, the trap will work till the ice is over a couple of inches thick.

In some locations where the water flows steadily, the log will tend to float out of the trap opening. I hold it in place with a piece of loosely wound wire.

Although I have never seen it, I believe it would be possible to use a conibear trap under the log to make the catch. Perhaps it would work as well as the wire loops with less trouble, but I suspect not.

The biggest problem with the stream trap, other than building it, is the fact that they are obvious. To a certain extent, they can be concealed. And after a few years in the same place, they no longer arouse suspicion. However, no landowner is going to come on one of these in his swamp and not be alarmed. But for the right place in the right time, the stream trap is an outstanding poaching device.

We had a stream trap on a tributary of the Des Moines River for a number of years. It was about 100 yards upstream from the main river between two large cottonwood trees. At that point, the creek was about eighteen feet wide and perhaps 5 feet deep. It was very difficult, because of the depth and the rock stream bed, to build the pen.

We made the mistake of trying to build it early in summer when the water was still high. Also, the pen had only one opening, a feature we regretted from the time the trap first went into use.

On the plus side, the trees and brush hid the trap nicely. Even the balance pole looked natural, cradled over a tree limb.

By fall the trap was aged and apparently no longer a threat to the animals on the creek. We set the trigger and started using it.

The catch was reasonably good. As I remember it, we got about twelve rats, two beaver, two or three mink and a fantastic number of sprung-trap and no-game situations. The trap was sprung so many times that we really became exasperated. More weight on the pole didn't help. Shortening the trap loops wasn't the answer.

All of this really had us beat till one day we checked the trap and found a large carp weighing about fifteen pounds fast in our loops. It was the most unusual critter we collected in the trap, and led us to believe that fish were in fact springing the trap.

Next summer when the water was low again, we removed all the larger carp away from the trap area. It helped some, but we never did completely solve the empty trap problem.

Over the years the trap was partially washed out a number of times. We always rebuilt it and were always happy with our catch, in spite of the many times it was thrown.

10

DEN TRAP

When I was a lad, my uncle—who was half Ojibway Indian—
showed me how to make a den trap. He used them extensively on
his trap line, so my revelation came more in the line of duty as I
followed him around the woods, than as a great unveiling of
eternal truth.

In retrospect it probably would have been better if I had
received the information via a great unveiling. I might have immediately understood the significance of what I had learned rather
than waiting six or eight years for its full impact to set in.

Consider this 11th wonder of the New World. We have at hand a
trap that will catch just about anything, including skunks, raccoons, fox, possum, weasels, mink, even beaver, marten, fisher
and coyote if set where these critters run. It will also catch food and
bait animals such as rabbits and squirrels with equal ease, and
generally in large numbers. I have captured pheasants and quail in
my den traps and even collected an owl and a snake on two
occasions.

No bait is required. Once it is in place, the trap is always set and
will often catch more than one animal at a time. I have even taken
two different kinds of animals at the same time in the same trap.

As an added bonus, the trap is permanent. Snow, sleet and rain
won't affect its operation.

As a poacher's tool, the den trap is beautiful. It can't be found,
stolen or destroyed. Animals it catches are safe and will await the
trapper's return without danger of theft, discovery or loss. At
times, six months elapsed between visits to my traps and its
inhabitants were always safe and well, awaiting my arrival.

Like many good things in this world, the trap is the essence of simplicity. All it really amounts to is an artificial den dug into the ground in a place where the sought after game is likely to use it.

Building the trap is not difficult, but there are a few considerations. Native rough sawn oak planks are the best material, but are often not available. They are, however, the wrong material if very many traps must be carried very many miles. My second material choice is 3/4 inch exterior grade plywood. Common pine boards are a poor third choice. Because of the nature of the set, untreated soft woods tend to rot. Use of paint or wood preservatives to protect the lumber will tend to spook game away from the den.

During the 1950's we made quite a few of these traps out of cypress. At the time, this wood was readily available, cheap, light, and durable. In the west, one can occasionally buy second grade cedar car siding which also works well.

Use any material that is convenient. Just keep in mind that the longer the trap is in the ground, the better it will work.

The den box should be no less than 2 feet square. Use screws or nails that are long enough to clinch over for added strength. A removable top is built that must overlap the box top and be cross-braced to withstand rough usage. A piece of dog chain or #9 wire is run through this lid and looped out again to provide a handle.

While building the den box, consideration must be given to the size of the tunnel that will lead to the den. A tunnel between 4 and 6 inches in diameter is suitable. We have used corrugated culverts, drain tiles, 2x6's or 2x8's nailed into a rectangle, and even old iron sewer pipe for the tunnel.

Whatever the tunnel material used, a hole must be cut in the side of the den box near the bottom corner that is slightly smaller than the tunnel itself. This is extremely important.

Later when checking the trap, a block on a pole will be inserted into the tunnel to close off the den. If the den tunnel hole is larger than the tunnel, the block will slip into the den and the animal may escape.

Placement of the den trap is important. Pick a well drained, gently sloping area that has a soil that will keep the buried wood dry as much as possible. Don't put the den in the bottom of a draw, or next to a stream. There are many great places to set a den trap along rivers and creeks, but they must be above any possible flood zones.

At times I have about a dozen den traps out. Two are in town, hidden in some ornamental hedges. The other ten are scattered within a couple of miles of my home. Some are at the tops of grassy, brushy draws, some by old, abandoned farmsteads, and some in little patches of woods. All are good producers. The only animals that frequent these parts that I haven't caught are bobcat, badger and otter.

When placing the trap, dig the den far enough into the ground to keep the top at least 10 inches below the surface.

Slope the tunnel slightly downhill and make sure it doesn't surface before the very end. Disguise the entrance with rocks, brush, grass or whatever. It takes an incredibly astute woodsman to find one of these traps, exactly the kind of people I always assume will try to catch me. It is best not to take chances. The farmer or rancher whose fur you are harvesting may also have a copy of this book.

Another critical portion of design is tunnel length. I honestly believe that a 20 foot tunnel will take more game than an 8-footer. However, 20 foot tunnels are impractical. It takes too long to haul the needed materials into the set, and it is virtually impossible to find a blocking pole 20 feet long. As a compromise, I make all of my tunnels 12 feet long.

Be sure there is enough space between the trees, rocks and hills to lay the pole down and push it straight into the tunnel.

Exact construction and use of the blocking pole is up to the individual. I don't like to carry a pole with me when checking traps, so I cut one for each set and leave it in the woods. The only thing I carry is a couple of blocks made out of 2x4's and 2x6's that have a hole drilled in the center and a wire stapled to the edge.

At each set I retrieve my pole and force the correct block onto the tunnel. The wire should be wrapped around the pole to keep the block from slipping off when pulling the pole back out.

My brother likes to carry a well-made permanent pole and block, but I feel this compromises him significantly in the woods. It's hard to run with a pole and will look suspicious.

If the trap will be checked infrequently, I bury the lid. If it is a good producer and will be opened often, I put leaves and brush on top of the lid. The hole and all fresh dirt must be camouflaged. Also, don't expect to catch much if light can shine through the den top.

I have never caught anything in these traps inside of six months, and usually it's a year or more before they really start producing.

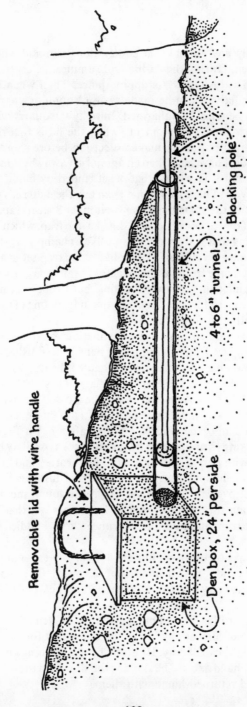

Removable lid with wire handle

Den box, 24" per side

4 to 6" tunnel

Blocking pole

DEN TRAP

Practically any animal that comes along can and will use the trap as a den. During the spring and summer the critters will be conditioned to use it as a stopping place. Then when fall rolls around, the harvest can be made easily. Young or unprime fur-bearers can be released unharmed. Initially the quarry will cower in the corner for a few moments when the lid is first removed, giving the trapper time to make a decision before shooting.

As an aside, I have never had an animal get away by jumping out of the top, and I have never had a set ruined by blood.

Over the years I have found that I can buy the materials for a den trap for about the same money as a Number 3 steel trap. It takes about a half day to construct and dig in a den trap, which isn't bad for something that will produce game like a champ year after year.

At one time my younger brother had a den trap set in a hickory grove about a mile from our place across a fairly large river. It was a long walk including the river crossing, but I believe he may hold the world's record for amount of fur taken from one of these traps in one month at a single location.

Brother assembled the den and tunnel out of some rough-cut oak planking left from building hog pens. The finished product was heavier than a dead priest, so he hauled the trap as near as he dared with a Jeep and dropped it in a large brush hole where the trap couldn't be seen. A few weeks later he crossed the river on foot from our side early in the morning. By first light he had the trap parts packed into the woods. Shortly after dawn the farmers started working their ground and planting corn. Activity hummed all around with nary a soul aware of little brother and his shovel.

About noon he sprinkled several shovels of duff over the set and threw the leftover dirt in the river. He ate his lunch and didn't see the trap again till the first week in December. At that time, he checked the trap, and found four prime skunks huddled together in the den.

Four skunks on the firing line are a lot of power for anybody to face. Brother did it with a single shot .22 pistol. One might guess that not even a crow flew through that part of the woods for quite a spell after. . . .

Normally brother hauled his catch home hidden under his long outer coat, but almost anyone would agree that four skunks are way beyond the call of duty. He didn't have a skinning knife along, only a small hand axe. So he skinned the skunks in the woods with the axe, and returned home with them.

A week later he and his skinning knife paid another visit to the den trap. This time there were three raccoons in it. In those days we made $.75 per hour and coons were worth $4.00 each.

Between Christmas and New Year's day, brother passed the trap for the last time. He was quail hunting and couldn't resist the urge to have another look. This time he cornered a mink, rounding out the month's catch.

11
CULVERT TRAP

When they were younger and going to school, my sons were chronically out of gas money. To help relieve the shortage without creating a scarcity of my own, I showed them how to set up a line of culvert traps.

It took about three weeks for them to really get the culvert traps rolling. But after that, hardly a day went by that they didn't collect game. Many times it was nothing more than a rabbit, but I remember one mink, many weasels, skunks, raccoons, possums and even a few grey fox which at that time were worth $3.00 for bounty. Three bucks bought about eleven gallons of gas in those days, so even these worthless little half-dog half-cat critters made them smile.

All of this game came out of not more than twenty culverts between our house and school. At times the boys drove the long way around to check the traps, but usually did it on their way to school.

Every country road has at least a couple of 6 to 18 inch culverts under it to allow the water to move from one side to another during heavy rains or thaws. Sometimes there is still water in the pipes, but usually the water table has fallen and the pipes just sit there empty except for the animals who use them for shelter.

The trick is to allow the animals to move into the culvert unmolested, but to get them out whenever the poacher wants them out.

Doing this requires that the poacher plan ahead in two regards. The first is locating the culverts. Finding the road drains may seem like obvious advice, but in many many cases the culverts are difficult to spot. They are hidden by grass, weeds, branches, sod

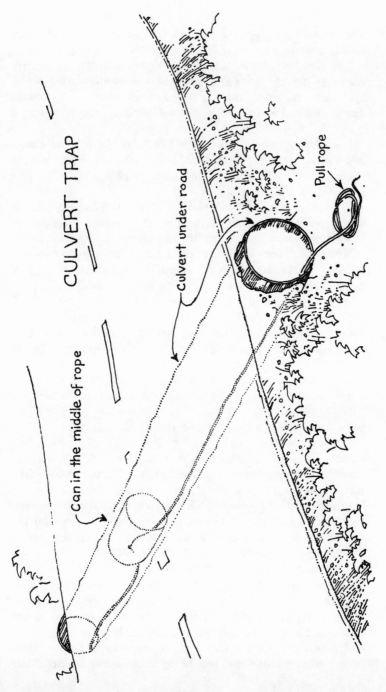

CULVERT TRAP

Can in the middle of rope

Culvert under road

Pull rope

113

and stones. New pipes are easy to locate but are not the ones that shelter animals.

The very best culvert location method is to check the country roadsides in early spring and late fall. My wife and I used to do this on long walks several days each year and nobody ever thought anything about it. In some places we found as many as twenty 8 inch culverts per mile.

Look for culverts wherever a road cuts a swale, or goes through a marsh or past an old drainage. Many farmers have culverts in the road ditches under their lanes into their fields. A cross or tee road is another good place to look.

During the winter when a skiff of snow covers the ground, it is often possible to see tracks to the culverts. Rabbits especially seem to visit every one in their territory sometime during their lives.

After the culverts are found, the poacher has to go to each and set them up. Doing this can be a problem if, for instance, a very good culvert is only a few yards down the road from Farmer Brown's house. Then the set up has to be made at night.

Take a long piece of Number 9 wire and coil it into a large open roll for transportation. The wire should be sufficiently long to reach across the road through the culvert. This is usually 30 feet or more.

Bailing wire is not the best material, but we have lots of it and it is free, so it's what we always used. Push the wire through the culvert from one side to the other, and pull a long piece of bailer twine back through the pipe with the wire.

Tie one end of the twine to something—a stick, bush, stone, etcetera—and cut the other end off at least one and a half times the length of the pipe. Leave the roll coiled inconspicuously out of the way on the ground near the pipe.

Punch a hole in a large juice can that will fit through the culvert. Don't make it a tight fit. The idea is to rattle the can through the culvert and scare the game out, not to dredge the whole length of the pipe. Some culverts are half-filled with dirt and stones, so the can may have to be relatively small.

Tie the can into the middle of the rope, which should be two feet from the end of the pipe, where all the extra twine is laying. By so doing, the poacher can pull the can through the pipe in one direction one time and the other direction the next.

Any critters in the culvert are scared out by the rattling commotion. You may then shoot the fleeing animals with a quiet .22. If

114

not, set a steel trap temporarily and catch them that way. Should the operation be a real "black bag" job, check the culvert at night.

The boys used to stop at several culverts near a brushy piece of bottom ground along a creek. The area was so overgrown that it was difficult to hunt conventionally, but they got all kinds of game from under the road. Early in the season they scared out dozens of woodchucks. Later, after the weather turned cold, the woodchucks went into hibernation and weren't a problem. It was funny to listen to their scheming about how they were going to find a market for woodchuck hides.

The only problem we ever have with culvert traps occurs when the bailer twine starts to rot. Some of the culverts flow water some of the year and that doesn't help. We have a bunch of old twine, and replace the line under the road when it begins to wear out.

Weasel Box Set

There is one other set that is related to the culvert trap. We call it the weasel box set. The two traps are related in the sense that we put them both out along a regular motor route to town, or to the office, and check them as we go about other business.

The weasel box set is an inexpensive, easy-to-build little affair that collects alot of weasels.

In some areas there are literally thousands of weasels. I am not sure what causes such a proliferation, but at times I have encountered areas with tremendous numbers of these miniature mink. Weasels have never been worth enough money to warrant a special effort to trap them. But where there are many weasels, it is possible to make gas money using one of these traps.

Build a square box about 12 inches on a side. Use scrap plywood, one inch stock or whatever else may be available, but build the box reasonably tight. Do not put a bottom in the box. Drill a 1 inch hole in the center of one end, about 2 inches down from the top.

Later in fall or early winter, take as many of the boxes as seems reasonable and a Number 1 steel trap for each, and set them out where weasels are known to be. Snow helps to spot large concentrations of them, and will not affect the trap.

Using a small staple, tack a piece of beef liver in the back of the box. Staple the trap chain to the box and set it right under the one inch hole inside the box. When the weasel comes for this liver it will jump through the hole into the trap.

The set is protected from the weather during the winter. It will remain operational no matter what. Birds won't get the bait, and nobody will see the trap. It's just a good simple little idea that makes good use of a normally neglected resource.

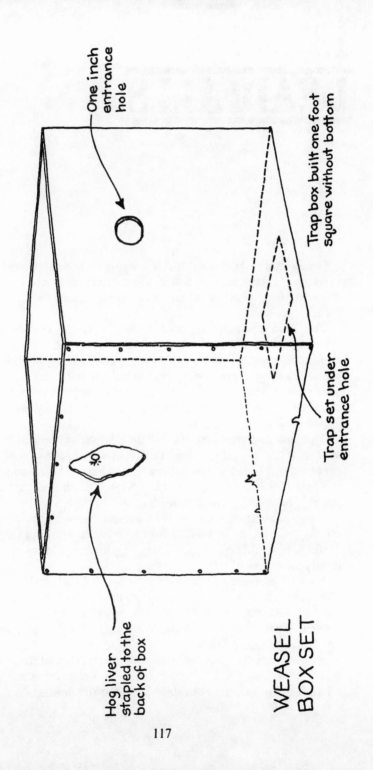

One inch entrance hole

Trap box built one foot square without bottom

Trap set under entrance hole

Hog liver stapled to the back of box

WEASEL BOX SET

117

12
DEADFALLS

Deadfalls are the most difficult kind of trap to master that I know of. It takes a great deal of skill and determination to build a good deadfall and get an animal to come in to it, take the bait and actually get caught.

Later in this chapter there is a long list of reasons why deadfalls are so tough to work with. But before launching into that, it is important to understand that there is one good compelling reason for at least knowing about these traps. Perhaps the average poacher who reads this book will never use deadfalls but, on the other hand, the information may be some of the best he ever acquired.

A general understanding of deadfalls is important because they are one of the few traps I know of that will work in a true survival situation. All it takes is a knife and an axe or saw to build a deadfall. If the emergency were truly great, a deadfall could conceivably be built *without any tools at all!*

A poacher with only a modest amount of ingenuity could conceivably take any animal on the North American continent with a deadfall. It would certainly be a long tough chore and not something that one would do for fun.

The first people to use deadfalls were North American Indians. This wasn't the only method the Indians used to catch game, but it was the most common. With deadfalls they could get any critter, whereas other methods might take beavers but not marten, weasels but not muskrats, and so on.

When white men came they brought a poor variety of steel trap and brass wire snares. The Indians fell all over themselves trading for these items but did not totally abandon the deadfall. About

118

1820 the Oneida Community started full scale manufacture and distribution of a superior steel trap, and that marked the end of deadfalls. By 1900 there were very few people left who knew how to build them.

I found out about deadfalls the hard way. When I was young, living on the farm, we were so poor that I only had two or three steel traps. I piddled around with snares, but for many land-sets a snare doesn't work that well. Raccoons, for instance, are tough for me to catch in snares, but I do collect one occasionally in a deadfall. Weasels, skunks, mink, foxes, possums, squirrels, bobcats, marten and rabbits are other animals that can be taken in deadfalls. Otter, beaver, muskrat, badgers and coyotes are some animals that are almost impossible to catch with deadfalls.

Bear and deer can be taken with deadfalls, although I have never done it. This is because a bear will come to a bait and a deer is a creature of habit. The trouble is that it would take me three days to build a bear deadfall, and I don't want to eat deer that have died of a broken back. If conditions were grim, though, I would reconsider very quickly.

It takes two men about half a day to build a small deadfall. By the time they walk into the set, cut the timber, make the trigger and build the trap, at least that much time will elapse. My older brother and I built three in one day years ago, but the last one was so poorly designed it never took a single animal.

Deadfalls must be extremely well placed. Unless one is a good woodsman and knowledgeable about the game in the area, it is easy to put the trap in a place where few animals travel. On the other hand, deadfalls should not be built in animal runs, right next to dens, or within animal feeding areas. I have tried placing deadfalls in runs, but was never successful. Putting in a deadfall is too disruptive to the environment. Even after two or three years the animals are reluctant to come back and use their old paths again.

Instead of routing a run through the trap, I have better luck putting the deadfall a few yards to the side of a known game run where I know the animals can see or smell the bait. With a little bit of ingenuity, deadfalls are easy to hide. Landowners and wardens don't notice them or are unaware of their purpose, so they can be set in places another trap could not.

Always build the traps in spring. This takes more planning, but is essential. The trap has a chance to acquire a weathered look.

Animals born in the spring will grow up accustomed to seeing the trap, and brush will grow up around it, providing additional camouflage. In fall the dead leaves will cover the trap to an even greater extent.

Other reasons for building the deadfall in spring are the ease of getting stakes in the ground, and of finding suitable logs for the trap.

After the trap is built, it should be propped open. Construct the trigger mechanism and leave it laying on the deadfall logs. More than any other part, the trigger has to age.

During the summer, walk by the set every now and then and spread some pieces of bait on it. The trap works fifty times better if the critters are used to stopping for a free meal. I use pieces of sucker fish.

The first step in building a deadfall is placing the base piece. The base piece, or log, is an even, sound hunk of log about 8 inches in diameter and 3 feet long. It should be of durable wood that will last a long time. All the knots and branches must be trimmed off the log so that it has an even side to act against the drop log.

Dig the base log into the ground so that only 2 to 3 inches of it remain above the surface. The ground on which the trap is built must be level.

Locate a suitable drop pole or log. The log should be about the same diameter as the base piece, and at least 6 feet long. Using three foot stakes driven in pairs on either end of the base log, construct the drop log guides. The drop guide stakes and the drop log should be clean and knot free. Often I peel the log and the stakes. This works well but it takes the set longer to age.

Finish the trap by building a pen of stakes around the back of the trap so the animals are directed through the front under the drop log for the bait. The pen can be up to 3 feet high and covered with branches or bark. Just be sure the covering doesn't interfere with the operation of the drop log.

At times it is possible to use a rock face or other natural feature in the construction of deadfalls. These possibilities must be developed by the alert poacher.

The heart of a deadfall is the trigger. Through the years I have seen an incredible number of ingenious triggers, all of which worked well. The most universal is the figure 4 trigger. It is fairly easy to make with a pocket knife and basically pretty foolproof.

Rather than trying to explain the figure 4 trigger, I suggest that the reader study the drawings of it.

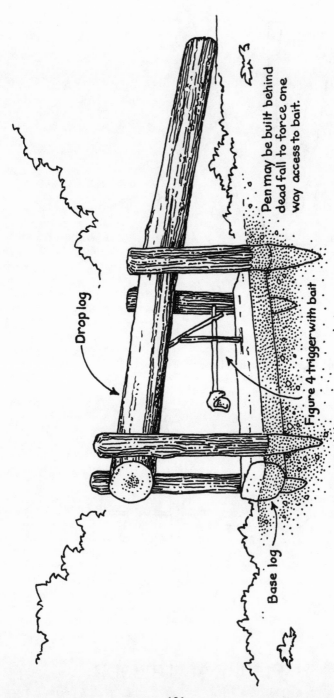

Drop log

Pen may be built behind dead fall to force one way access to bait.

Figure 4 trigger with bait

Base log

LOG DEAD FALL

121

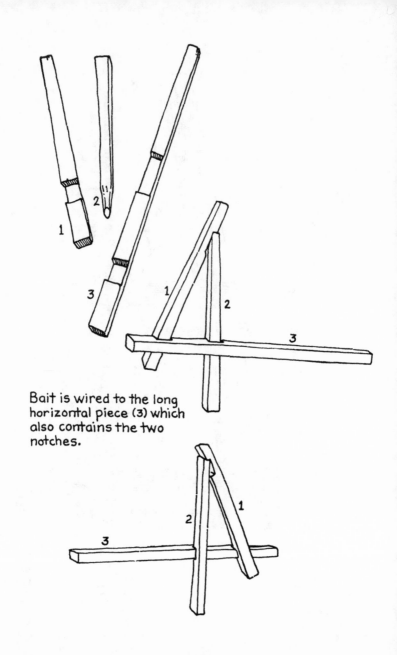

Bait is wired to the long
horizontal piece (3) which
also contains the two
notches.

FIGURE 4 TRIGGER

Deadfalls can be made in just about any size. I recommend a fairly large one that will kill at least a coon-sized animal. The drop log should fall sharply and have enough height to gain the necessary momentum to kill the animal. By so doing, the poacher can take smaller mink-sized critters on up to and including coon and fox with the same trap.

Set the trigger on the narrow side of the drop log and point the bait stick into the trap at a slight angle. The log should fall easily on small as well as large animals. If the bait is under the log, the animal may just pick it off without getting caught, or the bait may keep the trap from closing properly.

The Indians used to split a large cedar or hickory log and use one half for the base piece and the other for the drop piece. I never was successful with this approach. Maybe the animals are smarter now.

Birds will pick the bait and set the trap off with maddening frequency. Putting a cover of brush on the pen will help, but it will still happen.

There are literally thousands of deadfall variations that can be built. I have seen everything from a guillotine made of 2x6's to a funny affair built on two stumps above the snow for marten. All of these are fine if they catch game, and I certainly applaud their originality. The trapper has adapted the environment and the available materials to the need at hand. This, I feel, is the name of the game. Anyone setting up deadfalls will have to do the same.

One deadfall variation that is especially noteworthy is made from stone. Should the poacher live where there are a lot of flat rocks laying on hard ground, it is possible to put in a number of these cheap and easy traps. Of course, in addition to the flat rocks there must be some game in the area.

The best rock set is one that is almost too heavy to lift. Set a figure 4 trigger under the rock and pile another stone on top. Usually this is enough weight to do the job. Point the bait stick under the rock and presto, the set is complete.

Of all the animals I like to catch in a deadfall, the best is a skunk. They are killed quickly and easily without scent which, in my book, counts ten points to start with. One fall day my brothers and I were running our traps when we came on a skunk caught in one of our deadfalls in our north woodlot.

He looked dead enough, so we threw the skunk in our pack basket and headed on down our line.

At the trail's end we'd built a tiny cabin that we used to spend the night in, warm and dry. There was barely enough room to move around past the stove and through the bunk beds, but it was much better than hiking home or sleeping in the open.

For some reason, we brought our packs into the cabin and set them inside the door while we warmed some beans for supper. After perhaps twenty minutes I went over to my pack and started pulling out the game I needed to skin. But instead of pulling out the skunk, it jumped out itself, full of life and vitality.

As soon as it hit the ground, it raised its tail and gave my brother a shot. He was so horrified he dropped the dinner all over the floor and jumped on the top bunk. I tried to follow him up, but I hit my head on the rafter and fell flat on the floor four feet in front of the skunk, which also let me have it.

My second attempt at gaining the high ground was successful, but my brother and I couldn't stand to be that near each other. It was really awful in that little cramped space. All the money I had in the world was about $3.00 and I would have gladly given every cent for a rear window in that cabin.

We held on a little longer, but the skunk gave us another shot. Our eyes burned so badly it was unbelievable.

The only weapon we had between us was my brother's belt knife. In sheer desperation and rage he threw the knife at the skunk and charged for the door. The skunk shot the knife and then shot at my brother departing the premises.

I couldn't take it any longer either and followed him out the door. The fresh air saved us from certain death.

Now it became a question of how to get the skunk out of the cabin. We didn't have a gun, and doing battle with a club or axe in that cramped space seemed pretty futile.

Finally after thirty minutes of banging on the walls and floor we got the skunk out of the cabin. It fled into the night, we know not where.

Now the fun really started. Quickly we gathered up our gear and threw the bedding over the fence. It was about three hours' hike home, but we had no choice. Nothing could live in that environment, and we couldn't sleep outside. Shortly after nine we made it to the farm, but our troubles weren't over. We stank so bad Mom wouldn't let us in the house. We took off our clothes and washed in a tub at the back door. I was never so cold in my life. She handed out clean clothes and blankets. We slept in the hay mow that night.

Next day I washed all our stuff in the stock tank and hung it on the line. Later Mom washed the clothes again and hung them again, but it took the smell three months to go away.

I only had one other pair of pants to wear and those got pretty bad. Even our teacher in school complained. The skunk definitely won that round. Since that day I always make my deadfalls plenty heavy.

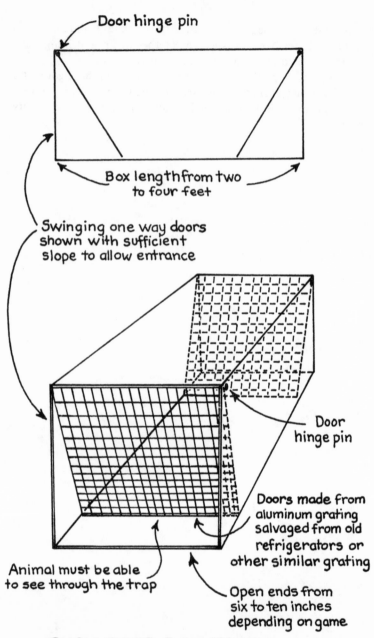

Door hinge pin

Box length from two
to four feet

Swinging one way doors
shown with sufficient
slope to allow entrance

Door
hinge pin

Doors made from
aluminum grating
salvaged from old
refrigerators or
other similar grating

Animal must be able
to see through the trap

Open ends from
six to ten inches
depending on game

PUSH DOOR BOX TRAP

13

BOX TRAPS

One of the great concerns I have is that many of the poaching techniques and devices that were common fifty years ago are being permanently lost to present outdoorsmen. At least two generations have come and gone since anybody knew anything about most of the poaching techniques I currently use. The reader will be my judge, but the standard simple push-type box trap fits that category. Nobody—especially the younger generation—knows anything about them, yet at one time it seemed that every other kid had at least one to catch rabbits with.

There are two variations of box traps. One has doors in both ends, the other has one door and a permanent grating fastened in the other end. The permanent grating, if used, should always be as open as possible. Animals are not nearly as fearful if they can see completely through the box.

Common box traps are constructed from any kind of solid material. This includes outdoor plywood, 1 inch boards, 2x8's and 2x10's, and even iron pipe or steel culverts, although this material is a lot more difficult to work with than wood.

Start by constructing a long rectangular box from 2 feet to 4 feet long. Size of the box will depend on the animals one expects to go after, but as a general rule the entrance should be no less than 6 inches square. Critters such as squirrels, rabbits, muskrats and mink work well in this minimum size. Coons, possums, cats, skunks, groundhogs and foxes need an 8 inch opening. Beaver, coyotes and badgers require a 10 inch trap that is the full 4 feet long.

I have seen a bear trap of this type made out of a piece of 4 foot steel culvert, but I don't think it was effective. The Fish and Game folks in Wyoming had one but I don't believe they ever caught a bear with it. There are other, more easily carried, and more effective traps for bear that will be covered in another chapter.

Doors for the end (or ends as the case may be) should be made out of very light steel or aluminum stock. In the larger traps, expanded steel is acceptable, but for the smaller 6 to 8 inch models I like to use a piece of aluminum grating, found in old refrigeration units. It is light, strong, and cheap. At times the stuff is hard to cut so that it still maintains its strength. I have remedied that by snipping off the piece I want and having the loose ends heli-arc welded back together. Cost is about $1.00 apiece when I have ten or twelve done.

The door is installed in the box so that it swings in but not out. It is very important that the door be angled quite a bit. Animals push in more readily if the door is sharply angled than if it is more nearly sraight up and down.

This trap is simply a box with one way doors. The critter pushes to the inside of the box but finds it can't push back out again, and is trapped. There are no triggers or pans. Everything is pure simplicity.

Application of the box trap is important. Animals will come to bait in them, but it is much better to be clever and use the traps other ways.

Easiest of all is to set them in the entrance to dens. Muskrats, especially, will swim right out of their bank den or reed house into one of these traps. I have caught as many as four rats in one six inch box trap in one night. By weighting the trap down with rocks, I was able to place it in front of a very active den and catch all I wanted.

Skunk and groundhog dens are other good prospects. Just be sure the trap is dug into the ground far enough so the critter has to come out through it. In some cases one might want to use two or three traps and cover all the exits. Caught skunks can be easily dispatched without odor by carrying the trap to a creek or pond and drowning them.

In town the box trap is beautiful. It encloses and hides the catch. Nobody will see an animal jumping around as they would with a steel trap. Also, few will know what they are. Even wardens have walked right by one of my traps set right out in the open without a question.

Traps in town can be set in natural runs where game is found to travel. A hole in a fence where rabbits run is a good place. They also can be baited with salt for rabbits and peanut butter for coons, possums, and skunks if there are any. Squirrels like buckeyes or acorns, if they can be found.

Out in the country we bait for coyote, mink, badger, skunks and coons with a live mouse in a jar. The lid of the jar should be punched and a handful of corn or wheat and leaves put in before the mouse is interred. When using bait, prop the door open an inch or two with a very small, thin twig.

On a farm the trap should be set next to a hen house or along the side of a barn. Wild creatures that visit a farmstead creep along the edge of buildings to hide. By piling boards on the trap to create a natural tunnel, one can catch everything that comes through the area.

When we used to raise pheasants, my wife would keep a box trap set along the side of their outdoor runs, right up against the wire. She managed to catch several fox, a number of coons and possums, and even a mink with her trap.

Beavers can be taken with these traps but it is usually too much work. I tore a dam out one time and, as the water level fell, put three big traps in the exit holes of the lodge. Next morning I had two beavers, but the dam was repaired. Evidently some of the beavers lived in bank dens. I had a devil of a time getting the traps out of five feet of freezing water.

Be sure to check the traps often. Some critters can tear up the box or ruin their skins if left too long in the trap. Badgers, especially, are very hard on box traps. Skunks may get impatient and give away their presence.

The only other word of advice I have pertaining to these very simple devices is to carefully judge the prey and use the right sized box. Too big is not effective, and too little will just keep the game out of the box. Should there be a chance of collecting a whole colony of animals, as with skunks or muskrats, use an extra long box.

14
DENS

The following are some quick and easy methods I've used to clear animal dens of their residents.

Digging

Digging is the most inefficient and wasteful way there is to clear a den. For example, the first fox I ever tried to dig out of a den was a killer. Actually the fox wasn't especially lethal, but the project sure did kill a lot of time and energy.

Three of us walked half a mile back to an open ditch that ran through the center of a section of prime northern Illinois farm ground. We timed our arrival to coincide with the coming of night so that no one would see us out in the middle of that flat open country.

Earlier in the day we jumped the fox near a pond we were checking for frogs. We followed it with our binoculars to a rough spoil bank area along the ditch. After some diligent searching, we located a den which we were reasonably certain held the fox. As a bonus, it seemed likely that the den might also have a family of little foxes in it. Fox were worth $5.00 each in Illinois at the time, making the project worthwhile from an economic standpoint.

We plugged the den with a large rock and left till dark.

That night, we hauled in a pick, an axe, two shovels and a lantern, which is quite a load to pack that far.

The stone was still in place, so I cut an 8 foot limb off a willow growing in the ditch and probed the hole. We should have been more alarmed than we were when the pole slipped in almost the full length at a pretty steep angle downward. It stopped at a bend which we assumed was the turn leading into the den chamber.

By taking turns, the three of us had the den dug out a full 8 feet

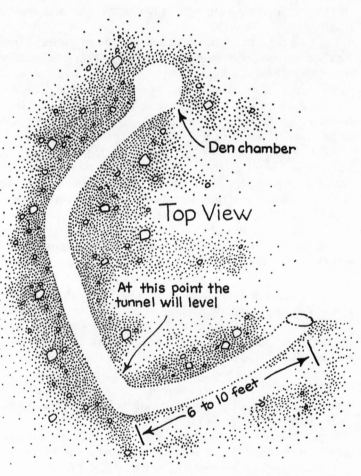

Den chamber

Top View

At this point the
tunnel will level

6 to 10 feet

TYPICAL SINGLE ENTRANCE
FOX OR SKUNK DEN

to the first turn by about 7:30. The only problem was that the trench was now almost 6 feet at the far end. It was very difficult to get the pole in the hole again. The cut we made was so narrow we couldn't work in it. However, after some additional digging and cutting, we finally got the pole around the corner and made a reading.

The hole turned at right angles and went down another 6 feet. This, we reasoned, was the end of the line. The next turn had to be into the den itself.

We continued on, digging like three demented grave robbers. Anyone brave enough to creep back and watch would have been scared out of their wits. The flickering lantern threw a sinister light on us, standing next to a pile of dirt the size of a car.

At 11:00 p.m. we called a halt to the project. There was still at least two feet to go till the turn, but as a result of some short stick probes it seemed very likely that the tunnel turned again. We strongly suspected that there was another 6 foot section of digging ahead. It was late, we were exhausted and the prospects of reaching the end of the tunnel seemed as dim as our smoky lantern. Before leaving I put a trap in the hole and blocked the passage with a pile of rocks. Next afternoon I came back. The trap was thrown, the rocks scattered about, and the fox long gone.

It was a valuable lesson in using half-assed methods to accomplish worthwhile objectives.

The next fox den I found a few years later was on my own property. Instead of piddling around, I called my friend who worked with his dad operating backhoes. We dragged a backhoe in with a tractor and had the foxes out in fifteen minutes.

As mentioned, I don't recommend digging dens. Some of the other methods of getting animals out are bad enough, but digging totally ruins the creature's shelter.

A backhoe can't get in where most dens are located anyway. Also, very few property owners will tolerate the disruption and mess that a backhoe creates. As a poaching tool, I would have to strike them from the list, except under unusual circumstances.

When digging dens by conventional means, remember that they are, as a rule, deeper and longer than one would suppose. Plan to put a lot of energy into the project. Be sure the den is occupied and that no other planned activities—like sleep—will interfere.

132

Barb Wire Den Snake

All options considered, the best method of extracting animals from a den relies on barb wire to do the job. Most den dwellers are long-haired animals such as fox, skunk, or wood chucks. A piece of barb wire will tangle in the hair of these mammals, and allow the poacher to pull them out without any significant damage to the hide or the hole. Using barb, the den is left intact for the next occupant, which in my book is important.

It is possible to pick up an old piece of barb wire and improvise it into a den snagging device. But a better, more effective design is available. I call it the den snake.

I use a double strand of #9 wire (not barb) about 20 feet long as the basic part of my den snake. At one end of the wire, put a 2 foot stick that is stout enough to withstand some rigorous turning, twisting and pulling. At the wire's other end, fashion a sturdy loop about 1 inch in diameter.

Attach 4 feet of barb wire to the loop. Now double it back so there is an effective double length of barb wire 2 feet long at the loop end of the #9 carrying wire. As the barb becomes tattered and twisted, it can be replaced. Use heavy duty barb wire and not the cheap, light foreign product that one often sees these days. The wire should have 4 pronged barbs, spaced every 8 inches or so. Some wire has the barbs so widely spaced that it isn't of much value.

Carefully work the barb bundle into the den, turning the handle and pushing the wire ahead as much as is possible. Moist, loose soil is hard to work with but not nearly so tough as a den in amongst tree roots.

Often when the wire comes to the end of the hole, and there is an animal there, it will feel like hitting a fairly solid sponge. Turn the wire quickly in one direction at least 10 or 12 times. Then pull it out of the hole. If there is an animal snagged, pulling it will be difficult.

The whole process is not unlike running a sewer router. The rig will hang up more and be more difficult to work into the den in the first place, but the similarity still remains.

About the most "fun" for a poacher using this device occurs when he ties into a skunk. They are in such a vile humor when they clear the hole all tangled in the barb, that there isn't time to shoot them before they shoot first. Working conditions get pretty rough at these den entrances.

In most cases there will be more than one animal per den. Be

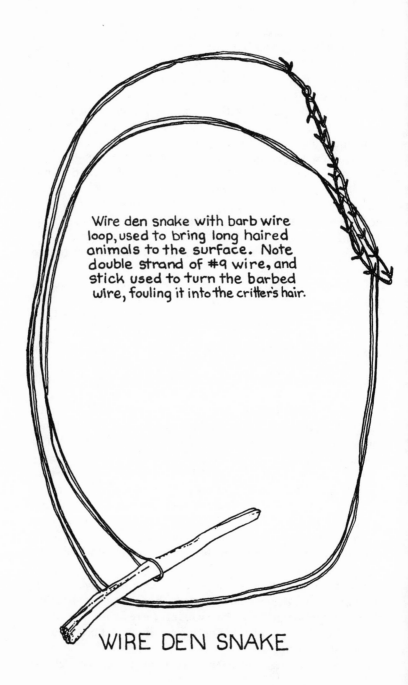

Wire den snake with barb wire
loop, used to bring long haired
animals to the surface. Note
double strand of #9 wire, and
stick used to turn the barbed
wire, fouling it into the critters hair.

WIRE DEN SNAKE

sure to run the wire back in and try again. I have in the past pulled five groundhogs from a den, or on another occasion, seven foxes. Since their skin is thin, rabbits are easy to take with barb wire. Often they are found in the same den with skunks.

The den snake can be rolled up over one's shoulder and carried without arousing a great deal of suspicion. Construction is cheap, and they are effective. At times it takes two people to hold the wire and twist it in the hole, but that is about the greatest hardship to using the device.

If the den has more than one entrance, the barb wire trick may not work. A variation is sometimes helpful.

Mechanical Ferret

Some years ago a company advertised and sold a device called a mechanical ferret. Its selling point was the fact that one did not have to house, feed, clean and train a live ferret if they had this outfit's handy dandy little mechanical device.

They are no longer available, but those who want a mechanical ferret can buy a 20 foot sewer rod and have about the same thing. Or if the reader is poor, as are most poachers, he can make one out of #9 wire.

The construction procedure is exactly the same as for the barb wire den snake, but the barb is left off the smooth wire. In the case of an all purpose mechanical den ferret, it is wise to use galvanized wire which is harder and more resilient than the #9 wire.

A well built, wire ferret is a good all purpose tool that can be used for many different poaching applications. It can be used with or without barb, with smoke cartridges or even with ammoniated rags.

When the den has many entrances, it is best to approach the area very quietly without broadcasting one's presence. Pick the most active hole and quickly work the wire ferret down into the hole. The sudden commotion will startle the animal out of the den sixty percent of the time.

It is best to either quietly set a trap at the other exit holes, or be prepared to shoot. Under these circumstances, a companion helps immensely. Often a trap will miss the fleeing critters, so it is wise to be ready to shoot.

Animals will not leave their dens if they know all the exits are covered. We spent two hours trying to get a fox out of a culvert one afternoon, but never succeeded. The fox knew instinctively that if he made a break for it, his chances were slim. The culvert was

135

about forty feet long and we could even see him in the pipe. Next day we came back with some barb wire but the animal was gone.

If the quarry decides to hold fast, and can't be snagged with barb wire, it may be necessary to try another method.

Smoke

Smoke bombs are one of the easiest, most efficient ways I know of for clearing out an obstinate den.

Before about 1954 it was easy and fun to make smoke bombs. All of the kids knew the secret, but about that time the film companies changed their method of making photographic film and the practice fell into disuse.

For those who want to remember the bad old days, I suggest the following method of making smoke bombs.

Take about five of the old, very flammable celluloid photographic negatives made before 1954 and roll them into a half inch tube. Tie the tube with a string to keep it intact.

Cover the negatives with 10 to 12 layers of newspaper and allow the ends of the paper to extend at least 2 inches past the negatives. Twist the paper ends up tight and tie it securely.

To light the smoke bomb, set one end of the paper on fire and wait till the celluloid film also catches fire and is burning briskly Lay the burning bomb on the ground and smartly stamp out the flames. The package will continue to smoulder, giving off clouds of dense obnoxious smoke.

Too bad the film makers changed their formula. We used to find these little devices of immense value at home, in school and on the farm.

For modern day poachers who need smoke to clear dens, and can't find any old film, I suggest the following types of improvised smoke bombs.

1. Collect some large corn cobs and put them in a place where they will thoroughly dry. After they dry, soak the cobs in kerosene for several days. Make a small holding basket for the end of the wire ferret that will protect the cob as it is pushed into the den. After putting one or two cobs in the basket, light them on fire and wait till they are going well. Run these as far into the den as possible. The lack of oxygen will add to the effect by causing the kerosene and cob to smoulder profusely, and by robbing the critter of its air in the tunnel.

2. Make smoke bombs. These are better than the cob business but they require a lot more work.

Use two parts of sulfur, one part of finely ground charcoal and one part finely screened sawdust. All these chemicals are easily purchased.

Mix the three together and pack into a toilet paper tube. Glue cardboard discs in either end to contain the mixture. I also glue 5 or 6 match heads in one end of the smoke bomb to make it easier to ignite.

To use the device, punch about 8 holes in the cardboard and put the bomb in the basket of the wire ferret. Light the bomb and as soon as it is going well, push it back into the hole as far as possible.

Whenever smoking animals out, be sure there is another exit to the hole. If not, the critters will probably elect to stay in the den and die of suffocation. They will not, as a general rule, come out past the poacher.

If the smoke comes bellowing out of the hole, it may be necessary to push the wire in the den further, or to plug the main tunnel forcing the smoke and the critters into other exits.

Thirty years ago we would occasionally run across a bellows contraption that poachers would use to blow smoke into a den. The operator cranked the machine to produce smoke generated from burning old burlap bags, sometimes sprinkled with sulfur.

As a poaching tool they were a complete bust. They were big and cumbersome, hard to hide and expensive to build. For these reasons, they eventually fell into disuse.

Ammonia

At one time when I was living near three large cities, I ran a successful animal removal business. I would remove unwanted animals from people's basements, under crawl spaces, or out of their garages. To get things rolling, I went around and talked to the police, offering to remove the critters for a fee. In all three cities they were delighted to let me handle a chore they didn't particularly care for. Later people called me themselves as my fame spread.

During that four year period, I removed perhaps thirty skunks from people's basements and never had one get belligerent. My method, which has a lot of application for poachers, was to use a squirt gun filled with ammonia.

At times it is possible to drive a coon or a fox out of a den, or from under a barn, with ammonia in a squirt gun, but usually it is best to use a small piece of cloth. Soak the cloth in ammonia and run it to the back of the den with the wire ferret and watch the action. No animal will stay in the den with that stuff near them. Ammonia is better than any type smoke in this regard and, with the correct procedures, easier and less obnoxious to handle.

Gas and Water

Some of the old farmers in our neighborhood used to mix 2 gallons of gas with 5 gallons of water to drive animals out of their dens. They would soak the mixture down the hole in what looked like an attempt to drown out the critter. After the ground soaked up the liquid, they threw a match in the den and started it burning.

The theory was that the water would carry the gas down into the den where it could be ignited for the desired effect.

I have never used the method myself but have seen it work fairly well on groundhogs, if the whole purpose of the effort was to ruin the den and kill the inhabitants. Invariably the fur of the critter is singed and worthless. Rabbits that came from burned out dens are especially messed up.

Dynamite

Blasting a den will work to rid it of any inhabitants. The method involved isn't as immediately obvious as one would first suppose, and it can be done in a manner that won't ruin animal hides; I am still reluctant to use it, though.

Blasting a den completely ruins the animal's home. There is one less place for them to live, cutting off a potential source of income forever.

The mess created by the blast is hard to clean up and is certain to create a problem later on. Land owners don't seem to like to have their pasture fields and woodlots cratered by bomb blasts. . . .

Dynamiting is also a lot of work. If the reader decides to try this method, he is well advised to bring along a couple of stout friends and some good shovels. There is a lot of spade work to do after the smoke clears.

For those who want to try dynamite, proceed as follows. First cap one stick and, depending on the depth of the hole, use three to six additional sticks for the main charge. The charge should be placed as far back in the hole as possible. If the operation is on posted property, be sure not to over charge the set. A muffled thump won't be noticed, but an overpowering roar is another matter.

Pack the entrance to the den with lots of moist soil. Now set off the charge.

After the shot, the hole should be cleaned out with a shovel and examined. It may be necessary to hit it again.

I haven't used dynamite in dens very often, but every time I have used it, the first blast has killed the critter instantly. In this day and age, with dynamite at $.90 a pound and caps costing $.75 each, I recommend one of the other methods of getting animals out of dens.

The Black Bag

Believe it or not, this method works—sometimes. I have used it as a curiosity procedure on several occasions and always got a good laugh out of the effort. In a slightly modified form it has value as a poaching technique.

Materials required are a square yard of heavy black cotton material and a rifle or bow and arrow. This is one of the few serious poaching applications I know of for a bow. Generally I consider bows to be clumsy, underpowered, inaccurate devices of little use to a poacher.

Black bagging only works for groundhogs. The poacher must be certain a groundhog inhabits the hole in question and that the critters haven't been hunted or harassed up to that time.

Carefully and quietly approach the den into the wind. Sneak in as inobtrusively as is possible. Lay the piece of black cloth on the ground over the hole. Pack it down lightly so that most of the large cracks are filled. The set can't be made light tight, but it should come pretty close. If a breeze is moving, weight the edges of the cloth down with small rocks.

As soon as the hole is covered, pull back from the set about 15 feet and sit down to wait. If it is a sunny day and the chucks have been coming out, one will butt its head against the cloth within twenty minutes. Be sure to remain perfectly quiet and stay down wind from the hole.

When movement is seen in the cloth, the poacher has two or three options. He can try and shoot the critter through the bag with a bow and arrow, or blast it with a gun. Most woodchucks that are stuck with an arrow under these circumstances will stay on the surface, but a gun shot chuck will invariably slip into its quarters below before dying.

My younger brother used to wait for hours beside some woodchuck holes back in our woodlot and try to club the chucks when they stuck their heads out. But, as far as I know, he never got a single chuck this way.

The black bag will not work on night animals such as skunks, coons or even rabbits. There is, however, a related trapping method that makes use of the sack psychology.

I have successfully set steel traps at the entrance to dens that I have covered over with a burlap bag or some other material. Apparently the animal doesn't know what to make of the dark cover over its hole and loses some caution. I have collected several denned-up fox this way that I believe would have eluded my trap without the burlap cover.

Den Trees

Once a den in a tree is located, the biggest chore is getting up in the tree to the den. One relatively easy way dictates the use of climber spikes. Climber spikes are used by utility servicemen, to climb poles, and by lumberjacks, to climb large trees. With one important exception, the spikes are the same for poles and trees.

Basically a climber spike is a steel strap bent in the shape of an "L." It is worn on the inside of the leg below the knee, held on by two leather leg straps and a strap over the boot piece. On most commercial models, the steel strap is padded so it won't dig into the user's leg.

A slightly angled steel spur is welded on the inside of the steel strap. The spur points downward. The spurs will dig into the pole or tree, allowing one to walk up the timber by first digging in one spur and then the other.

If the above description sounds confused, I suggest stopping next time a utility truck is seen and talking with the linemen. This is the easiest place to get information on the device and to see them first hand.

A word of caution here. When ever I have needed climber spikes, I have been able to buy them from utility company servicemen. They sometimes have an extra old set that is for sale. That is the easy way to acquire climber spikes. But the spikes used for poles are significantly different from those used on trees in one respect.

The tree variety have much longer spurs. The longer spurs are needed to dig through the bark to hold the climber. Utility poles are always peeled and require relatively short spurs.

In some cases the utility servicemen have climber spikes with changeable spurs. Usually the poacher will have to take the climbers to a welding shop and have the spurs lengthened. They should be stretched to at least twice as long as regular pole spurs.

140

People who climb poles use a safety belt hooked around the pole and to a harness worn like a belt by the climber. Unless a tree is relatively limb free, it can't be climbed with a safety belt.

To use the climbers, spike the spur very soundly into the tree at what seems like a lot of angle. When weight is applied, the angle will decrease, and the spur should be embedded in the meat of the tree. Climb up one notch and spike the other foot, proceeding up the tree in that fashion as far as needed.

Practice initially on trees from 14 to 24 inches in diameter. It is easier to climb a smaller tree where one's legs can be wrapped around and the spurs pushed in on opposite sides. A very large tree must essentially be climbed on its face.

Climber spikes worn under loose pants are hard to detect. It is mildly clumsy to wear them walking, but not severely.

Once up to the den hole, I use a smoke bomb, squirt gun with ammonia, or a rag soaked in ammonia to run the critter out. Many dens in trees are so small that a short two foot piece of barb wire will do the job, or the animals can be dispatched in the day with a handgun.

Ferrets

Up until about twenty-five years ago it was common to use ferrets to run rabbits out of their burrows and as a control measure for rats. Probably because of strict state laws regarding use of ferrets, and the advent of good commercial rat poisons, ferrets are now unknown to most people.

Domestic ferrets originally come from Egypt where they have been trained for thousands of years. The ferret is a small brown animal, weighing about three pounds. A large one will measure thirty inches tip to tip. To a casual observer, they look like a large mink. Ferrets, however, have hair and not fur.

Not only do ferrets look like mink, but they also act like mink. They are ferocious carnivores and have the same scent glands a mink or skunk does.

Ferrets have been bred in North America for well over 100 years now and have, to a certain extent, acclimated themselves to our colder climate. But they still do better in the southern states where elaborate precautions to keep them warm are unnecessary. Apparently they will not live in the wild in North America or will only do so in limited numbers. Many have been "liberated" or have escaped but there are no records of sizeable native populations.

Animals such as rabbits and rats are inherently fearful of ferrets and will flee from their dens immediately if one enters. Some ferrets can also chase out mink, skunks and coons, but that process is far from certain. Most ferrets are used to scare rabbits out of their dens where they are subsequently collected with shotguns or a .22 rifle.

It used to be common for one of us to carry a trained ferret in a special large pocket in an old overcoat. No one knew we had the ferret with us, and we could merrily go about our business as soon as everybody was out of sight.

To work well, a ferret must be handled extensively. They are by nature very feisty and difficult. I never handle one without some kind of leather gloves. With constant personal attention, they will eventually settle down enough so that it is practical to move them around, but it isn't always easy.

Ferrets and mink require a similar diet. I believe there are several commercial dry feeds on the market today that would be much simpler than the ground fresh meat preparations we had to contend with in years past. Ferret chow in any form is expensive and should be considered as part of the cost of keeping them as a poaching tool.

Hunting rats with a ferret is good sport, but not of much economic benefit to the poacher. The best animal to use is a female with a litter. She will hunt for several hours at a time and drive out or kill a tremendous number of rats.

The primary poaching use of ferrets comes when collecting rabbits. If there are a large number of rabbits living in dens in one's territory, a ferret is an incredibly efficient way of collecting a lot of them very quickly.

The system is very simple. Carry the ferret along till a den is spotted and then release it at the entrance. After a few minutes of sniffing around, the critter will go into the hole and proceed to clear it. We stand back a few feet and shoot the escaping rabbits with .22 shorts.

At times a ferret will kill a rabbit and stay in the hole to eat it. If this happens, there is no choice but to sit and wait it out. Some poachers use a harness with a cord on their ferrets, but I prefer to feed them well before the hunt and take my chances.

Another hazard with ferrets in the north is that they don't like to come out in the cold from the warm hole. I carry some food in my coat pocket as well as some old rags. My ferrets usually come right out and get in the warm pocket.

142

Perhaps this short piece on these interesting little animals will renew some interest in raising them. I hate to think that running ferrets will become a lost art.

There are perhaps 100 ferret breeders left in the U.S. Most of them advertise from time to time in *Outdoor Life*, *Field And Stream* or *Popular Mechanics*. A matched pair is not particularly expensive. A pen can be constructed in a matter of hours, putting the poacher in business simply and easily. I suggest that readers give ferret raising serious consideration before the art is forever lost in this country.

White-Tailed Deer
Odocoileus virginianus

144

15
DEER

Probably the single most sought after big game animal in North America is the white tail deer. White tails are very abundant, extremely prolific and are about the largest animal the average hunter is likely to encounter. As a result, they are the ultimate game as far as most hunters are concerned.

Tons of information have been written about hunting deer. Most of the information is pretty much the same. If it is the reader's goal to stop hunting deer, and start reducing them to possession, I urge a careful reading of this chapter.

There aren't a great many tricks to poaching deer. On the other hand, it doesn't take a great many techniques to get all the deer one could possibly use in a year. For the most part, the information here is simple and straight forward, but is not found in any other text.

At one time I lived where deer were the only hoofed animals. It took ten per year to feed my family, but taking those ten wasn't a particular chore. On one memorable hunt we got four deer, and a few days later we went out again and got three more. In preparation for this chapter I glanced through my diary. According to carefully kept records, there were eleven days in the last ten years when I got three deer. On another hunt I managed to bring down four mule deer, but that was a special case.

Often the biggest problem a poacher has is getting into the places where the deer abound. Farmers fall in love with their deer, land owners want to have them around to look at, or to save for themselves during hunting season. State and national parks have tremendous deer populations, but it's against the rules to hunt them. All of these factors work both for and against the poacher who wants to live on the natural fruits of the land.

Rather than bridling against these limitations, I suggest that the reader go back and review the chapters on *Protecting The Resource* and *Exit and Evasion*. Environmentalists and Save-The-Deer types play right into the hand of the skilled poacher who is willing to take a little time and properly learn his trade.

Other than traditional deer hunting during the season business, reducing a deer to possession is incredibly easy. Seasoned poachers will certainly agree. Some might even go a step farther and say they aren't that difficult even during the hunting season. Yet for the average hunter, bagging a white tail continues to be a big deal.

It's a big deal because on a *quid pro quo* basis the white tail is much smarter than the average hunter. It might be surprising and helpful to list the ways a deer is smarter. Here they are:

1. A deer knows the country better than the nimrod pursuing him. There is no reason a hunter can't learn the country as well as the deer that live there, but most don't. But if one is to become a successful poacher, he will have to make a start at it, if only to keep from getting caught.

2. A deer has a far better sense of smell than a hunter. True enough, but what good is a superior sense of smell if the poacher is moving toward the deer with the wind in his face? Also, most methods poachers use do not influence quarry having a superior sense of smell.

3. Deer have better eyesight than hunters. This isn't necessarily true. Deer are color blind and can't change camouflage suits to match the seasons. I believe it's about a tossup with the trained, alert poacher.

4. Deer can run faster farther. So what. Ninety-nine times out of a hundred deer escape by sneaking away, not by outrunning the hunter. On short sprints around hills or through a patch of woods, it's a tossup. The hunter should be able to move fast enough to get himself into position to shoot, otherwise any marathon running ability is unnecessary.

5. Deer can hear better than a hunter. Perhaps true—perhaps not true. At any rate, the poacher should not try to imitate a storm trooper in heat moving through the woods. Most poaching techniques have nothing to do with anything's sense of hearing.

6. Deer can hide in the woods better than the average hunter. Maybe they can hide better than the average hunter, but the average poacher had better be able to hide as well as a white tail or his ass is going to be grass. Hiding in the woods has nothing to do with catching deer, only with not getting caught.

There are other attributes of deer and of hunters that could be reviewed. I think, however, my point is made. Don't be so dumb as to try and match deer one for one in the woods. Under those circumstances they *will* be smarter. Instead, use techniques that do not affect a deer's senses, and play on all their failings. Then it will be easy to bring home the venison.

A couple of falls past two of us set out on a deer hunt. We were dropped off at 3:00 p.m. and were a mile or so from the road by 3:15 p.m., when we received a call on our radios that one of my boys had returned home and wanted to join the hunt. He was on the road talking to us from a mobile unit, so we arranged to meet him in the field.

The two of us originally on the hunt worked around a large hill. Shortly before dusk started, with the wind in our faces, we headed toward an old orchard. In the mean time, my boy crept up to the same orchard from the side and was sitting, watching the deer eat.

With only fifteen minutes of light remaining, he shot a fat old doe in the head. The noise alerted the other deer as well as a farmer who came to the window of his house to see who might have made the noise. The poached deer fell perhaps 500 yards from his back window in an almost open field. Quickly my boy pulled it behind a small pine and lay on it to help camouflage it. He was wearing a good set of camouflage coveralls and a camo jacket. The jacket was vital as an additional cover for the deer.

Although the pine was very small, no bigger than a Christmas tree, the farmer didn't appear to see either my boy or the deer.

In addition to the deer already on the ground, there were at least six others. Two of them came running through, contouring the hill above us. One very nice buck stopped dead still when it got down wind of me. I spotted it in a small clearing about 200 yards away, and put one round through its middle. It ran about ten feet and collapsed.

Quickly I pulled it into a thicket. We were about 800 yards from the farm house and I didn't like the idea of firing a second shot. Fortunately, the wind was blowing away from the house, and in a few more minutes it would be fully dark. The buck was a nice big one, well worth expending a little time to take.

After dark my boy came up and told us what had happened. I sent him down with my friend to get the first white tail out whole. "No sense leaving a pile of guts on this farmer's door step," I told them. In the interim I snuggled under a tree on a high open point where I could watch with my binoculars. It wasn't long before they were back with the deer, but the farmer and his boy had apparently decided to drive the roads to look for a car or other evidence of the shooters. I could see their truck moving slowly along the country lane below us.

We gutted the first deer, took off the head and feet, and put the rest into a package to carry. Leaving the head and feet makes sense since they do weigh something and are hard to carry. At home the head and feet are tough to dispose of. We scattered them on the hill in very heavy thickets.

I went ahead and scouted above the buck I killed. As soon as I knew for certain the coast was clear, my friend packed the doe north about a half a mile to an old farm road. My boy and I gutted out the remaining buck and packaged it for transport. It was a very large heavy deer.

Soon we were ready. "O.k.," I whispered in the radio. "O.k.," came the response from the watcher sitting on the doe.

In a few minutes we were together again. I took all the rifles and two of the three radios, leaving the porters with one radio between them. It was my job to move out on point a hundred yards ahead and be sure the way was clear.

We walked for about a mile straight north along the old farm road, towards our pickup point. It was getting close to seven, the appointed time for our ride.

All of a sudden I saw lights coming over a small hill ahead of us. I raced back to the fellows and hurriedly boosted them over a low fence to our left. We were right out in the open in the middle of a large wheat field. The only cover was the high grass along the fence.

Quickly we lay the deer out in the furrow along the fence and tried to flatten ourselves into the ground.

Seconds later the truck passed within ten feet.

As soon as it was down a little hill away from us, we picked up our gear and game and ran up the fence row another 150 yards to a place where there were some bushes. It was a more screened place to hide, plus I could see the road from that point.

148

"Two two," I called on the radio. "Twenty two, can you copy?" There was no answer.

Behind us the truck growled in low gear as it pulled off the little grass lane. The farmer was obviously trying to swing the lights around in the field.

Far in the distance I saw car lights turn onto the gravel side road that wound up past the farm lane we were pinned down on.

"Three three eight," cracked the radio.

"This is three three eight," I whispered. "Hold your present position. Do not come in till we are all clear, do you copy?"

"I copy," came the reply, and far in the distance we could see the lights flicker out.

"Well, bless her heart," my friend whispered. "This isn't a job for a dumb broad, is it?"

We were indeed thankful for a knowledgeable, alert pickup driver.

The farmer's truck rumbled back to the lane and started out. We flattened behind the bushes.

As soon as it was past, we were up and moving. My boy and hunting companion carried the two deer, and I took the three guns, three radios, pair of binoculars and two jackets.

By the time the truck got to the road we were 300 yards behind and winded. There was no time to stop, however. The truck turned east, away from our waiting pick up car and moved on slowly.

"Two two," I called, "come in immediately." "Roger, three three eight. I am rolling," came the immediate reply.

Quickly, I sent the fellows racing for the road while I stood watch. Farmer Brown's pickup disappeared around a bend into the trees.

"Can you kill that light switch," I called. The lights on the pickup car went out.

The pickup gal pulled into the farm lane below just enough to get off the road. My boy stopped her and immediately unlocked the trunk. Both deer went into a large plastic mattress cover. The trunk was shut in less than twenty seconds.

Usually I don't like to send hunters home with game, but in this case the two jumped in the back seat and got on the floor. The car, already in motion, headed back out the way it came in. I started walking parallel to the road, 200 yards out in the field.

At home the two deer were hung in a tree behind the house at a place where they could easily be moved if need be.

All of the bloody clothing went into the washer immediately, and the two men took a shower in the basement. The car was checked for blood and hair.

About forty minutes later I got a call. "Three three eight, this is 300."

"Three hundred, pick me up at the red barn," I answered, and they did.

That night we butchered and wrapped the two deer. Using our own efficient butchering technique we were able to put the deer in the freezer in forty-five minutes using three trained people. We had five, so it didn't take that long.

In logical order, here is how I feel one can go about easily reducing many deer to possession.

Does

I mention doe deer not as a technique, but because there are still poachers who have an aversion to shooting them.

In a surprising number of places in the United States and Canada, the deer population has expanded to the point where the environment cannot accommodate any more. This problem is intensified by the increase in state and national park lands, monuments, game preserves and the no-trespassing-save-the-animals mentality. This phenomenon has already been discussed at length.

The point is that if the poacher takes only bucks, there will still be an incredible number of doe deer, especially young that will die the next winter. In places where only bucks are customarily shot, it is my observation that the herd often lacks vigor. Too many bucks are killed, and often the does that remain are barren, wormy and poor.

My rule of thumb is to start taking deer in the fall as soon as the young can take care of themselves. This is generally when the adults reach sixty to ninety pounds, depending on the continent and the type of deer. For example, coastal black tails are smaller, and a sixty pound black tail would be plenty large. On the other hand, mule deer are hardly big enough to care for themselves at ninety pounds.

Each poacher will have to decide for himself what that date is for his area.

After I know the young deer can care for themselves, I start shooting deer by size. I take only the larger third of the herd, regardless of sex. This precludes some methods of taking deer, which is fine that early in the year.

The only exception to this rule is that I never shoot doe deer with twins. Invariably the doe is in marginal health from nursing the two. I also feel that such doe are a very valuable part of the breeding herd and should be left.

By being size selective only, it is surprising at how many barren does one comes across. In many areas I believe they outnumber the bucks, especially where it is illegal to kill does.

Baiting Deer

Recently a farmer in our area discovered a mineral block that I put out for deer. In many cases it is a foolish waste of time and money to pack salt in for deer, since they can get all they want from blocks set out for cattle. But in this case a nice little woods with an abandoned apple orchard lay especially far from anything else, so I thought it was worth the effort.

The farmer called the warden who went out to examine the situation. After a close scrutiny, our intrepid warden decided that the salt was indeed set out for deer and that he had better stake out the location. It was the middle of September. Our warden waited patiently five days for someone to show up, his truck parked right out in the open on the road. We all laughed about the possum sheriff's stupidity, but at least he wasn't snooping around someplace else during that time.

In case the reader does not know this, deer won't generally come to salt in the fall. They may stay in the area, or come by the lick every week or so, but salt is not the magnet for them in fall that it is in the spring. This holds true for elk, moose and bear as well.

Should the poacher decide to put salt out, I recommend a location that is high and dry, yet near to water. The ground should be clay, if possible, and the location sheltered by trees or heavy brush. It is best to find a spot that is used by deer at present, or plan to wait at least three years before activity builds around a new lick.

If detection is a problem, use rock salt rather than blocks. The deer will eat the ground after the salt is melted, and is therefore not as easy to spot.

In fall the best locations for deer are around old apple or pear trees, or in orchards. Deer just can't leave apple trees alone.

I locate every apple tree in my deer territory early in fall and check them regularly for activity. One old tree stands in a little horseshoe clearing in the midst of a fairly large woods. I think that fifty years ago there was a farm house there, but now the tree stands alone. Six or eight years ago we went back and pruned the tree out so it would produce many apples again. Since that time we have killed no less than twenty deer there from a little stand six feet up in a near pine.

Sorghum, wheat or corn work well for a bait in some places. I often bait a grain set up for birds and find deer visiting it. Sometimes farmers will leave a few rows of corn or a small patch of oats or wheat for local deer. Watch these especially late in the season. The deer may hang around, allowing the poacher to get them using other methods.

Another bait that is often overlooked or dismissed as unimportant, especially in the west, is a green patch of alfalfa, clover or grass. Early in fall before the snow flies, these little spots that stay watered have a tremendous appeal to deer. I know of two within five miles of our present home that I have seen a high of nine deer on, and several more that are consistently used by four or five.

Early Hunting

It is very important that the deer poacher get out and make his harvest early while the critters can still be taken easily. "Early" varies from one section of the country to the other, but is usually from September first through the end of October. The deer are much more relaxed, there are few people in the woods, and the days are longer.

When the days are long and hot the deer will get hungry and thirsty before dark. If they have no reason to be suspicious, the poacher can be sitting there waiting for them at dusk, and have his pick of good shots. As an added bonus, early hunting will eventually alarm the deer. They will be shy during the regular season, protecting the resource for the poacher who can easily collect all he needs after hunting season ends.

Early deer hunting is more than just hunting. One must know the country, be able to enter unnoticed into the best areas, inobtrusively make the kill, and get the deer back out again—without getting caught.

Spotlighting

Almost every poacher in the country has used a spotlight for deer at one time or another. If there is a universal method used by poachers, spotlighting has to be it. Kids in school go out spotlighting, farmers occasionally shoot deer from combines, men too old or lazy to walk spotlight, to the extent that half of what most wardens do is try to catch spotlighters.

For this reason I seldom spotlight deer, and if I do, it is only under the most cautious and controlled circumstances.

Spotlighting deer involves driving around in a car or truck at night and sweeping a light across a meadow or clearing where deer might be feeding. A hand-held spot works best with the driver operating the light as well as the vehicle. Hand-held spots are less obvious and are much more flexible than permanently mounted lights.

The light should be at least 200,000 candle power unless other factors preclude one that bright.

Spotlighters should be careful to keep the light down and off when not in use. Don't flash it around indiscriminately and arouse the suspicion of farmers or ranchers.

When the light hits the deer, they will often freeze. If they have been hunted before, or there are shadows from brush, or the light hits them from behind, the deer will not hold. Previously shot over deer, for instance, will run as soon as the car stops and will duck and crawl under the imagined barrier at the edge of the light beam.

All shots for deer in a spotlight should be made at the head or neck. By so doing, they are either got or not got. Looking for a wounded deer at night is no fun.

Use a quiet gun and only ever shoot once in an area. Some people use .22 rimfire rifles for deer, but I never felt this cartridge had enough power. They aren't even all that quiet.

As soon as the deer is down, kill all the lights and dump out the pickup men. There should be two—one to gut the deer and the other to help. Use two way radios, if possible.

Having dropped the men, the driver should continue on up the road for five or six miles looking for potential problems. If it is practical and won't arouse suspicion, I like to come back past the kill and check out the back road too.

Assuming the coast is clear, pick up the deer and hunters and head out.

Spotlighting is full of dangers, to the point that I don't feel it is worth the risk. But if the reader is determined to try it, here are some suggestions. Not all are always practical, but they will help keep one out of trouble.

    1. Spotlight remote meadows with only one access, or on private ground where no one will know or care what is happening.

2. Post watchers on the roads with radios. If necessary, use more than one rig.

3. Never hit the same area twice. This still won't keep the good poacher from falling into a trap set for a sloppy poacher who was there the night before, but it will help.

4. Watch closely for cars, campers, farm houses and anything suspicious.

5. Consider picking up the deer the next day rather than taking it home that night.

6. Don't carry the rifle and light in the same car after a shot is made.

7. Gut the critter back away from the road so there won't be easily found evidence left that a deer was spotlighted at that location.

Shining deer works best early in fall. In some areas of the U.S. it works right through winter, but generally the deer are in the deep woods later on. It helps to have a silenced firearm. But if one is caught with a silencer, his future will be very grim, and it is quite likely that one *will* be caught while spotlighting deer.

Dogs

Using dogs for deer is common in some places in the U.S., but is mostly unheard of throughout the rest of the country.

The ideal dog for deer is a yappy little beagle. Beagles follow slowly, have a good nose and make lots of noise. Deer won't be unduly frightened since they can always hear the dog and tell where it is. In addition, a beagle won't move the deer very fast and the poacher can move around to crossings and trails for a shot. Beagles on a deer track sound exactly like beagles chasing a rabbit.

Rather than a beagle, I have always used a semi-silent airedale for deer. Airedales move a bit faster through the woods, making the deer harder to circle, but they have great stamina and intelligence, and they are quiet.

A poacher's dog must be quiet and intelligent. He must stay with his master unless on a track, and always come when called. A stupid unruly wild dog is worse than worthless. It is a hindrance. So is a dog that makes too much noise. I want my dog to give a little bark every twenty to thirty seconds when on a hot trail, and absolutely shut up when I tell him. It won't do to have a barking crazy dog while trying to sneak up on deer, or away from farmers.

The poacher should only put the dog on a good fresh trail of a deer headed someplace where he knows he can get a shot. As soon

154

as the dog is off, start working in to known crossings. Coordinate with others in the party. Keep track of the dog, and always try to guess the deer's direction of flight. Radios are almost a necessity.

A good dog is a wonder to behold, but sometimes the hound may have trouble training its master to get around ahead of the quarry and do his part.

Fresh Snow

If the country is fairly open and not too hilly, deer can be taken from snow shoes on a fresh deep snow.

The trick is to pick up a fairly fresh track, and the skill is to be able to snow shoe long enough to get up with the deer.

I have used this method in Wisconsin, Michigan and Pennsylvania. Usually it isn't necessary to worry about a warden in the woods, but they can be a problem waiting on the road.

This really is a very easy way of getting a deer when the snow first gets too deep for them to run. Just be sure that plans are well made to get it out.

Deer Yards

In some sections of the country, deer will bunch up in sheltered areas where there is a good supply of food. These yards, as they are called, can be found and identified in spring and summer. Yards will have brush and trees that have been eaten off, many deep game trails in a small area, and at times, the skeletons of animals that died there.

During the winter it is easy to walk into the wind right up to a yard and shoot at least one deer. After that, they may scatter and not return. Often that is not all bad, since deer will tend to yard up and not move till they eat all the available browse.

In my estimation, deer shot from a yard are poor tasting and inferior. By the time they get there, all their body fat is gone, and they are just holding their own through the winter. At this point in the season, I aim to have my harvest completed.

Water

A plan that is seldom used is to spotlight deer from a boat. It sounds risky, but I have found that in general it is a much safer plan than using a light from a car.

There are several areas where I can run a boat far from any homes or main roads and make a good harvest. By using a quiet gun, I've been able to take several nice deer and have them in the boat before anyone knew what happened.

One of these was at a public camp ground and lake way back in the boondocks. There was only one access road to the area. We pulled our boat into a small cove about 11:00 p.m. and spotted a deer with our light. My partner shot it with his .25-.20 and we gutted it in the dark right on shore.

Quietly we loaded it on the boat and made off using his trolling motor. About a mile out we fired up the big motor and were gone before anyone knew what had happened. People were sleeping in their campers not 300 feet away.

If your poaching territory does include some water, also watch for swimming deer. It is surprising how often we run across them in lakes. One time I killed one with a hammer. It is better to shoot them, though, because when the boat gets close, the deer will start to lunge and make quite a commotion.

Snares

Anybody who hasn't gotten his meat by the onset of bad weather and/or the middle of winter may have to resort to snares. They are simple, effective and easy to use. No one should have any trouble snaring deer, even if they are a Class C woodsman of the klutzy kind.

Deer snares should be of the correct length and weight. Full instructions are given in the chapter on snares. Readers are encouraged to go back and look this chapter over again.

Snares are set in regularly traveled deer trails. If you don't know where these are, wait till it rains or snows, then find the places where the trail is beat down by two or three sets of fresh tracks.

Look for a narrow place through light brush between larger trees. Slight brush will help hold the snare in position, and force the deer to put its head down and plow through the tangle. The large trees can serve to force the deer into a constricted space, and may be rigged with a spring pole.

I believe more deer are missed as a result of too small snare loops than from those that are too large. As far as I am concerned, the ideal size is about the diameter of a bushel basket, or in the neighborhood of 18 inches.

The center of the loop should be about belt buckle high on a six foot man.

Snares set for deer must lock, and should have a stop so they don't collapse past about 7 inches in diameter. A strangled, bruised deer is only good for dog meat.

My ideal snare set for deer always has a light spring pole with

156

enough tension to hold the deer without allowing it to thrash itself to pieces. Some people put bells on their snares and sit in a tent or cabin and wait for the deer to ring. I never wanted to make that much noise, nor have I ever been where I could camp near the snare.

Human tracks in the snow are sometimes a problem. To get around this handicap, I may make my deer snare in fall without actually activating the trigger. Then in winter I walk by and cock the trap spring pole and tie open the snare. I use long strands of dry grass to lightly tie my snare to the bush. The grass looks natural and is easy to use.

By having the set ready to go early, I don't have to trample the snow flat while rigging it. Later, after the set is going, I may check it by walking 20 feet to the side. I am more concerned about two legged creatures catching me, than about four-legged critters not getting caught, because of my fresh tracks in the snow. Everything is more comfortable after a little new snow falls and obscures the trail.

Coastal black tails are difficult to get any other way except with snares. On the other hand, mule deer are almost impossible to catch with snares. And once a poacher has seen how a white tail sneaks away in heavy cover, he will never have trouble setting an effective snare loop for white tails again.

Snares are cheap, easily set, hard to detect and very effective. Snaring deer is easy, but obviously works best after the poacher has some experience at it. Remember that deer vary in size tremendously. If the deer breaks your snare, get heavier cable. If it tears itself up, check the set more often and rig a better spring pole. If it slips through the snare or misses it, set the loop larger or smaller as the case may be.

Flying

A lot of game can be spotted from the air. Game officials know this and consistently promulgate regulations regarding hunting from a plane. But the problem in this case is not evading the game department, but capitalizing on the information acquired flying around. The game wardens can't tell intent even if they are fortunate enough to catch up with the flying poacher after he gets back on the ground.

To work well, the plane used to spot game should be a high wing type that can fly very slowly. Other than some old J-3's or perhaps a Luscombe or two, there aren't many of these kinds of planes around any more. Few airports have them to rent.

157

The next best alterantive is a Cessna 150 or a 172. Both are common planes that can be flown by anybody who has a license. They rent for between $20.00 and $30.00 an hour.

The pilot should stay well in control of the plane and fly at about 500 feet above ground level. Even these slow planes cannot be safely flown at these altitudes much under 70 m.p.h., so going lower is self defeating. It is dangerous, the ground moves by too quickly and the game may be spooked.

Flying is an ideal method of locating mule deer. Unless someone scares them, they will stay in the area at least until the weather changes. If one knows the conditions on the ground, it is much easier to spot mulies from the air.

Earlier in the year, look high up on grassy benches or in saddles next to patches of trees. If it has been dry, the mulies will be lower. Snow also forces them down into the canyons and so on. A good poacher must have some "feel" for the animals, the weather and the terrain, or he will have to spend a lot of time cruising around locating the deer in the first place.

In spring, bears can be located from the air. They look like black stumps that ripple or shine in the grassy meadows below. Once located they can be trapped, or dogs brought in. I have never had much luck spotting bears from planes in the fall. Bears seem to roam too much at that time.

It is easy to plane-spot white tails working an orchard or an alfalfa field in the early fall. Later on in the season they can sometimes be spotted on an open hill or, if there are many, in the yards. I have never been able to locate deer in heavy timber from the air.

Moose and elk are the two animals that I think are best spotted from the air. In fact, I usually won't hunt them without at least trying to spot them from a plane first.

Moose are especially easy. They are big and black and sometimes come right out in the open in a muskeg or along a lake shore and stand. After spotting one, the pilot should climb to a couple of thousand feet and circle till a hunt can be planned.

Planning a route into the country is the core of the hunt. I believe I could find at least two or three moose in a morning of flying over reasonable country every time I went out, but getting into the area is something else again. Often there are rivers, swamps, bogs and lakes in just six or eight short miles between the nearest road and the moose. It may be possible to slip in and get it,

158

but then again maybe it isn't. Good air reconnaissance can show that.

A recon flight for elk is an immense help. These animals can move tremendous distances over mountainous country in a short time, so it is often futile to start "hunting" elk on foot. Better to fly over an area first and examine the saddles, open hillsides and grassy meadows near the creeks.

Since they are large and light colored, elk can often be spotted in heavy timber. During the heat of the day they lay in the saddles or at the edge of high meadows like cattle. Early in the morning or late in the evening they may be found contouring the hills nibbling grass.

The idea is to locate an area where the elk are known to be, and plan the route in, rather than trudging over a lot of empty country in vain.

Driving Deer

A trained, expert crew of deer drivers can get a white tail any time any place they choose, as long as deer live in the country they are working. It is so easy it is shocking. The only problem is that, as far as I know, there aren't a dozen good deer driving teams in the entire U.S. I have lived in a hundred different places in my lifetime including the middle west, the south, the north and the far west. I have hunted over much of the U.S. with a great number of people. I still say most hunters don't know how to drive deer, fox, bear, or many of the other species that easily fall victim to this method.

Driving game is a labor of love with me. There isn't anything much that I would rather do than organize a hunt and drive something past a shooter.

The older I get the more I am convinced that driving game is an art and not a science. Although it is easy for me to take one or two novices and quickly blend them into my regular hunting crew, it is very difficult for me to tell someone how to drive deer. Perhaps the greatest value to this book for the average poacher is to know that it can be done. Deer or anything else can be driven with impunity by a trained crew. Knowing this, the poacher can strive to perfect his techniques, and eventually use two or three people in a drive and get results every time out.

There are two kinds of deer drives. The most common is the *line-up*, where 8 to 10 men position themselves shoulder to shoulder and attempt to push the critters out of the cover to waiting standers. This system works o.k. during the hunting season if there are enough bodies, but as a poaching technique it is worthless. It is impractical to hide that many people and the wagging tongue syndrome is impossible to overcome after the hunt is completed.

Most poachers start learning to drive deer from these mass exercises, so I'll offer a few pertinent tips by way of an example. Seasoned poachers will laugh at the simplicity of the advice, but on reflection will probably agree that for most beginners, it is much needed.

When I was living on the farm, our county was inundated with stray dogs. The county lay in the center of a triangle formed by three large cities. City people who wanted to rid themselves of unwanted pets drove out into our area and dropped them off by the hundreds.

A build-up occurred, principally in numbers of dogs, and the results were catastrophic. Packs of these starving hounds started roaming the country, attacking farmers' livestock and decimating the wild game. One man who lived a mile or so from us lost thirty-six sheep in one night. Another a few days later had four full grown sows killed. Other damage occurred but nothing much was done about it. Philosophically it's hard to come out in favor of shooting dogs on a county-wide basis.

Winter came to the midwest along with a stretch of bone crinkling cold. The wild dogs became bolder, since the cold cut off their source of native game and domestic stock. The situation culminated one morning when a pack of about ten dogs attacked and almost killed a six year old girl waiting for a school bus. Only the timely arrival of the bus prevented her death, but she was terribly disfigured.

As a result of the incident, a hue and cry went up through the county. Farmers and small businessmen volunteered their services and the national guard sent up a number of large trucks.

Giant drives, a section in size each, were organized. Fifty or more men lined up and marched in unison with similar numbers on all four sides of a section till they met in the center. Each carried a shotgun and a dozen shells issued by the organizer. All ammo issued was #4 shot, to preclude anyone from using larger, more dangerous buck shot.

By sundown the group had covered 7 sections and had killed almost a whole pickup load of wild dogs. It was a grisly sight, but the dead dogs are not my principal memories of the occasion. I think of the dog hunt every time I see a line of men moving out to drive a woods in Michigan or Pennsylvania. They are doing the job by brute force and not finesse, with actually very limited results. It's an exercise in regimentation, not hunting.

For starters might I offer the following simple advice for drivers just learning the game:

1. Try to determine if there is any game in the country one proposes to drive. If the deer have moved elsewhere, it does very little good to tramp the woods in search of them. I realize full well that I harp long and hard on the theme "know your territory," but if it seems bad now, wait till the end of this chapter.

2. Try to drive the deer down wind. More expert hunters can drive into the wind and may shoot the deer on the drive itself, but for now the driver should reconcile himself to the fact that he is nothing but a brush beater.

3. Allow plenty of time for the standers to get around through the woods to their stations. Many, if not most, drives start too soon, without giving the stander time to take his position.

4. Use plenty of standers. Remember we are substituting muscle for brains. No one knows where the driven deer will emerge.

5. The drivers should take their positions on the drive line *silently*. At the start of the drive, there will be plenty of noise to scare the game, if the human scent hasn't done the job already.

6. Space out the drivers just far enough so they can see each other through most of the cover. Require them to stay in visual contact. Don't worry about noise on the drive, and don't let them go through too fast. Deer will be more fearful of slow moving noisy drivers and tend not to lay down and try to slip through the drive.

7. Everyone should wear bright hunting colors. No camouflage on these hunts.

8. One person should be the group leader and be responsible for getting the people through on line and formed up for the next drive. Use of radios is helpful but not essential as it is when three or four people drive deer.

By following the above guide points, reasonably successful deer hunts can be organized. Of course they will have to be undertaken only during the regular season by people with proper permission, licenses and all that good stuff.

The real test of a poacher is his ability to pull off the same drive with three or four people and pick up twice as many deer.

My biggest problem in directing drivers is finding enough people who know the country. It is virtually impossible to send someone around a field, or over to a point if he doesn't know where that field or point is. Also, how is someone supposed to be able to drive a woods or brushy draw if he doesn't know how the country lies? It is impossible. Deer will get past the driver, or will run to an unexpected place and escape.

In my opinion, 90 percent of driving deer quietly and successfully is knowing the country. Even if the deer get past the standers, the group can analyze the hunt and decide how to work it differently next time. All else failing, the poachers can at least observe the tracks on the drive through and decide where the deer went, but again they "gotta know the territory."

As with mass drives, silence for the standers is golden. A stander must at times go to great lengths to creep silently around the woods to get to his station. The drivers must also be silent getting into position. True professionals don't need to make noise talking or snapping sticks on a drive. They know how their counterpart driver will handle the country, how long it will take them to get through an area and when to turn, wait or whatever. Similarly, standers will know when game should appear if it is going to, and how long it will take the drivers to reach various places on the drive.

Professional drives can be made with the wind or into the wind, depending on the circumstances. Deer can be bagged either way. If with the wind, the driver's movement should be calculated to push the game to the stander. If against the wind, the stander may float in order to hold the deer in place till the driver can arrive and make a shot.

This is an important technique since it isn't always practical to poach a deer at the edge of a woods or by a stock crossing. At times the team may want to drive the deer away from a house or barn, to a place where a shot won't disturb anybody.

Poachers should realize that among their own team there will be some who are better drivers than standers, and vice versa. As I have said before, a lot of driving deer is an art, and some people have more of a feel for driving and others for standing.

In summary the important elements of a skillful professional deer drive are:

1. Knowing the country, where the game is and how it will react;

2. Being able to understand how all of the team members will handle the country, where they will be and what they will do;

3. Being able to handle that portion of the task which is assigned on the drive.

As I said at the start, I know I cannot tell a person how to handle a professional deer drive any more than an artist could tell me how to paint an apple. It can be done, however, and that's the point. A good three or four person poaching team can move in just about anyplace where there is game and put it on the grass in a very short time. My wife calls the system the incredible poaching machine.

As a help I have listed four actual drives that we regularly run. They are typical of many that poachers are likely to encounter. Studying these situations or case studies will help the average hunter get a handle on the concept of driving game.

Situation I

The area to be hunted is about 1500 acres of heavy timber and brush with a few openings located in the center of rolling pasture and grain fields. It is about a quarter of a mile to most of the farm houses from the woods, but one home is located back in the trees and must be avoided. There are many farmers who own pieces of the country and almost all of the ground is posted.

An 8½ mile road loops around the field and woods.

The tree covered portion of this country is moderately rolling to rugged. In the woods it is possible to see 100 yards at the most. In some places narrow fingers of cover extend almost to the road.

This is a very typical set up. Hundreds of deer live in the mixed agriculture forest region, but few hunters get on the ground because of posting. The few who do amble through the woods see nothing. Because of the size, fifteen men or more would be needed for a mass drive. However, three good poachers can get deer every time they go in.

Hunt the woods as follows:

The cover extends about two miles to the north and averages well under three fourths of a mile wide. A prevailing westerly wind blows across the narrow direction. Hunt the downwind portion of the woods first for obvious reasons.

Put the best man 400 yards into the woods walking quietly parallel to the average edge. A second hunter keeps about 100

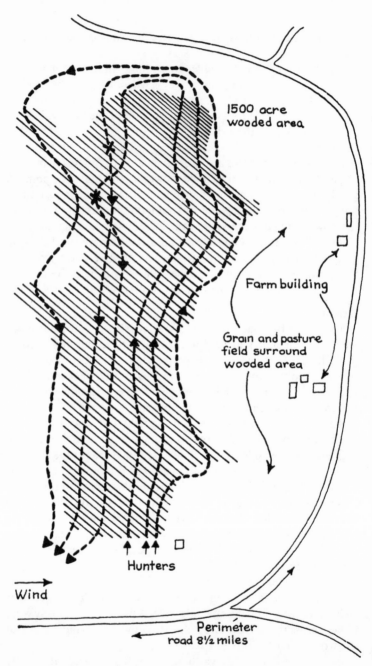

1500 acre
wooded area

Farm building

Grain and pasture
field surround
wooded area

Hunters

Wind

Perimeter
road 8½ miles

SITUATION I

yards from the edge and the third hunts right at the edge in the open fields but walks up and through the fingers of brush as he comes to them.

The outside man has a lot more walking to do, and is expected to stay ahead of the other hunters about 100 yards. Sixty percent of the shots will be made by the man at the edge as deer jump out of the small fingers and try to escape through the fields.

The other 40 percent of the shots will be made by the hunter in the center, as the wise old deer try to come around through the woods past the center into the deep woods.

At the end of the woods, swing around and run the upwind side back the same way. If there is an especially wide or long finger, the two inside men should stop and become standers while the outside person runs the cover.

Deer in the very center of the woods are missed on this drive but few stay there anyway. It is a typical big woods situation that most hunters can't handle.

Situation II

People continually ask me how to drive a big heavy woods that is part of a whole mountain. How, they ask, is it possible to get deer out of so much country? Other than some coastal rain forests where the cover is very thick, it is always possible. Consider this simple little problem.

A heavily wooded hill in the middle of a large forest. The hill rises perhaps 300 feet, covers four to five hundred acres and has a few clearings. The top is tree covered.

By previous scouting we know there are many game trails on top of the hill. Most lead to a saddle that connects to the next hill.

We put one man on top of the hill and the other two contour around at 100 yard intervals. Most of the deer run uphill toward the saddle. Ninety nine percent of the shooting is done by the man on top, regardless of the wind direction.

Situation III

This is a draw in a large woods. Deer come into the draw to drink. The draw is about 1000 yards long and 500 yards wide. Heavy brush covers the bottom that at its deepest is 100 feet below the surrounding forest.

Hunt this by putting one man down in the draw's bottom. He should bust through the brush, moving from side to side. A second hunter stays up on the ridge to the right of the brush beater, slightly ahead. The third man moves 200 yards ahead to the left.

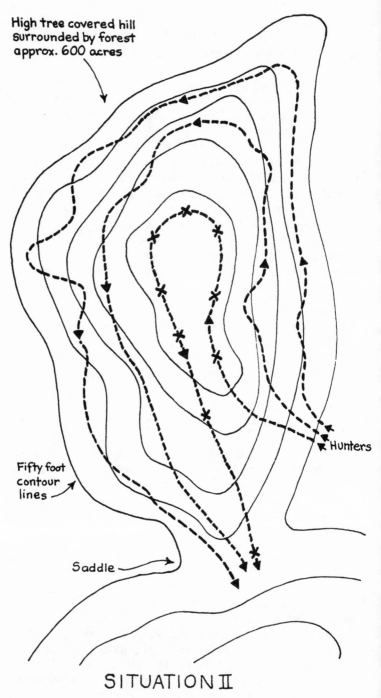

High tree covered hill surrounded by forest approx. 600 acres

Hunters

Fifty foot contour lines

Saddle

SITUATION II

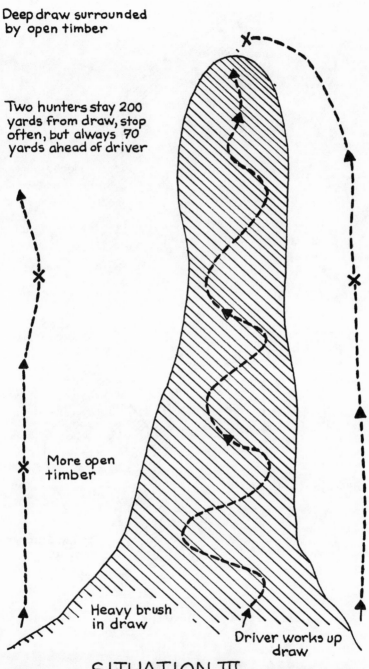

Deep draw surrounded by open timber

Two hunters stay 200 yards from draw, stop often, but always 70 yards ahead of driver

More open timber

Heavy brush in draw

Driver works up draw

SITUATION III

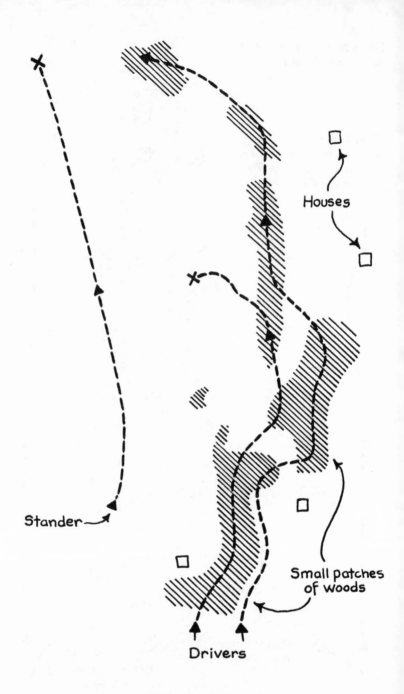

Houses

Stander

Small patches
of woods

Drivers

SITUATION IV

168

He should stay at least 250 yards away from the brush buster up on the flat ground. Since the third man will get most of the shots, he should work through open timber as much as possible.

Situation IV

At first glance, Situation IV seems to be simple. Small woodlots surrounded by acres and acres of open fields. The ground may be gently rolling, but for the most part visibility is very good. Even if the wind is all wrong, the novice will at least see game no matter where he stumbles into the woods.

Another plus is the fact that deer thrive on the small woodlot in a sea of pasture, corn fields and wheat environment. There are bound to be lots of them around.

The big problem involves the fact that there are so many houses. Without special planning, mixed with an unusual portion of skill, the poacher will be spotted out in the open, or be discovered when he shoots.

To correctly handle the situation, the deer must be moved from woodlot to woodlot till they are at a place where they can safely be shot.

The hunter on the left is actually a floating stander. The two on the right hold to the right, continually attempting to move the animals toward the stander. Both drivers must make use of every scrap of cover to shield their activities from the view of people in the houses.

Smart deer hunted under these circumstances will move out many hundreds of yards ahead of the drivers. If done properly, the direction of the wind is not critical. But again the floating stander will have to be prepared for a long shot.

Most of the real life deer drive situations are not nearly as complex as the ones shown. Every one requires study, planning and a knowledge of the terrain, no matter how simple or how complex.

The first time through, the poacher is likely to handle the country all wrong. More important is how he will handle it next time. That's what separates the real deer drivers from the folks who stroll through the woods with a high-powered rifle.

16

BUTCHERING DEER

One of the hardest animals to handle is the untagged deer. Something has to be done with them quickly—this is the what-to-do chapter.

Over the last forty years, my family and I have been able to collect all the deer we need to feed ourselves. However, we have never killed more than we needed.

It was only logical for us to develop a quick and easy method of preparing untagged deer for the freezer. One can't, after all, take that many animals to the local custom butcher or even dawdle around putting them up with a pocket knife.

Briefly, our system is as follows:

As soon after the deer is shot as is safely possible, gut the deer. I don't want to waste my energy carrying guts home and I don't want to have the trouble of disposing of them in an urban surrounding. So leave them in the bush.

The deer should be pulled sideways to a slight hill and rolled on its back. Only one man should do the actual work. Wardens look for blood on the poacher's hands or knife, so it is best to allow only one poacher to gut the deer.

While someone holds the deer upside down, slit the deer's belly from the bung hole all the way to the adam's apple. In the crotch the knife will only cut to the pelvis bone, but cut as far as possible.

The pelvis itself must be cracked or sawed. I don't like to carry a saw or the noise a saw makes. Instead I drive my knife point first into the pelvis with the palm of my hand. Some people use a rock, but that makes an awful lot of noise. By inserting and punching the knife three or four times, the pelvis will be severed.

Next drive the knife into the bottom of the rib cage, twist and cut. Older, larger animals will have tough rib cages. Push the knife through slightly off center and the job will be slightly easier. The ribs can be split even on a large old animal without making much noise this way.

Cut out the trachea and sever it from the body right below the head.

Roll the deer on its side and pull the trachea out. The intestines should follow. Cuts will be necessary around the diaphragm, but basically the guts will just roll out.

Save the heart and liver from the pile. Scatter what's left out so the birds and foxes can quickly eat it. If necessary, throw the entrails in heavy brush, down a canyon or in a river. Try to make sure no one will find them.

Cut the legs off at the first joint.

Most hunters waste part of the neck. I cut the head off as close to the neck as possible. There is a lot of burger on a neck. Before hiding the head, take the tongue out. I skewer the tongue on a forked stick, then the liver and last the heart. It is easier and cleaner to carry them this way.

We always pack the deer over our shoulders Indian style. It requires two people to load a deer this way, but one person can carry up to a 175 pound load Indian style. The only drawback is that the packer can get bloody on the shoulders and neck. On the other hand, there is no trail or hair, and the hunter can move the deer great distances very quickly and quietly.

We cut heavier mule deer in half so we can still pack it on our shoulders.

Try at all costs to keep the meat clean on its journey out to the road. I don't like sand in my hamburger and doubt if anyone else does.

Once home we hang the deer in the garage and skin it immediately. The skin is disposed of in a place where it can't become an embarrassment. Bury it, store it in an out building or in the neighbor's garage, but don't leave it laying around.

Split the deer end to end. A common wood saw works fine for this job. Start at the tail and follow the white line right over the backbone down through the neck. One person holding the carcass and the other sawing works efficiently.

Once the carcass is skinned and halved, we refer to it as being on the rail. I believe this is standard butcher terminology. It should take no longer than fifteen minutes to handle this part of the job.

Speed is of the essence. I want the deer wrapped and in a freezer as soon as possible. Just as bringing a deer to the road is the weak link in that chain, a half-butchered deer in one's basement is the weak link in the butcher chain.

Since speed is the order of the day, we have developed a very fast method of handling a deer from rail to the freezer. The method has no correlation to standard butchering techniques and may make some pros wince.

Take two good sized tubs, a knife and a saw and proceed to cut as follows. Remember, speed is the key. We want to reduce the animal to easily handled small pieces as fast as possible.

1. Saw the two front legs off just behind the remaining joint. These will later be boned for hamburger.

2. Pull the shoulder out and cut it off the carcass, taking as much meat as possible with the shoulder.

3. Saw the two necks off at the bottom of the ribs.

4. Cut in at the flank just down from the rear quarter to within three inches of the backbone. Saw down through the ribs all the way to the bottom, severing the ribs from the backbone. Be sure to stay at least three inches from the backbone or the loin will be ruined.

5. Saw through the back bone just below the rear quarters.

6. Saw off the hind leg below the joint. Put the hind ham and the shanks in the pan, completing that part of the operation.

Boning the Meat

Our family has a shortage of freezer space. With all the birds, deer, fish, berries and apples that go into our freezers we have become accustomed to freezing the deer meat without bones. I've been in some lively discussions regarding the speed of boning versus the speed of sawing bones, and time it takes to wrap boned versus unboned meat. It still seems to me that there is only five minutes difference in methods. If you also need to conserve freezer space, bone your deer meat as follows.

1. Working from the hoof end, bone the four shanks. Throw this meat into a hamburger box and the bones into a bone bag.

2. Filleting right next to the bone, remove the loins. On large deer there will be four. On small animals the inside loin may get lost in the shuffle.

172

3. Starting at the shank or narrow end, cut as many round steak wheels as possible off the rear hams. These should be about one inch thick. Split the remaining chunk in two, working the meat into two roasts. Meat remaining on the bones should be removed for hamburger.

4. Bone out the neck. This is a tough job, learned only after practice on a deer or two. The neck bones are ripply and it is hard to arrive at a system. A novice may want to make soup out of the neck bone if very much meat remains. After the poacher learns the task, this operation can go very quickly.

5. The last operation is another tough one requiring a lot of skill. I don't know an easy method of either doing the boning myself or telling someone else how to do it. Start as follows and stick with it.

Lay the front ham on the boning table with the hide side up. Rotate the piece so the leg points away from the worker and, using the back of the knife, tap the chunk till the long thin bone separating the shoulder blade is located. This bone forms a T with the shoulder blade.

Cut down on either side of the vertical bone to the shoulder bone and work the meat off into two roasts. If one is skilled or the critter is small, the piece can be taken off as one roast. Often we roll these roasts and tie them up with bakery string.

All the hamburger meat is put in one package and frozen. Later in the year we pull all the packages out and grind them at once. Many years ago we bought a large commercial meat grinder at an auction. The grinder takes about two minutes to grind a deer, but because it is so heavy, about 15 minutes to set up.

The best division of labor we have found is to have two people boning, with one person wrapping the meat as it comes off the boning table. Many many times we have done a deer—rail to freezer but no grinding—in forty-five minutes. On larger deer or elk we like four or five to help, but after that point there is no additional efficiency gained by adding people.

Be sure to wash up everything thoroughly when the job is done. The fish and game department has a test they can used to determine where—in what drainage—a scrap of meat or drop of blood came from. Should the deer be one you claim came from an open area, when in fact it did not, they may challenge you. I believe the test is not accurate enough to hold up in court but the F&G people may want to go through the motions anyway. After the meat has been frozen a few days, the test is even more tenuous.

In some areas the game commission will obtain search warrants and check freezers. Never, never label any meat with a date. Use a red marker one year, black the next and so on. Simply write an "H" for hamburger or "R" for roast in the appropriate color. If there is deer, elk, bear or moose mixed together, it may be necessary to use an "EH" or a "BR." Be sure to have a convincing story put together regarding the source of all that meat.

An accumulation of hearts and tongues can be an embarrassment. Within reasonable limits it is tough to reconstruct a deer from a bunch of boned packages in a freezer. But four hearts are something else again. One time my wife gathered seven deer hearts, and put together a giant roast heart dinner. The eating was great, but what if the warden had walked in just then?

17
NAIL CAN BEAR TRAP

A surprising number of people live within easy driving distance of black bears. The reason these bears continue to roam at will is that the average bear is smarter than the average person.

When I was young, my uncle made me promise that I would never tell anybody about his secret bear trap. That way, nobody else could ever use his method. More important, the wardens would never get wind of it and discover how he got so many bears.

Uncle is dead and gone now, so perhaps he will forgive me for telling you about his secret bear trap. If I don't tell someone soon, I am going to be dead and gone too, and nobody will be around to pass on the information.

To start with, trapping bears can be a problem for a poacher. Good numbers of bears exist that are fairly easy to trap, but other factors confuse the issue.

Steel traps, for instance, are illegal in almost every state, and are not really a viable poacher's tool. Old original steel bear traps have antique value, and are far too valuable to set out in the bush. Modern bear traps available from HERTER'S are still too expensive, in my opinion, and are dangerous in the woods. If a person ever got caught in a poacher's bear trap, there would be merry hell to pay before that incident blew over.

Large jaw traps are hard to pack into a set and difficult to dig in and make operational. If there is even a hint that there might be a large jaw trap out, souvenir hunters and wardens will descend *en masse* and look for it with metal detectors. Besides all this, bears don't like to put their feet in steel jaw traps. They *do* enjoy putting their feet in my traps.

Since jaw traps are not practical for bears, this leaves the

175

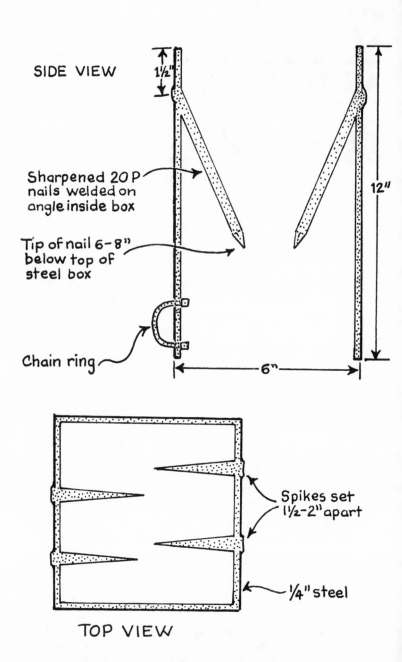

SIDE VIEW

1½"

Sharpened 20P
nails welded on
angle inside box

Tip of nail 6-8"
below top of
steel box

Chain ring

12"

6"

Spikes set
1½-2" apart

¼" steel

TOP VIEW

NAIL CAN BEAR TRAP

aspiring bear poacher with only snares and nail can traps. Snares are covered in a previous chapter. They are certainly a good way of catching bears and are much less expensive than nail cans or anything else. However, nail cans are far easier to set and much more effective.

Building a bear trap of this type requires the use of an arc welder, a cutting torch and a drill. Cost will run from $10.00 to $40.00 each, depending on how much of the trap is scrounged and how much work is done by the poacher himself.

Start by neatly cutting two pieces of 1/4 inch sheet steel 6 inches wide and 12 inches long. Cut two more 4½ x 12 inch pieces and weld them up with the first two into a box 4½ x 5½ inches inside diameter, 12 inches deep. Both ends should be left open. Do a very thorough job of welding the box so it is extremely sturdy.

Weld a four foot length of log chain to the box one inch from the bottom. The chain must have at least 1/4 inch links, be securely fastened to the trap body and have a ring on the end of it. I make the ring out of 3/8 inch bar stock. Don't try to skimp on the chain length or quality.

Drill two 5/32 inch holes one and a half inches down from the top of each side of the trap, slanted downward. Later the spikes will have to be adjusted, but it is easier if the holes are angled to start with. Drill the holes so they offset each other as shown in the diagram.

Sharpen four 20 penny nails needle sharp and push them into the four holes. The ends of the nails must extend down no less than 5 inches into the trap. This gives them a great deal of angle and removes the impression of their being an obstacle. Weld the nails in solid.

Adjust the nails so that there is 1½ inches of distance between the points. This size trap will miss the small one year old bears but will collect most larger bears.

Carefully dig the trap into the ground along a path or trail where bear sign is abundant. Shovel extra dirt into an old gunny sack and dispose of it away from the set.

When completely dug in, the top of the trap should be even with the ground. The chain should be dug in and hidden. It is well secured to a stout 8 inch drag log 6 feet long. Keep the set neat and tidy and minimize the amount of human scent left.

Bait with old honey and/or bacon grease. Pour the bait in the trap, allowing some to spill around the top. Use a lot of bait. A half gallon of either is not too much.

177

Rain has little effect on the set other than washing the human scent away. There is no need to shelter the set, although the poacher may want to cover the trap slightly with dry leaves or grass.

Check the trap once every four to seven days. Try to do so without approaching too close or leaving human scent. Be ready to replace the bait since bees, coons and skunks will work on it.

Modern bears are used to playing around in dumps looking for food. They are also, by nature, used to pushing their paws into openings to pry out goodies. At first he will smell around the trap. Then, after a bit, the bear will try to push his paw into the goodies and lick it off. Once that paw is in the trap past the pad, the spikes will hurt the bear, causing it to relieve the pain by pushing in farther till it is hopelessly caught.

A caught bear is a fearsome creature. They are so powerful it is unbelievable. Often I have found my trap and drag 600 to 800 yards away, tangled in a pine thicket. Staking a bear trap-fast is foolish. The critter will either break the stakes or tear the trap apart.

These traps won't catch humans, but they will grab onto a deer leg or a young domestic cattle leg. Be very careful not to put the trap in a trail so as to avoid hoofed animals. Even if the poacher can use a deer, it is an inefficient method of getting one. The deer will end up thrashing itself to death, ruining its meat.

18

BEAVERS AND MUSKRATS

An excerpt from my diary begins this chapter:

Shortly after lunch we started the three mile hike into the beaver ponds. It was mostly downhill, but what little trail there was twisted and turned tortuously through the rocks and trees. The ponds were on a small stream that lay at the bottom of a steep, short canyon. Not the kind of place I would have walked into daily to check traps.

A few minutes before we got to the bottom, the sun set behind the mountains. A good ninety minutes of daylight remained, but the sun was no longer in sight.

There were two nice ponds lying back to back at the bottom. We moved around with extreme caution so as not to alarm the beavers. There were no beaver in sight, but their tracks and droppings were everywhere.

After a few minutes of scouting, we decided that the first two ponds we came to were the best for our plan. Large fresh lodges sat in each. There was an open spot up the hill where we could watch both dams, but it was 300 feet or more to the down stream water.

We searched on for a time, but it was obvious that we weren't going to do much better without making a lot of noise. My pard finally settled down in the clearing, cradled his silenced .25-.20 on his lap and started to wait. I slid down the hill to the first dam.

People who have never tried it have no idea how difficult it is to untangle the sticks and branches in a beaver dam. By working diligently, I finally opened a three foot square hole in the wall.

By the time I got to it, the lower dam was just about flooded out as a result of all the additional water from above. Again I set to work and in twenty minutes had an even larger hole in the bottom dam.

Carefully I snuck back up to my friend who was watching the ponds intently.

Twenty minutes or so passed, and it was getting dark. Suddenly there was a small splash and a "V" on the upper pond. A medium-sized beaver glided into the dam with a branch in its mouth. He poked the twigs into the breach while we continued to watch.

In a few minutes, a second, much larger beaver broke the water and also swam for the dam. When it climbed onto the pile of sticks we could definitely tell it was a large one, worth taking. The .25-.20 grunted quietly, and water splashed on the beaver. A miss. It looked around unafraid. Partner's next round hit solidly, knocking the fat beaver off the dam into the stream below.

A second beaver "V" shone in the water, but there was also a beaver on the dam below. Carefully my partner took aim and fired at the far target. The water splashed, but the beaver just sat there. We shot twice more, but couldn't hit the damn thing.

Almost out of disgust, my pard pulled down on the close beaver in the near pond and dropped it stone, cold dead with one shot. It lay on the dam.

Another beaver showed up on the far dam. It was so dark we couldn't tell for sure, but it looked like all shots missed.

We killed one more beaver on the close pond and called it quits. At least two more beaver splashed a warning as we broke our way down to the water.

Using our small flashlight, we retrieved two blanket beavers from the first pond as well as a nice two year old. At the second pond, we were both delighted and surprised to find a second blanket beaver floating face down next to the dam.

We elected to carry the beavers whole to the road, which may have been a mistake. It took us till 9:30 p.m. to get out and it was a tough, heavy pack. But we made it home safely.

In a situation like these remote beaver ponds, breaking out the dam makes a lot of sense. We could have trapped the ponds and eventually caught the same beaver, but we would have had to haul the traps in and out, as well as walk in ourselves four or five times. By breaking the dam, and being quiet, we were able to select only the most mature animals. It's a good system, but remember to always be very quiet, watch the wind, tear the dam out late in the day, and expect to shoot most during the last five minutes of daylight.

Pen Trapping Beaver

This is a common trapping method that the Indians of North America used. It was at one time almost universally known, but in just my lifetime has become a lost art.

Pen trapping works well when the conditions are right and not at all when the conditions are wrong.

To work, the method requires an axe, ice chisel, steel rod and a good dog. The beaver pond must be frozen over and solid enough to walk on. If the ice over the pond is new and clean, the dog is not essential.

The trapper must be sure the beaver pond is active. Assuming that it is, set a line of one inch wood stakes, cut from the thickets around the pond, in front of the dam spillway and upstream where the pond ends. Chop a line in the ice through which to set the stakes. The ice should help hold the barrier, so don't chop too wide.

Jump on the beaver house and chase the critters out of their home. If the pond is small, the noise made while staking the pond will have scared them inside. Put a line of stakes in front of the beaver house entrance as soon as the beavers have left it.

The beavers will swim under the ice for a time, but will eventually have to go to one of their bank dens for air. Watch for their mud and bubbles along shore, or let the dog find them.

When a bank burrow is found, take the iron rod and probe into the bank till the borrow is located. Usually the probing drives the beavers out, but if not, chop out the ground to the hole and the beavers will leave. Stake this burrow shut.

Keep working around the lake till all the beavers are in one or two burrows. At the last burrow, set up a solid line of stakes back from the entrance about 4 feet. Now chop all the ice out in front of the burrow up to the stakes.

Probe the bank and, when the beavers come out, shoot the two largest ones and let the little worthless beavers go till next year.

It will take two men about three hours to stake a pond if they both work at it. Many times there are more than two large beavers, giving a fair return for the labor on the project.

Spearing Muskrats

On a good open marsh where there are a lot of muskrat houses, it is possible to spear rats.

The spear head is made of a single tine of one quarter inch steel 24 inches long. A shallow barb is cut in the shaft back about 2½ inches from the end, and the point sharpened needle thin. The spear shaft is mounted securely in a piece of 1½ inch dowel rod that is at least 2 feet long.

To use this method, one must be able to ice skate proficiently and ice must cover the marsh.

Skate quickly and quietly up to a muskrat house and plunge the spear into the house at a 45° angle down into the living chamber. The best way to locate the muskrat living chamber is to pull a house apart and look.

If a muskrat is impaled, there will be thumping, scratching and tugging on the pole. At times the spear will impale two rats, since they pile up in the house.

Don't tear the house up if there is no obvious victim. It is to the poacher's advantage not to destroy the places where the rats—which are his income—live.

It is very easy to slip into a distant untouched marsh on a cold blustery day and make a very nice harvest using this technique. The ice skates and spear can be carried in a bag, as can the rats.

Tip Barrel

This trap is described in a later chapter on frogs, turtles, etcetera. It works well in summer for turtles and just as well in winter, before the freeze, on rats.

To work, the rats must come to bait, which is often not likely in streams or sloughs late in the year. I use raw carrots or corn for bait, but often I can't get the rats to come to it.

Blasting Beaver

Beavers have proliferated to the point that the are pests in many places. When a farmer from afar calls about problem beavers, and he doesn't care, I blast out the dam about an hour before dark and shoot the beavers with a .22 rifle. The sudden drop in water level brings them out immediately, or it may be necessary to scare them out of their house or bank den.

Dynamiting beaver dams is like shooting ice. Set out as much powder as you think necessary, and then double it. This is an old rule of thumb of the powder monkey's.

I usually start with eight sticks of dynamite and go up to twelve or fourteen. Push the charge down in the mud, upstream from the dam, 3 to 5 feet. It's tough to get the charge deep enough, but the deeper the powder, the better the shot.

It won't be difficult to get the beavers out of their houses, but it may be necessary to dig or punch the burrows with a steel rod.

Beavers will escape on even small streams, so often I set steel

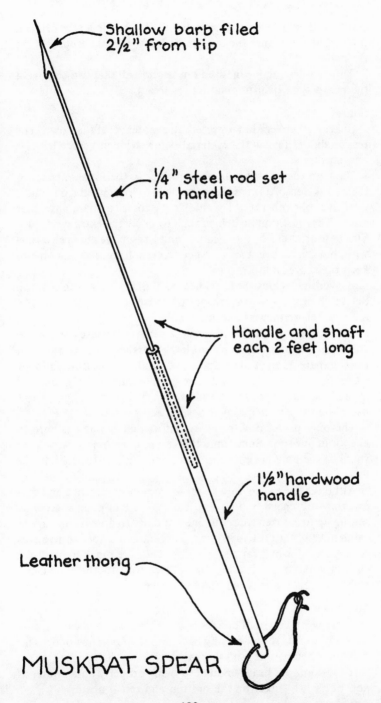

Shallow barb filed
2½" from tip

¼" steel rod set
in handle

Handle and shaft
each 2 feet long

1½" hardwood
handle

Leather thong

MUSKRAT SPEAR

traps for them in a narrow spot 100 yards or so from the original pond. Then, if I miss the critters with my rifle, the traps will get them.

This is a destructive method but is often all that can be done if the beavers are over populating an area.

Snares

Snares are covered in a preceding chapter all of their own. The reader should review the material before trying to snare beavers and muskrats.

Rats are easy to snare in the entrance to their grass houses or their bank dens. At times a good run can be located far from where they live, but otherwise I wouldn't try to set a snare any other place. They just don't catch enough to make the extra work pay. Snares for rats can be the cheap, simple ones made out of electrical wire, but must have a small bush or branch for a spring pole to keep the snare snubbed up.

Beaver snares must be fairly heavy, of the type used on coyotes. Set these in the runs in and out of houses and burrows, and in marshes where they have built canals.

In the winter it is difficult to snare beavers because the water is cold and deep and they don't work the marshes. One solution is to put the snare on the end of a pole and push the pole down into the water in position over a run. The pole becomes a drag and will immediately snub the snare and drown the beaver. A lighter pole using the same principal works very well on rats.

The only problem with the system is that the pole is hard to anchor in one spot. Sometimes this can be overcome by wiring the snare to the pole back a foot or so, and pushing the rig into the mud.

Although snares are only about forty percent effective on beavers, they are cheap and easy to set. I have had good success by setting up to a dozen snares in one pond. By so doing, I manage to catch most of the critters in one night. Snares are not as obvious as steel traps, so won't raise suspicions. They are much lighter than conventional traps, lending themselves well to the in-and-out technique, even if it is only half effective.

Box Traps

These work very well on rats, but aren't so hot on beavers. Box traps set for rats should be dug back into their burrows or dens far enough so the critters can't work their way out to the side. Also, be sure the doors are heavy enough to swing properly under water. If not, put a fish sinker on the bottom and test it again.

At times, an old gunny sack laid over the trap works well to channel the rats into the chamber. If there is more than one escape route out of the den or house, use more box traps. Leave them there two days and then move on to the next house. By systematically working through the marsh or creek, a poacher can make some very easy multiple catches.

Under most circumstances, box traps for beaver are too big and clumsy. They will work during the summer, but at that time the pelts are worthless. Also, beavers will just raise hell with a box trap. I have seen some Fish and Game department traps left two days that the beavers turned to shambles.

Ice Hammer Method

This is certainly one of the most unorthodox ways of collecting muskrat skins, but on four or five different occasions it has worked well for me.

When the weather turns cold very quickly in fall, I make it a point to run out to some of the larger marshes and the river to check the ice. If it is frozen solid a couple of inches deep but is clear enough to see the bottom, there is a chance to pick up some easy rats.

Roughly the procedure is as follows, but please try the method before laughing too loud.

Quickly run out on the ice over to a rat house and jump on it. Stand there on the reed structure for a moment or two, watching intently for rats leaving their home. If one is spotted, follow it on the ice. After a few yards, hit the ice with the hammer side of an axe. Smack it sharply right above the critter. A blow or two will slow it down and bring it up to the surface where another sharp rap on the ice will stun it enough to cause it to drown. Then it is a simple matter to cut through the ice and retrieve the rat.

During the early 1950's, I drove past an extremely large marsh in Nebraska on my way to California. The late fall ice had just thickened to the point where it was possible to walk across the marsh. It was new and beautifully clear.

We parked the car. The only tools I had were a tire iron and a hammer, but we went to work anyway.

My wife scared out the rats and I followed, hitting the ice with the claw hammer. Slowly, but surely, we worked around the swamp till it was almost dark. When we counted the rats, we had about twenty.

That night we took the critters to town. We found a fur buyer there who bought the rats whole for $1.75 each. A motel in those days was $5.00, so we felt like we had put together a fine day's work. As I remember, we made it to L.A. on the money we made that day.

Hunting In Spring

A very old traditional method of gathering rats involves shooting them in the spring. This plan only works during the flood periods when the rats' burrows and houses are covered with water and the critters are forced to sit on the bank.

Rat skins stay prime long into the spring, and in times past the animals were so abundant it didn't matter when they were hunted. I don't like the system unless it is used south of the Ohio River where the winters are less severe and the population doesn't naturally die back as much by spring.

A silenced .22 helps, but standard velocity shorts or even BB caps work just as well. Muskrats are easy to kill and will float when dead, so a bunch of firepower is not necessary.

Simply float down the river or stream, or through the marsh, in a canoe or small rowboat. Be very quiet and if there are rats around, they will soon be seen eating, crawling or sitting on the bank, or swimming in the water. Glide the craft over to within 30 feet of them and start collecting.

One should be very certain he doesn't glide his boat downstream right past some fishermen, or the warden checking fishing licenses, however.

Spring rat skins are very nice, but are easily spotted by fur buyers. If there is no spring season in the state, be sure that you have your story straight.

Shooting In Dens

I don't use this method because, unlike spearing rats, it destroys the den. Also it is very costly and obvious, unless a silencer is used. And it's quite expensive to run up to each den and shoot six or eight times into it.

For beavers this method is a complete waste of time. A rifle won't penetrate the house, and it's too darn difficult to pull the house apart to see if anything was taken.

Spearing

In spring during flood times, it's possible to chase down rats with a canoe and spear them. I prefer shooting or clubbing rats to spearing them, however. They aren't torn up so badly as with spearing, and are worth a lot more on the fur market.

Spearing beavers next to their dams or houses is an old Indian trick. Use a spear similar to the one designed for rats, only make it larger.

One night I was spearing trout in a beaver pond with the aid of a canoe and lantern, when I spotted a beaver swimming for the dam. I quickly glided the boat into position near the dam. When the beaver passed near, I took my five tined fish spear and put it right in the beaver's back. I did this by leaning with all my weight on the spear.

As soon as the beaver was hit, he rolled over and flipped me right out of the boat into four feet of icy water. I jumped up onto the bank for fear the beaver was going to treat my leg like an aspen limb, but the critter just struggled around on the bottom.

After a few minutes my now-broken spear pole floated to the surface. About thirty minutes later, the beaver came to the top. He weighed about forty pounds, and was one of the bigger beavers I have ever taken.

Hooking

In some sections of Canada this method is well known. In the rest of north America, it is virtually unknown, and unused.

From a practical standpoint, I believe that hooking would work for muskrats. But to my knowledge, it is only used on bigger, more clumsy beavers. It is a very good method under heavy ice and snow when trap platforms and snares are virtually impossible to set. A hook set is inexpensive, effective and can be hidden through a very small hole in the ice.

On the other hand, a hooked beaver will often be worthless to fur buyers because of the tears the hooks make in the hide.

A hook set-up is made as follows.

Using ten or more 10/0 fish hooks, put one hook every eight inches on a piece of #12 or 14 wire. Do this by threading the wire through the hook eye and twisting the hook twice to set it on the line.

This string of hooks is bent slightly from side to side to form a more formidable mass. Set this right in front of the lodge opening, being sure the wire is limp and that the tangle is pushed down far enough to obstruct the den entrance.

Fasten the other end of the wire to a chunk of wood and lay this on the ice. The branch should be long enough so the beaver can't pull it through the ice hole, but short enough to be handy. The wire should be slack in the hole. Pack snow in the hole and over the branch to hide the set.

187

The hooks must be kept needle sharp. I use a whetstone to do this.

Apparently the beavers may pass back and forth several times before getting hooked. But once they are snagged in one hook, they roll around and snag themselves in many. When I check my hook sets, any caught beavers are always drowned. The hook line is twisted up in an incredible fashion.

The hook line is an effective deep water set in winter when nothing else will work. Otherwise, I wouldn't use it.

19

FISH

There are literally hundreds of quick easy ways of reducing large quantities of fish to possession. In a pure survival situation, it is my recommendation that after cereal grains, fish be given first consideration as a source of food. There are so many fish in so many different and diverse places that they are usually the easiest meal to get.

All of the methods described in this book work. However, most take time to build or set up and even more time to begin to actually catch game. It is said that humans are only three meals away from the onset of starvation. Obviously three meals is only one day. It will take at least that long to build three deadfalls or set out a string of culvert traps, build some snares or even set out a bird trap. But fish are immediate. A shrewd poacher living just about anywhere outside of the extremely large cities could collect 100 pounds of fish in a matter of hours. By so doing he could buy a significant breathing period wherein other poaching options and plans could be implemented. For that reason alone, I believe fish techniques are the most important to master.

Because so many good fish methods exist, some of the descriptions have been abbreviated. An entire book could be written about this subject alone.

Dynamite

Dynamiting provides the quickest and easiest method of checking quarries, lakes, ponds and sloughs for fish. It is a relatively cheap method that, when done properly, is not particularly destructive to the environment. In fact, many of the small midwest farm ponds we hit became more productive because we killed forty to fifty percent of the tiny stunted fish they contained.

Salmon
Oncorhynchus

Shooting (or dynamiting) a pond requires a fair degree of skill, most of which can only be acquired by practice. My best advice is to read this chapter and the one on dynamite. If it then seems wise, get out and buy some powder and make a start at it.

Virtually all shots made for fish are done with non-electric cap and fuse. There is simply too much fooling around with electrical caps to make them practical in water.

Most fish shots are made with either a half or a whole stick of dynamite. Less powder is impractical and more is harmful. This depends, of course, on the depth and the size of the pond. Experience is the only practical way of determining size of charge.

Fish are sensitive to an explosive shock. Too little explosion will scare them away. Too much will rupture their air bladders, allowing them to sink to the bottom and be wasted.

My usual plan when dynamiting fish is to first survey the target water for depth and total area. It is important to locate all the deep holes if at all possible, and to have an idea how many sticks should be capped to properly treat the area of water at hand. In many cases I have been hitting the same ponds off and on for many years, so I know about how the program should run. New ponds require good common sense and a bit of luck.

Use half sticks for water in the 4 foot deep range, and whole sticks for water over 5 feet. Try to put one charge in each deep hole, or string them out in the pond about 20 feet apart, 10 feet from the bank if there are no obvious holes. One person can light three or even four charges if he is cool. More than that number should be handled by at least two people. I never set more than 8 charges, even if it is in Lake Michigan with 100 helpers!

Lay the prepared charges on the bank near the target areas of the water. The first charge lit should have a slightly longer fuse than the last one. Don't leave the fuse trimmings on the bank for other people to discover, if the length must be cut.

Some dynamite floats and some sinks slowly. The slow sinking stuff is o.k without a weight. It is actually better if the dynamite goes off a few feet above the bottom rather than in the mud. Remember that after about 20 feet, ignition with cap and fuse becomes very tenuous. For deep sets I put my powder in a good sound plastic bag. While not totally waterproof, the explosives usually stay dry enough to allow the shot to go.

Dynamite that won't sink must be tied to a rock or scrap of iron. Allow about a foot of twine between the weight and the powder so the blast won't occur right on the bottom and lose some of the effect.

191

When shooting the bay area of a large lake from a boat, stack the prepared charges on the seat and run through the area at about 8 miles an hour. Light and throw out the charges as fast as possible but, again, don't try more than six or eight at a time.

In theory the best shots are those that go off one, two, three, then a pause, then a fourth. The fish are either stunned on the first shot, or escape up the line of charges, where they concentrate and are hit by the fourth (or last) shot. In real life I have been able to plan a string of sets this way on several occasions. All produced excellent results, but the ideal set-up is often hard to put into effect.

A correct size charge, properly set, will generate a muffled "thump." There will be a great silver flash and the water will boil like a witch's cauldron. It will not be obvious to people even fifty yards away what has happened.

Small fish will often be killed outright in large numbers. Larger fish will most often be temporarily shocked, allowing the natural air in their bladders to carry them to the surface. As they surface they must be immediately speared or many will revive and dive down again.

The only fish blasting I have ever done in salt water was in the Gulf, off Key West, and in the Inland Passage east of Vancouver Island. The charges were a little harder to sink and had to go deeper but otherwise the situation was the same as in fresh water.

In both cases we chummed extensively before dropping the charges.

Rock Trap

This is an inobtrusive yet effective trap used to take fish traveling up and down a stream or small river. The trap does not have to be made out of rocks, but usually is. Besides this, I don't know what else to call it except a rock trap.

As with many other kinds of traps, this one works best if it is blended into the natural environment rather than fighting against it. As a general rule the best location is one where the creek is uniformly 6 to 8 inches deep, as narrow as possible, with a gravelly, sound bottom. There should be a good supply of large but carryable rocks at hand for use in constructing the trap.

Sometimes there are suitable rocks scattered out in the creek that can be collected and arranged with little effort. Even at the best, however, these traps take a lot of time and energy to build. Usually I figure about two days for two people. On the other hand,

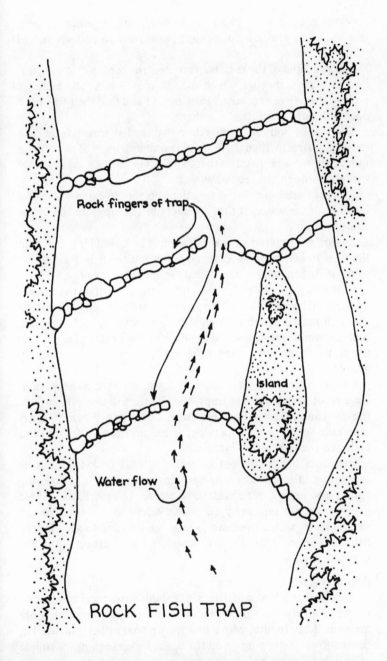

Rock fingers of trap

Island

Water flow

ROCK FISH TRAP

they will last for years with only minor repairs, require no expensive materials and are not obvious, especially to college-trained game wardens.

The principal of the rock trap involves the construction of pens in a "V" shape through which the fish must swim. The pens are built so the fish cannot easily turn around and find their way back out. Two pens is an ideal number.

The V must point in the direction that the fish travel. If they are moving upstream, then the V should point upstream. If two V's are used, they must be offset so that fish finding one exit cannot swim straight through the second as well.

All rocks used in constructing the pens should extend at least a foot out of the water. If that is impossible, lay logs on top of the stone work.

Be sure not to build a dam. There must be lots of large cracks in the lines to allow the water through but not the fish. Raising the water level behind the trap defeats some of its purpose.

At the trap's upper end, a solid line of rocks is put up that makes up the final barrier. Many migratory fish are excellent jumpers, so this wall must be built high enough to discourage such jumping. Shallow water is not a particular problem, but deeper places where the fish can get up a head of speed for a run must be closely guarded.

I have taken pike, bass, suckers, carp, salmon, walleyes, and large trout in one of these traps. Usually the fish came through in the night and were waiting there the next morning. When the run is especially heavy, I sometimes slept on the ground near the trap and collected the fish with a lantern.

Getting a big feisty bass or pike out of a rock trap can be interesting. They will ram around any deep water at surprising speeds and jump great distances to escape. Usually it takes three people who are unusually quick and adept with a spear to get them. One guarding upstream, one down and one to go after the fish itself. Remember not to throw the spear, especially in the gravelly, shallow water.

Bow and Arrow
A sixty pound bow with fiberglas fishing arrows works reasonably well for carp. Most other fish are more easily taken with other methods. I like to hunt with a bow from a boat rather than wading the shallows or creeping up on the bank. To make things as simple as possible, I use a pole with a spin casting reel rather than a bow

194

reel. Use 20 pound line. At times three of us have used two poles when we were in amongst a lot of carp on a reservoir. We kept busy all day with one person shooting while the other two reeled them in.

Chumming

Chumming is not really a technique meant to catch fish. Its purpose is to *attract* fish to a place where they can then by reduced to possession. The technique is especially useful when fish must be caught by conventional hook and line methods, but the poacher still wants the competitive edge.

It is impractical to list all of the chumming possibilities here, but major ones include salmon eggs for trout, where there is a good source of fresh salmon eggs. Canned corn for bluegills, perch, sunfish and rock bass. Chopped liver for carp and bullheads, chopped crayfish or minnows for bass and so on. Be sure to keep chumming in mind anytime one must use conventional fishing methods in a confined area.

One of the best chumming techniques I know of works on trout. This is another secret my uncle never wanted publicized, but future generations may want to share it. At any rate, Uncle has used it all he ever will.

Whenever Uncle came across a porcupine in the woods, he always killed it. He then tied the carcass up in a tree over a small pond in a trout stream. If possible, he would also wrap the body in chicken wire to better secure it to the limb. In places where there was a likelihood of it being discovered, Uncle put the porky up as much as 10 feet or more in the air over the water.

After about ten days he would sneak back to the little pond and fish it with a #10 hook and white corn. He always got every large fish for hundreds of yards up and down the creek this way. They were all there waiting under the porky for the maggots to fall off it into the water. Uncle called them his welfare fish. The ones waiting for a free handout.

Chicken Wire Fish Trap

At a guess I would say that one outdoorsman in a thousand knows about these traps. The rest of the world doesn't have the foggiest idea what they are. Those that have them seem to catch most of the fish, so perhaps it's time to spread the word a bit.

A fish trap is a cylindrical chicken wire enclosure. One end has a hinged door for access to get the fish out, and the other is fitted with a funnel to allow the fish to swim in. A good chicken wire trap will take hundreds of pounds of fish from waters just about anyplace in the country.

Most people build their fish traps smaller than necessary. Smaller traps are harder for the warden to find, but they miss a lot of fish as well. Wardens find fish traps by noting the stay wire tied up to a root or branch on the bank of the pond or river. Rather than tying it up to anything, make the trap big enough and you can just throw it in the water. Mark the spot on the bank and pull it out with a long handled rake.

A good sized trap for the beginner is 4 feet long, and made of 1/2 inch chicken wire. If the heavier half inch fur farm wire is available, that is even better, but this material is getting so expensive it probably will pass from the scene.

Cut a 4 foot wide piece of wire 7 feet long. Wire this length will roll into a tube a little more than 2 feet in diameter. Securely fasten the ends together using light wire or hog rings.

Construct an end panel for the trap. I use a piece of 1/2 inch chicken wire bordered with a hoop of #9 wire. Fasten this to the cylinder with light wire so the end can be taken off to remove the fish.

On the other end of the cylinder construct a funnel that reaches into the trap 2½ feet. The small opening in the funnel should measure three inches and be comprised of cut ends. Don't leave a finished factory edge or the fish will get out more often.

The funnel must be securely and evenly wired into the cylinder. Most of the time I use a piece of #9 wire around the funnel end of the cylinder to stiffen the trap.

Hog liver and corn in a light cheese cloth bag is by far and away the best bait. Scraps of meat, fish heads, and a cob of corn are also good.

Be very cautious when approaching and checking a fish trap that has been in place for a while. Somebody may have found it, and be waiting in hiding for the owner.

Snag Lines

I have had reasonable success using half a dozen or so #2 treble hooks rigged on a line to snag walleyes, suckers and salmon.

Use 40 pound line and tie the hooks on the line about three inches apart. At the end of the hook line, rig a piece of rubber tubing and use a piece of lead wire hung down at right angles, heavy enough to hold the line. Cast the whole rig out across a stream or channel through which the fish are working.

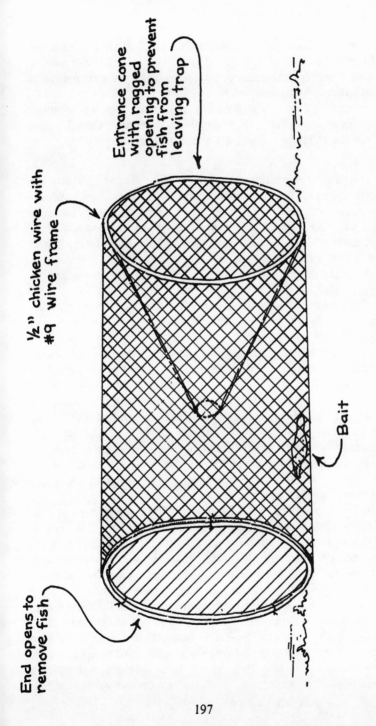

Entrance cone with ragged opening to prevent fish from leaving trap

½" chicken wire with #9 wire frame

Bait

End opens to remove fish

CHICKEN WIRE FISH TRAP

197

Every 20 seconds or so, pull the line sharply till it is worked out of the fish area. Cast it back and start over. If the fish are moving through the stream at that point, the poacher will be surprised at how often fish are snagged.

In rocky places or those with many sunken logs, a substantial number of hooks can be lost snagging objects other than fish. But given the right conditions, it's a method worth trying.

Gill Nets

It would be interesting and probably a lot of fun to list all of the applications for fish net a poacher could get involved with. Admittedly, many of them are pretty far out and not all that practical in this day and age. A book twice the size of this one would be necessary to list them, much to the consternation of people who don't give a damn about fish.

For this reason I have limited discussion to one net and its application.

Gill nets are by far and away my favorite type of fish net. They are relatively cheap, light and compact, even with floats and weights, and very effective.

My older brother bought our first gill net when we were still at home. He used to string it across the river on heavy line rather than using floats. People paddled over the top of it in their boats, walked by it on the bank and even swam around it without ever knowing it was there. To hide the net, he used to release the top line tension and sink it out of sight on the bottom. All that was necessary to reactivate the net again was to pull the line tight.

By setting the top line about a foot below the surface, he managed a masterful job of concealing it, although some fish probably escaped over the net as a result.

Gill nets are made out of thin nylon lines tied into rectangles. They catch fish by snapping shut behind the gill cover of any fish trying to force its way through the mesh. Size of the mesh varies between one inch and 4½ inches. Obviously any gill net will sort for size, since only one size fish can get caught in any given size net.

Smaller fish slip through and continue on unharmed. Larger fish are turned back as the net becomes a seine for their size range. The trick is to buy the correct size net for one's area. The most ideal is to use a net that will take the middle third size range, turning back the big third and allowing the smaller third to get through. Obviously, this size varies from species to species as well as from area to area. However, there are usually more fish worth catching in the middle than either end of the range, so it is the size the average poacher should try for. If more than one species is targeted, deciding on the net size is even more of a problem.

When living in the midwest, I used a 1½ inch net and took suckers, some carp, red horse and bass up to about two pounds. In northern Wisconsin, I used a 2½ inch net principally for pike. In Georgia and Alabama I again used a 2½ incher, mostly for bass. In the west I use a 3½ inch net for salmon and steelhead and have occasionally taken some large bass. One use for a smaller sized gill net is to rig it with poles on either end and pull it like a seine. We have an old net that we fitted with floats that is a wonder for that purpose. It works well on whitefish, squaw fish and suckers as well as smallmouth bass.

The best plan when using a gill net for a seine is to cut off a shallow inlet or little arm and corner the fish into the land. We can drag through a deep creek hole with only half the effort it would require with a regular closed-mesh seine.

Gill nets should be set any place fish will travel. One winter we chopped a hole through the ice in some of the Rainy Lakes near Fort Frances, Ontario, and dragged a line through to a second hole 200 feet away. Then when the ice got thick we were able to pull a gill net back and forth under the ice. During the course of the winter we probably took 200 Northern pike this way.

Other than in a straight line on lakes or across ponds, the best place to set gill nets is in a barrier position on rivers and streams. Although not as many fish are moving then, I like to set the net out in August or September when the water in the rivers is low.

Some fantastic catches are possible in the rivers in early spring. But many times the water is so high and wild it is a problem. One big log can sweep down and rip out an entire net, causing more damage than the potentially large catches are worth. In spring, if the water is high, it is usually best to stay right there with the net. Often, this is time well spent. As the net fills rapidly with fish, it may be emptied often, and saved from floating debris.

All gill nets these days are made in Korea or Taiwan. They cost between $28.00 for the 1½" inch model to $45.00 for the 4½ inch kind. If possible, order the net without floats and weights. They are much cheaper. The weights on the net are easily installed by the poacher at great savings.

Nets are both easy and difficult to buy. Several net companies advertise in the various sporting magazines. Even better, look in the yellow pages of phone books for larger cities on the coast.

Boston, Portsmouth, Charleston, Galveston, San Francisco and Seattle all have net companies. Some do not want to sell to small private users but usually something can be worked out with them.

Electric Fish Probes

Of all the fish collecting methods, shocking is probably one of the best. It gets all the fish, big and small, top feeders and bottom. It requires a minimum of effort and, once the generator is purchased, is very inexpensive. The big advantage to shocking is that any unwanted fish can be left to recover while all others can be harvested or otherwise disposed of.

With the advent of light, quiet, easily carried generators such as the Honda portable, the method is even becoming practical. In the past we have occasionally tried to use a hand crank generator from an old telephone, but they never had the poop to do the job. The other alternative was a big tractor drawn generator, which were not practical wherever stealth and surprise counted for anything.

Use of a portable generator is incredibly easy. First, run either one lead from a 110 or two from 220 depending on the need and the generator's capacity, using as much 12-2 wire as is required to get to the pond's corners from the generator. Push the first wire's lead into one side of the receptacle socket, and tie its other end to an 8 to 10 foot pole.

The second wire need only reach to the water's edge. It acts as a ground. Plug this into the other side of the receptacle. Turn the generator on and probe the water with the pole. Anything between the two wires—the ground and the wire on the pole—will come rolling to the surface. The best plan is to work along the bank to the extent of the probe wire, and then move the generator. A 2½ KV generator will operate through water for about 25 feet.

The procedure is exactly the same for 220V except two probe poles are run simultaneously in opposite directions. With two probing a good pond or lake, the fish roll out of the depths in great numbers and kinds. One man is easily kept busy collecting them all with a net or spear.

A generator can be put in a boat and used with long leads as the boat moves across the lake. Trail a lead out the back about 25 feet and mount the ground on the front with a pole. To most people, the generator sounds like an outboard, so there is little danger. Just be sure no one falls in the water near one of these generators.

Snares

I thoroughly enjoy snaring fish and often go after them using this technique for recreation. Depending on the conditions and time of year, an amazing variety of fish can be taken with a snare.

The proper snare for fish is the copper wire model described in the chapter on snares. Obviously a snare for salmon will be larger than one for bass, but other than the size of the loop, everything else is the same.

Suckers, squaw fish, carp and gar are the easiest to snare. It is probably best to practice on these before tackling the more difficult game fish.

Set up the snare so that the loop is large enough for the intended fish to easily swim through. Tie it to a length of 12 to 25 pound monofilament line, depending on the size of the game. The line is then tied to a fairly stout 8 to 10 foot pole. Old cane poles work very well for this purpose. Leave enough length in the line so the snare just touches the end of the pole.

The trick now becomes one of creeping up on the bank close enough to hang the snare in front of cruising fish. By working the loop around, it is possible to get just about any fish to go through the noose, provided the poacher does not show himself or otherwise alarm the quarry.

As soon as the fish enters the loop, whip the pole smartly. If the snare misses, it should be completely collapsed from the momentum of the pull. If it connects, it will cut into the fish slightly and hold it, unless the pole slacks. Fish fight harder when snared than when hooked in the mouth. Don't expect to pull the critter right out of the water unless it is fairly small.

The method will work from a boat or a bridge as well as from a stream bank. Any place where the fish can be seen cruising or laying undisturbed is a good prospect.

Bar Of Soap Or Detergent

I have used this method a number of times right next to people who were fishing conventionally. I believe there was enough difference in our respective catches to attribute it to my technique, and not to my imagination. At any rate, this method contains a bit of alchemy, but other poachers might like to try it to see what they think.

In a large bay of perhaps 8 to 12 acres, it is possible to get the fish to start biting by dumping a large box of concentrated detergent in the water. Run into the bay at half-throttle and meter the soap into the wake behind the boat. Criss-cross the water several times, and then wait fifteen minutes for the detergent to sink.

The detergent technique works best on pike, perch and walleyes that have quit biting in an area. Perhaps it works for bass—perhaps not. I am also not nearly so certain about its use in southern waters.

A big box of detergent is expensive, but some time when the fish have quit feeding for some reason or other, give it a try. Dump the soap and then fish the area by conventional means. I am betting the average poacher will be very pleased with the results.

In the west I have tried floating detergent into some good trout holes. Whether trout bite or not is generally dependent on whether they see the fisherman. For this reason I couldn't really tell if the action picked up because they didn't see me any longer or because of the detergent.

One place where I am certain soap has a positive effect is ice fishing. To take advantage of this method, drill a hole in a bar of soap and hang it in the ice hole right along side the tip-up. The soap should be on the bottom or, if the bottom is very deep, about 12 feet below the bait. Perch and walleye definitely react to this technique. People who use it always seem to get more fish.

Trot Lines

In times past it was very common and popular to set out trot lines. I remember several as a kid that were a mile or more long that took two men in a boat ten hours a day to tend. They were set for sturgeon in some northern Wisconsin lakes.

Today few people seem interested in trot lines, even though they are legal in many places in this country and Canada.

A trot line is comprised of a single main line on which a number of short hook lines are fastened. The ends of the main line are anchored on each side of a river or bay, and the hook lines allowed to hang down where the fish will find them.

A small 50 to 80 foot trot line that is ideal for most smaller rivers, lakes and ponds can be made as follows.

Begin with a piece of 100 pound test line 100 feet long. Starting in the center, tie an 18 inch drop line on the main line every two feet. The drop lines can be 18 pound monofilament. Work out from the center, but leave 10 feet of line free of drop lines on either end. The end is used to anchor the trot line.

Tie an appropriate size hook and a small sinker on the end of each drop line. Hook size depends on the fish in the area, but I generally use a #4 or a #6.

Bait the hooks with worms, liver, crayfish, hot dogs or whatever attracts the fish. Set the whole thing out, being careful not to tangle the hooks any more than necessary. For bottom fish, let the line sink down to the bottom. If surface feeders are the intended game, stretch the main line tight and keep it up off the bottom.

Some poachers put a float or two on their main lines to keep the bait up. There are several reasons for not doing this. Floats broadcast the rig's location, and often the best target fish for a trot line are the bottom feeders. If it is necessary to keep the line up, tie it tight but don't use floats.

In even mediocre waters, it isn't uncommon to take one bullhead for every three trot line hooks day after day. It would never pay to sit on the bank and try to fish for these guys. But a fifteen minute trip each day to a 40 hook trot line can be extremely rewarding.

Trot lines are fairly inexpensive, highly portable and generally easy to hide. They are a simple little tool that poachers should use more.

Set Lines

Poachers need a good fast and easy technique to get the bigger game fish in large bodies of water. Fish such as large pike, muskellunge, lake trout and salmon can be a real problem to the poacher without some special advantage.

After years of trying this and that, the best method I have come up with is a sort of modified set line.

We take used plastic bottles from outboard oil and tie about 100 feet of 25 pound line on them. The hook is somewhere between a #1/0 and a #3, depending on the game.

The bottles must be red or white, or they can't be found again and set. This constitutes something of a hazard. Usually wardens will pick them up rather than wait for the owners, so the danger is not as great as one would first suppose. If a warden does come along while a poacher is checking his line, the poacher can always maintain that he saw the bottle and stopped to pick it up.

I like to bait the hooks with a chunk of sucker about one cubic inch in size. This much bait requires a little bit heavier sinker, but that is no problem.

In large lakes for big fish, I let out 40 to 80 feet of line and tie it off at the bottle. Set the line out in very deep water and allow it to drift into the shallows where it will hang up and hold the bait at the correct level. The bigger fish will often take the bait in the open water, or in the shallows where the bottle stops.

A knowledge of the currents and winds will help when checking the bottles a day later. But if a big fish is hooked, it is anybody's guess where the rig will end up. I have retrieved my lines plus some huge lake trout as far as two miles from the place where I dropped them a day earlier.

Dip Seine

See the chapter on crayfish for instructions on how to make dip seines.

These outfits can be used successfully to catch blue gills, sunfish, carp, suckers and an assortment of smaller fish. If one is very patient they even work fairly well for bullheads and smaller catfish.

In spring when the creeks are flooded, it is often productive to walk the banks and dip the seine every few yards or so. This plan works especially well near the mouth of larger rivers and places where creeks run into lakes.

A dip seine is a fairly versatile tool for a poacher. People in the business should have at least one of them.

The Mix Master Method

Here we have an ancient trick that northern guides have used for years to get the pike to start biting. Usually they use it when they have dudes out and the action is slow. It works best early in the morning and later in the afternoon, but try it anytime and it will start things rolling to some extent.

The technique is simply to use your outboard to chop and mix up the shallow weed buds. Pick a spot where the weeds are growing up out of the water for 300 to 400 yards along shore. Run the boat parallel to shore at the edge of the weeds, working back and forth into the weeds. Keep at it, going deeper into the weeds till the boat won't go any more.

The idea is to chop and mix as many of the weeds as possible. This usually requires 30 minutes or more of running. After finishing, troll a minnow along through the chopped up area. Invariably the pike will have started feeding and some will hit the bait.

Rotenone

The best pond fish poison is Rotenone, or its close relative, Pyrethrins. Both work very well and are fairly easy to purchase, but must be used very prudently.

Rotenone functions in water by coating the gills of fish, robbing them of their ability to take in oxygen. Almost all of the fish in a pond or pool treated with Rotenone will die. The poison dissipates quickly, but those pond fish that are originally dosed will succumb.

The material has the advantage of being very portable, but the disadvantage of being a bit expensive. Under certain circumstances it is a good method, but the individual poacher will have to make that determination for himself based on conditions in the field.

Rotenone is the principal active ingredient in many bugs sprays and vegetable dusting powders. These sprays are available from all garden supply stores, hardware stores and even places like K-Mart.

The trick when purchasing Rotenone is to look for sprays that have a high percentage of it as an active ingredient. To do this requires that one read the label. At times I have been able to find a five percent solution of Rotenone, but in many stores the highest concentration offered is two percent. One percent mixtures are common and usable in large quantities, but the higher concentrations are much better.

Dairy farm suppliers are especially good places to look for the high concentration Rotenone materials.

Rotenone must be thoroughly mixed with the water in a pond or pool in order to work. Sometimes this is a problem, especially at levels below five feet. Rotenone doesn't sink well, being basically a buoyant material.

In creeks I mix a can of bug powder into a slurry in a bucket and meter it into a ripple above the target pool. This way the material has a chance to mix a bit before going into the deep water and is very thoroughly distributed. The results are good, even on fairly large pools.

Ponds are a bit tougher. The best plan is to slurry the powder in a bucket, then pour it into old pint milk cartons. Put a few stones in the cartons and punch holes in their tops. Now quickly drop the cartons overboard into the pond's deepest holes. It will take up to 30 minutes for the stuff to seep out of the containers, but at least they will be on the bottom where it can do some good.

Use about four pounds of 2 percent powder or 64 ounces of liquid per acre of pond unless it is very deep. Rotenone takes about ten minutes to start working. A sign of success is fish skimming the surface for air.

Generally we spear or net the fish as they come up. Throw the trash fish on the bank for the coons.

Rotenone is ineffective in very large bodies of open water.

Spear And Light

Perhaps it is well to end this chapter with a word about a method that to many is the most traditional way of poaching fish.

Jack lighting, or spearing fish with a light, works just about anyplace. The only thing that changes is the fish, and even some of these are pretty consistent from one section of the country to another.

Jack lighting is done by blinding fish at night with a powerful light at a time when they are in shallow water or on the surface. I have used the technique successfully for everything from gar fish in Mexico to salmon off Vancouver Island.

To work well, the poacher must determine when his target fish are likely to be moving upstream or laying on the surface of a lake or pond. This requires a knowledge of the resource that is best acquired out in the field.

Other than migratory fish, one can usually catch pike, blue gills and sunfish in the early spring with a light in shallow lake water. Carp and suckers are easy targets in streams and rivers anytime in summer. In some places, a few bass can also be picked up along shore.

Spotlighting fish can be risky. To minimize our exposure, we use a lantern with a hood. The hood keeps us from being blinded, concentrates the light in one place, and doesn't give our position away as easily as an unhooded light.

As an added precaution in populated or dangerous areas, we work two with the light and one away. It is the duty of the man in the dark to stay ahead of the action and to listen and watch intently. He should be prepared to warn the others immediately if there is danger. Most wardens will station themselves on a creek ahead of poachers and allow them to work their way into his hands. A good point man out ahead of the light can stop that.

Creek bottoms and marshes are low and generally tree protected. If the poachers will just be quiet and not swing their lights promiscuously, everything will generally be o.k.

Work upstream in rivers and creeks. Splashing and other noisy movements should be avoided. When a fish is seen, throw the more powerful flash light on it and work into spearing position. Often deep holes can be probed with a light. There may be bass or trout lying in them that can't otherwise be seen during the day.

Some of the Mexican fishermen I fished with hung their light out ahead of the boat on a pole. The procedure worked well enough, but I guess it's too much trouble for us lazy gringos. We set the lantern on the bow and stand in the boat, directing the paddler or motorman.

Pintail Duck
Anas acuta

20

GAME BIRDS

There is no one, all encompassing, surefire method of poaching large numbers of game birds that I know of. Instead there are a number of interesting and effective tricks that can be employed, depending on which bird and what the weather and other conditions are at the time. The skilled poacher will have to sift through the suggested techniques and use the ones that best fit his situation.

One of the funniest things that ever happened to me in all the years I have been poaching was the time we collected nearly a half a pickup load of crows with dynamite. This story has been repeated so often it has either happened in substantially the same form to other hunters, or it has entered the public domain as a tall tale. At any rate, the following account is true and may be the origin of a number of similar stories.

When I was a young man living in Harlan County, Kentucky, there was an old gent who loved to set off dynamite. He blasted stumps and rocks for a living, sold powder and supplies for additional income, and taught me much of what I now know about explosives.

One fall day he came puttering up in his old black '39 Ford truck with the startling news (for him it was startling) that a whole passel of crows had made a roost back in a large cottonwood on the river. Old Dan wondered aloud about the possibility of stringing dynamite in the roost tree and firing it off after dark to try and get some crows.

I didn't have anything better to do, so I agreed to go along to help, which meant crawling up in the tree to place the charges. Dan was too old for that business, but he did offer a lot of encouragement from the ground.

By twilight I had 6 four-stick charges strung around through the tree. We connected them electrically so they would all fire at once and pulled back about 300 yards till pitch black arrived. It was obvious from all the screeching and hollering that there were a number of crows using the roost.

Quietly we pulled the truck up to the drop wires again. It was too dark to see for sure, but it seemed like our movement wasn't bothering the crows.

Old Dan got out of the truck and lifted the hood. Gingerly he touched the two drop wires to the truck's battery.

The explosion, uncontained and unmuffled high in the tree, was deafening. Bits and pieces of leaves and twigs showered down on the truck. Dan and I tried to shine the headlights on the tree, but the tall grass obscured the light so much that we finally gave it up and went home.

Early next morning Dan and I drove back to the river to have a look. It is impossible to tell how many crows got away, but there sure were a lot of them that didn't. We filled about a third of that old truck bed with dead crows, which is a whole bunch of the black critters.

Other than the dead crows, we were very impressed with the state of the bombed out cottonwood. It looked like an umbrella after a tornado. Several smaller trees that happened to be standing near were also very tattered. The leaves were already falling when we hit the crow roost, so it wasn't too surprising to see the trees defoliated. What was surprising was the number of leaves that held on tenaciously but were shredded into tiny waving threads.

For those who would like to duplicate this experiment, use 60% dynamite with electrical caps. String it out away from the trunk of the tree as far as possible and as high as possible. Also try to get the powder set as early in the day as possible. I always felt we were a bit late with our operation.

The only application I know of using explosives for game is blasting holes in the ice for ducks to come in to during the winter, or setting a charge at the surface of a pond where it might get feeding ducks.

During a severe winter an open watering hole is a good magnet for ducks. They will come in by large droves to get a drink if everything else is frozen. The problem with shooting a hole in the river or a pond is that the blast wakens the neighbors and scares the ducks in the vicinity. By the time they get settled down, the hole may be frozen over again, not to mention the humans that might wonder what is happening.

A charge hidden in a marsh for ducks isn't practical. It makes too much noise, is always in the wrong place, gets waterlogged quickly and really gets very few ducks even if everything else works perfectly.

Snares

Game birds can be taken with simple electric wire snares if the poacher can get them to start coming to bait. Early in fall, the best time to collect game birds, it is often very difficult to get them to come in to bait. Later in winter bait works well, but the allowable harvest may have already been made.

The best, most effective game bird snare I have ever seen is one developed and used by African bush natives to catch birds around their kraals.

It is made using a very light, five strand electric wire snare mounted in gangs of four to six on a small wooden "X." The bait is placed in the center of the X, the bird then either fouling its feet or neck trying to get the food.

We use them in two sizes. The smaller is about 6 inches across and has its loops opened to the diameter of quarters or a little larger. These work extremely well for quail and hungarian partridge type birds.

The larger size is 10 inches across and may have as many as seven snares on it. Set the snares about the diameter of half dollars or more. I have caught many pheasants and grouse in this type snare. They are very effective.

Bait should be smaller grain such as wheat, oats or barley. Corn is o.k. but the critters can gobble it up too quickly before getting tangled in the trap. Put a half a handful of grain in the center of the trap and scatter it around the edges of the snares a bit.

It is very helpful if the area has been baited for a week or two before hand so the birds are coming in well.

I believe a larger version of this snare would be dynamite for turkeys, especially late in the season. Unfortunately, I have never lived around these creatures long enough to give the plan a try. About the only upland game bird that can't be taken with a snare trap is a chukar.

The trap is very handy, very easy to set, and hard to detect unless there is a bird in it. Pheasants, for instance, flop around a lot in a snare. Anybody who sees this will be alerted to what is happening.

211

Poachers should also be warned that pheasant/grouse sized birds will carry their traps for short distances.

I use 3/8 inch exterior plywood cut into 1½ inch strips 6 to 10 inches long to build the trap base. Nail these together in the middle, fasten the snares on the cross members and set them as shown in the drawing.

Call

Many seasoned poachers don't realize that they can use a call to locate and attract some upland game birds. Bobwhite quail, in particular, can be fooled with a call that sounds like a bird lost from the covey.

I work weed patches and fence rows with my call, listening for a response. If I get one, I sit down and continue to talk to the critters for a while. After ten minutes or so, a few will usually start to show. They can be shot with .22 BB caps or a silenced long rifle.

Olt makes a commercial quail call. From time to time I have seen other home-made calls. The best bet is to watch for them in local sporting goods stores.

Shooting With A .22

A good quiet .22 can take hundreds of birds in the winter. I watch baited places, roosting areas and other areas of cover that have a concentration of birds due to snow, rain or cold when using this method.

The only real tricks are to be patient, and learn to shoot at ranges slightly greater than that of a shotgun. Pheasants will run down corn rows or along a fence at what they feel is a safe distance. The shrewd poacher can peck away at them and, if he is a good shot, often bring home some meat. Quiet .22's won't raise the hackles of landowners and usually won't spook the birds.

One technique that is often overlooked in late winter is driving birds. This requires at least three hunters, one of whom is very good at pass shooting. The drivers should allow plenty of time for the stander to get into position. Standers should move very quickly and should try to obscure their position behind brush or weeds while waiting.

There is a difference of opinion here, but I like to drive with the wind if it isn't howling at gale force.

The shooter will have to use a shotgun under most circumstances, but in vile weather during the middle of winter it is possible to get away with the extra noise of using a big gun. This is especially true if the poachers are well camouflaged and don't hang around all day after making the kill.

212

SIDE VIEW

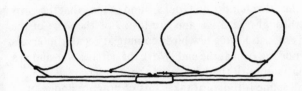

Six strand copper
wire snare made
from electric wire

Bait scattered
on lath

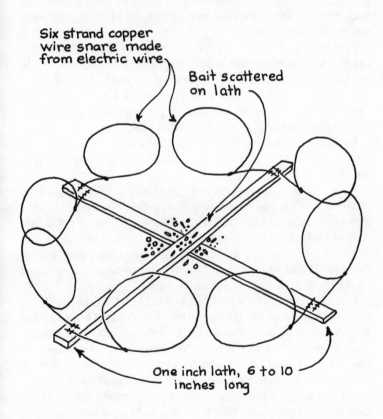

One inch lath, 6 to 10
inches long

AFRICAN BIRD SNARE

The drivers should know what they are doing. Don't drive too fast, but on the other hand, don't fool around so long that the birds filter back through the drive and are lost. For the sake of the shooter, it is nice to have a few birds coming at regular intervals rather than one big rush at the end. Work the patches well and in a direction that will push the birds over the stander.

Driving all game is tough. It takes lots of practice and a lot of savvy. Best to get started and learn the art as soon as possible.

Nets

Nets are an important method of getting both ducks and upland birds. I use 3½ inch gill net for ducks, 2½ inch for pheasant and grouse, and 1½ inch for quail. For the upland birds, chicken wire is o.k., but it is more expensive and obvious than gill net, and really not quite as effective.

Fish gill netters know only too well how many diving ducks they catch inadvertently trying to ply their trade. The secret here is to set the net across the middle of a small bay or inlet where the ducks have been seen feeding and actively try to take fowl rather than fish. Many poachers are satisfied to get both and set their nets accordingly, but that's up to the individual.

I buy my nets unrigged, having neither floats nor weights. The nets should be at least 4 feet deep (unless the water averages less) and about 100 feet long.

Longer nets are a problem, in my estimation. They are easier to discover, too expensive and will usually catch far more than the average poacher could ever use. One night, for instance, I caught thirty-one ducks in one gill net 100 feet long, plus a number of nice jack fish. I left the net out one more night and then I took it in for the year. It had produced all I needed in two days, and it wasn't worth the risk to leave it out any longer.

I rig my nets myself. If possible, I use 3/4 inch nylon line strung through the top of the gill net rather than floats. This way I can stretch the net a foot or two under the surface of the water where it can't be seen or hit with a boat. Net weights must be installed. I find it is much cheaper to make my own lead sinkers and put them on the bottom of the net than get them factory installed.

Ducks caught in the net will drown and be nicely cooled. If one likes diving ducks in the first place, the taste does not seem to be impaired.

Scout the locations during daylight, and then set the net after dark. Usually I place the net one night and pull it in the next, without awaiting to disentangle the catch. Better to fold up and sort everything in a secluded cove than out in the middle of a lake in front of the whole world.

An old tattered piece of gill net will work fine for upland birds, if the holes can be repaired. It must be at least four feet square. Anything bigger than about four feet by six feet is a waste of effort.

Stake the net taut about 4 inches from the ground for quail and 6 inches for pheasant sized birds. I do this with four good, solid stakes and use a piece of 120 pound monofilament fish line on the four sides and in an X across the middle. The line supports the net, but is pretty much invisible to the birds. The area under the net must be level and clear of long grass or brush.

Make the set in a small clearing with good bird cover on all sides, preferably obscured from human view. It is helpful to be able to see the approaches to the trap in case someone has found the set, and is waiting for the owner to return.

Use millet, sorghum, wheat or barley for bait. If these grains are not available, then use cracked corn. Sprinkle the grain lightly all around the trap and heavily in the center. It helps immensely if there is a light layer of duff and dirt to mix in with the grain. More birds are caught when they have to scratch around for the feed.

The principle the trap works on takes advantage of a common weakness of feathered creatures. They will hunt and peck along for feed in a forward direction, working themselves under the net. But as soon as the quail or pheasants put their heads straight up through the mesh, they are trapped. A bird will not pull its neck down out of the net to release itself.

Although I haven't tried the trap on every kind of upland game bird, I believe it would work for all of them, including turkeys.

Pole Trap

This is an old, old system used by control trappers to catch predatory birds such as hawks and owls. When I was a lad, farmers who let their hens run in a yard often had a pole trap around to protect the flock.

To construct the trap, put a 4 inch pole securely in the ground. The pole's height should be at least 2 feet above any roofs or fences within 60 feet. Nail two 8 inch 2x4's flat on the pole, providing a square platform.

Fasten a long piece of baling wire to the chain of a No. 1½ steel strap and nail to the pole, allowing enough lead so the trap can be set on the platform.

Any predatory bird contemplating making a meal of the chickens will land on the pole either coming or going.

Problems with the trap are its obviousness, unless it is concealed in some way, the fact that small birds will set the trap off and the difficulty one encounters climbing the pole to set it.

Damaging or killing hawks, owls or eagles is a federal offense.

Baiting

A good poacher is always on the lookout for new and better ways to bait game birds. Successful baiting brings in large numbers of birds in such a way that they are exposed to conventional methods of harvest. Baiting is cheap and easy, and in most cases hard to detect.

The best bait as far as I am concerned is sorghum. Wheat and barley are a poor second and the bait most often used—corn—is a no-no as far as I am concerned. Corn is easy to get, attracts game birds as well as anything, but it is too obvious. Sometimes it is possible to get dried peas or black beans, which also make good bait material, but don't use yellow corn unless there is some other mitigating circumstance.

The secret with bait is to get it out early in small quantities over a long period of time in areas where the birds are known to feed. Don't try, for instance, to attract turkeys to a suburban Memphis lot and then blame the bait when nothing shows up.

As winter sets in farther north, baiting becomes a real winning proposition. If the bait has been there long enough, the birds will become accustomed to it and even dig it out of the snow.

Set dryland bait stations up in small semi-cleared areas near major game bird cover. The birds have to feel they are protected coming to the grain or they won't eat it until there is a dire emergency. Be sure the bait is set in a place where hikers or farmers are unlikely to stumble across it. Using dark colored grain helps, as mentioned. The average farmer will walk right over bait and think nothing of it unless his suspicions are raised by the obvious presence of spilt grain.

Another trick is to put out a hat full of rock salt along with the grain. If the ground is well drained, the salt will dissolve in the ground and last for several years. The combination will attract many times the birds just grain alone will.

Baiting ducks is easier than upland birds, but it's easier to get caught at it as well.

Be sure to put the bait in water no deeper than two feet, in a sheltered area where the ducks are likely to come even without bait. Bait at night or when it is certain no one will be around to watch. Bait early and keep the bait replenished. One of the best places is over warm springs where the ice won't form till everything else is frozen up tight.

Some of the readers in Indiana may want to look up this next episode and verify its authenticity.

A few years back we learned that a U.S. Senator from Indiana and a couple of his cronies were in the northwestern part of the state hunting a marsh near the Tippecanoe River State Park Reserve. Their hunting grounds were on private property, but a significant number of the ducks they intended to shoot came over from the reserve.

At 11:00 the night before the senator's hunt, we snuck in with two bags of shell corn and scattered it all over the marsh in front of their blind. Using a fictitious name, we then called the warden and reported that the senator was shooting ducks over a baited marsh.

The warden reached a federal marshal and they visited the senator in the blind next morning, shortly after daybreak. We watched for a while and finally concluded the bastard might talk his way out of it, so we ran to town and called the newspaper in Logansport.

A reporter got to the farm an hour later just as the wardens were leaving. I don't know what finally happened, but for a few weeks there were a number of very lively news stories about the senator having been caught shooting ducks over a baited marsh.

Duck baiting works best if the ducks can see the bait from a long way off. It is better early in the season than late, and, of course, requires open water. But we have at times put out bait out on low muck flats adjacent to the water and had good success.

Spotlighting

Most birds are paralyzed by a beam of light shining directly at them.

Pigeons can be hand-picked right off their perch if a light is held on them till the poacher can get in position and make the grab. I have removed or collected a good many pigeons this way. We got them out of old feed mills, barns, an old church loft, from the eaves of commercial buildings, and even out of the rafters of houses.

Our usual procedure was to find them after dark with our flashlights set at low beam. When one is spotted, we would turn the light all the way to bright and either grab it or shoot it.

Spot lighting also works on ducks if the light is bright and is focused on the bird before it spooks. I have never gone out specifically looking for quackers with a light, but many many times we have come home from frog spearing with a mallard drake or two in the bag. Should a poacher have a liking for mud hens, many of these could be collected with a spot light.

Doves are another easy bird to take off a roost with a light. They hold as well as pigeons do, but my question has always been "Why bother?" I won't even invest a .22 cartridge in a dove, because they provide so little to eat.

Den Traps

These are covered in the chapter on den traps and the reader should be sure to look over the information relative to game birds presented there.

Pheasants, quail and owls occasionally work their way into den traps, and are often part of the general catch. Although I would never set a den trap primarily for birds, it should come as no surprise when one is picked up.

Box Traps

Occasionally I have used a standard swinging door box trap to catch game birds. They work on ducks in secluded marshes and on pheasants in brush, if the snow is deep and the pheasant is hungry.

Bait the box with corn and expect it to stand for a long time between catches, even in places that have been pre-baited and are heavily used by birds.

Generally I don't view box traps as being of much value to the bird poacher. The yield is too low.

Steel Traps

Game birds can be taken quite easily with steel traps set in runs late in the season and around baited areas.

Expect to check the traps often and to find a preponderance of mutilated birds that may be unfit to eat because they have flopped around in the trap so much. The bloody struggling bird will also scare other birds away.

Use a number 1 trap for quail and pheasants to try this method. But my bet is that the average poacher won't continue to use steel traps for birds. The only exception might be on turkeys.

Hooks

Many game birds can be reduced to possession by using 12 pound monofilament line and #12 hooks baited with soft canned corn. Pheasant, grouse, hungarian partridge, chukars and especially ducks can be taken with this method.

I put two hooks on each line about one foot apart. The line should be 4 to 6 feet long and tied to a light drag. Two feet of branch will do very nicely.

Put the hook and bait in a previously baited area and check once a day. Birds that are caught will pull the drag twenty or thirty feet away and hide.

Hook and line for birds is a most inconspicuous, cheap and effective method. It works best on ducks, then pheasants and other upland game. Ducks, however, are at times caught right out in plain sight where their struggles with the drag invite trouble. This does not preclude using this method for ducks, but it does require that one exercise additional caution.

Most fishermen or landowners who find hooked birds will assume they are fouled in a line intended for fish. Wardens won't be fooled for a minute and may decide to sit and wait for the owner to show up and claim the bird. Use caution approaching any trap. Look around. Notice tracks, trails through the grass and muddy water.

If it looks like a setup, walk right on by, and don't stop unless the bird is very obvious. Then pause long enough to let the bird go and keep right on walking.

Flight Traps

There are several very excellent flight traps that the poacher can build. One of them is diagrammed on page 221.

Flight traps are of no value for upland birds, and of limited value for ducks. They are big, conspicuous, expensive and hard to build. But they can be ideal for taking sparrows, blackbirds, crows, robins, starlings, and hawks. I use the traps principally to easily rid farm areas of pests. Farmers will love you for it, and permission to use their property is more readily forthcoming.

Bait should be something the target species likes. In the west I use a dead rabbit for magpies, for instance. Corn is good for crows and mixed cattle feed for starlings.

Usually one need catch only the first bird or two for the fun to start. The trapped bird will call all his buddies, who will then drop through the opening en masse to their own destruction.

I wait till after dark to clean out the trap. Often I use a burlap bag and a light and just grab the critters out of the enclosure. Later I drown the bag or throw it in a dump.

219

Leave a few birds in the trap from day to day to keep calling the catch in. Fresh bait won't be as important, but should still be offered in the trap.

Cost of building a flight trap is at least $20.00 even if most of the materials are scrounged. Bigger is better, but I hardly feel it is worth making a crow-sized trap for sparrows. A big trap with small 3/4 inch to 1 inch mesh is dandy if there are a lot of starlings around to get rid of. At times a good-sized flight trap will catch 100 or more of these pesky critters in a day. A flight trap for sparrows can be as little as 2 feet square. The opening should be about 1½ inches around.

At one time I owned a large trap that I used for crows. It worked fine with a stuffed owl decoy, but when the crows tore up the decoy, the trap was no longer very effective. It was 6 feet square and ridiculously heavy. After a few years I sold it to a feedlot operator who killed thousands of starlings using it.

Cone Traps

These are mickey mouse little affairs that were even sold commercially at one time.

A cone trap consists of a light chicken wire funnel, flat on one side, with a thin tin bottom on which to put the bait. They are made out of light 2 inch chicken wire and tin, lighter than flattened cans if possible. Skirts on the inside of the funnel pressure the birds into the trap and keep them there till the poacher returns.

These things are inexpensive and fun to fool around with, but they generally don't work well. I first saw them in Ontario, Canada, on a moose hunting trip. Our guide set some around the cabin for fool's hens and occasionally got a ruffed grouse. Later I tried them for pheasant with only limited success. Several times I lost the traps, either to pheasants that got in them and ran off, or to farmers who thought they were dunce hats.

Duck Pen Traps

Almost any duck hunter has at least heard about duck pen traps. They are very, very effective, especially after the first duck gets in the trap. On the other hand, they are so obvious it's awful. The ducks quack and carry on and anybody within a half a mile can tell what's going on.

The pens are fairly expensive and can be difficult to set. They are not something that can be stored in a pack and secretly taken to a duck marsh. Still in all, they are so effective that I have used one for three days to catch enough ducks to last our entire family a whole year.

220

FLIGHT TRAP

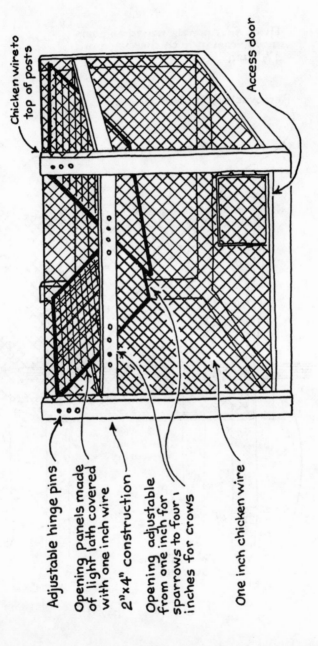

Chicken wire to top of posts

Access door

Adjustable hinge pins

Opening Panels made of light lath covered with one inch wire

2"x4" construction

Opening adjustable from one inch for sparrows to four inches for crows

One inch chicken wire

221

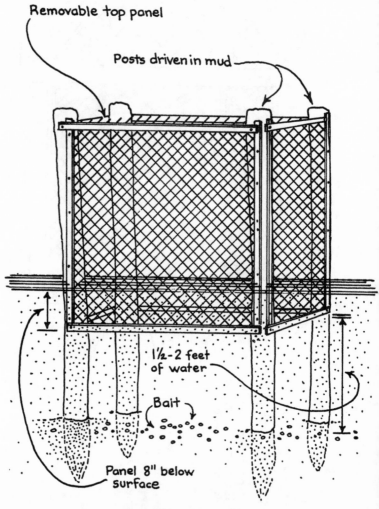

Three foot panels nailed to posts made from inch chicken wire and 1½" lath

Removable top panel

Posts driven in mud

1½-2 feet of water

Bait

Panel 8" below surface

DUCK TRAP

The ducks were caught in a tiny clearing on the south end of giant refuge. A lake of perhaps 600 acres made up the main body of the reserve. There was a road around the lake to the west, north and east, back perhaps 150 yards from the water.

To the south there was nothing for several miles because of a large marshy area which gave way to trackless desert. Trees lined the bank around the road, and there were other clumps of brush extending to the south.

We cut out the pieces for a pen trap but didn't assemble it. Later we carried the collapsed pen and a hog ringer in a car to the end of the road where one of the gals dropped us off. By staying in the brush we were able to wade the swamp unseen till we were more than a mile from the nearest road. At times the water was above our waists and cold as ice.

Eventually we found an ideal sheltered spot of water about twenty inches deep and set up the trap. We used the hog ringer to put the stiff wire together. Since the enclosure was so obvious anyway, we used shelled corn for bait.

The next day two of us went in again and collected about twenty ducks from the trap. Their quacking and splashing didn't arouse suspicion because there was so much quacking and splashing in the rest of the reserve.

Yet a good woodsman could have easily seen that someone was wading the swamp on that end of the lake.

By the third day we felt we were pushing our luck. Also it was getting bitter cold. We took the trap apart and sunk it, carried our last batch of ducks out and called it a good job.

To work properly, a duck trap should be made out of 2 inch fur farm wire. Hardware cloth is stiff enough but is too solid. The ducks see it and avoid getting in the trap. Chicken wire will catch ducks but is too light and flexible. Some poachers make their duck traps on wood frames, as shown at left. It is then possible to use lighter, easily found chicken wire, but the wood-and-wire traps are very obvious. They also don't last in the water, and won't sink as easily. See page 224 for more details on this trap.

Doves

Many times doves nest in cities. Some people like to eat them, but I always felt they were too small to warrant the trouble it takes to collect them, unless it was an emergency situation.

Doves are best taken with a light at night out of the trees in which they roost. Pin them down with the light and shoot them with BB caps, or grab them.

They also can be trapped and snared, or taken with bird lime.

Ducks

I have been in on two of the wildest duck hunts in my life right in town. The ducks were staying on city ponds in large numbers and had become so tame they came up and begged for bread.

We walked into the park shortly before light early in the morning and bagged a number with .22 BB caps. It was a vile, blowy, rainy day with nary a soul in sight. After fifteen or twenty minutes all of the ducks were either scared off or floating in the pond, so my friend folded up his .22 rifle and headed out.

I waded out and picked up the ducks, putting them in a bag I carried inside my rain coat. Both times the bag got so heavy I couldn't carry it, so I threw it over my shoulder and simply walked home.

Cars whizzed by, dogs smelled me, but no one paid anything but fleeting attention to the wet, dirty, derelict walking down the sidewalk.

Other than shooting, it might be possible to set a chicken wire trap for ducks, or even better a hook and line.

Set the trap on sturdy stakes in water not over 2 feet deep. The bottom edge of the trap should extend down under water about 8 inches and the top of the trap should be at least 16 inches above the water. Put it in a clear area with at least 4 feet of open water all around the trap.

If the set is to be checked by boat, it is better to wire a door in the top. A poacher wading to the trap may not mind reaching under the trap and pulling the ducks out, but from a boat, this can be a chore.

Bait the surrounding area liberally. I use a bushel (60 pounds) of shell corn per set. Initially the ducks come in for the corn. As they dive down to scoop it off the bottom, some will come up in the trap. As soon as one is caught, it will squawk and holler, calling in the whole flock till the trap is full.

I make my traps 4 feet on a side and 2 feet deep. The wire should be fastened together with small hog rings. Wire the pen to the stakes after they are securely set. In some marshes I drive the stakes three feet into the mud, necessitating poles 5 to 6 feet long. A load of ducks in a pen can easily dislodge poorly anchored stakes.

Catching ducks in a pen is no problem if there are ducks around. Not getting caught at it may be something else again.

Punt Guns

No book on poaching would be complete without mentioning punt guns, although most punt guns are now impossibly obsolete.

Late in the last century, poachers used to mount large bore shot guns on scull boats and use them to flock-shoot large numbers of ducks. The guns were too big and cumbersome to use on upland game (except for passenger pigeons), but could be moved about on boats.

Sizes varied, but ranged from 8 gauge shoulder-held shotguns throwing three ounces of shot, to 1 gauge cannons loaded with a full pound of shot, nails and other miscellaneous junk propelled by a quarter pound of powder.

It is possible for the average poacher to build or have built a muzzle loading punt gun, but it's not practical. The cost would be prohibitive, both to build and to shoot. A gun of this nature would be impossible to keep hidden, and everything—even the earthworms—within a mile would know every time it was fired.

As a compromise it might still be possible to find an 8 gauge magnum shotgun for sale someplace. Navy Arms imported them from Italy about fifteen years ago. They weighed 16 pounds, had 36 inch barrels and threw 3½ ounces of shot per barrel. The shells were handloaded on Remington Plastic 8 gauge hulls used in industrial Ram-Set tools.

Perhaps it would be possible to sneak one of these into a remote duck blind. Just don't shoot more than you need.

Food Color

Here is another crazy idea that can work if one can keep from laughing long enough to try it out.

Mix about four packages of bright blue food coloring in five gallons of warm water and spill the dye out on the ice in front of a good duck blind. Put the decoys out in the blue, propped up with snow. During certain times of the year when the ducks are crossing lakes looking for water, they will be attracted to what seems like a small patch of open water.

For some real fun, allow the ducks to actually land. Most of them won't, flaring at the last second, but it sure is funny to see them come in.

The dye works best on an inch or two layer of snow over the solid ice.

21

FROGS, TURTLES, CRAYFISH & SNAKES

I always felt that frogs, turtles, crawfish and snakes were valuable but, except for frog legs, not valuable enough to spend a lot of time trying to collect. The methods that follow are in many cases ancient techniques that allow one to gather up these critters with a minimum of effort. They make collecting them a lot more interesting and personally profitable.

In some cases the methods are common knowledge. Others are well known but only in isolated localities. There are many other techniques in addition to those listed, but this chapter is a good start at passing on some ancient traditions.

Bullfrogs

The worst way to collect the big frogs is during the day with a .22 rifle. Yet I have at times seen dozens of people out trying to shoot them with their .22's. If the truth were known, most are probably using the big croakers for targets without really caring if they get to eat the legs or not.

In my estimation this is an unconscionable waste of a valuable resource as well as a wanton frittering away of poaching opportunities that are among the finest in our country.

The *best* way to collect frogs is to wade out in the ponds and sloughs at night with a powerful flashlight and a good spear. In new territory, it is best to start out on a warm early summer evening, then drive around and listen for their deep throated "harrumpf." The best place to stop is near the small one and two acre farm ponds, but the big frogs can be found in small creeks, in sloughs and bayous and even in larger lakes and reservoirs. I have encountered them as far north as Milwaukee and Spokane, and all the way south to the Gulf. All bullfrogs are large compared to the lesser tiger frogs, but the real monsters live down south. I have taken frogs up to nineteen inches in length in Tennessee, Kentucky and Texas.

By referring to an area map, the various frog ponds can be identified and a coordinated hunt planned. Set up a drop off spot, a pickup point, an alternate pickup point, and a walk out contingency plan. The drop is made at least two hours after dark.

Wear a pair of gym shoes or Viet Nam jungle boots, dark loose cotton pants and a long sleeved cotton shirt. We usually travel in a team of three. Each carries a spear and a light, plus a good hole-free gunny sack to put the frogs in.

At each pond we quickly check to make sure there are no other people present.

A few summers back, we crept into a pond after dark and came upon a car parked at one end. Three of us waited for twenty minutes or so and then decided to surprise the occupants. It seemed likely that they weren't going to leave, and we had a lot more ponds to tend to without worrying unduly about this one. In retrospect it was probably dumb to risk giving away our presence, but we were in one of those moods and didn't intend to hit that pond again till next year anyway.

I crept up silently and swiftly to the car and threw my flashlight rheostat on full power. My intention was to surprise and embarrass the inhabitants, and then fade into the bush and be gone.

As it worked out, I faded into the bush o.k., but they were not the ones who were surprised and embarrassed. As far as I know, the couple never missed a stroke and probably never knew I was there. The whole thing was a dumb maneuver, as I keep telling myself over and over.

In a tightly controlled situation it is wise to keep one man up on the pond bank while the other two wade around the edge. Frogs don't generally sit in water deeper than three feet, and many stay right on the bank, so it isn't necessary to get out in the middle of most ponds. Keep about six feet apart, one man searching the bank while the other checks the pond shallows.

When a frog is spotted, blind it with the light. Then using the correct spear technique, collect it.

A variation of this method substitutes a rifle or pistol with either BB caps or a silencer for the spear. Frogs must be shot between the eyes at the base of the skull, or the round will have no effect.

Blind them with the light. Shoot, and then run over and pick them up before they revive.

I seldom try shooting frogs since so many are usually lost. In forty years I have seen perhaps two or three people who could consistently shoot accurately enough to collect frogs without wasting the resource.

A bow and arrow can be used on frogs, but in my estimation this is another dumb technique. The bow is clumsy and inaccurate, the arrows expensive and it takes forever to scare away all the frogs in a pond.

Frogs can occasionally be taken in a chicken wire fish trap but this is more by accident that design. See the chapter on fish for more information about these traps.

One method that works for frogs very well during the day is virtually unknown in many parts of the country. It is the only way I know of hitting a pond during daylight, if that is the most expeditious time to be there.

You'll need a long pole. At times I carry one in, but generally I cut an eight foot willow branch on the way or at the target pond. Tie an 8 foot piece of 12 pound monofilament line to one end of the pole. Tie a number 8 treble hook on the other end of the line. Put a small piece of bright red nylon cloth or a wind or two of red yarn on the hook.

Stay back about 6 feet from the water's edge and dance the hook with red material 6 to 8 inches above the water. Work it through the grass, around the cattails and over the lily pads. Be sure to be silent and cautious walking around the pond.

The red bug will attract the frogs which will jump after the bait. Most of the time the frog will miss on the first pass. They miss the bait so often I wonder how they ever catch enough bugs to live. In any event, the jump will signal the poacher to stop and work that particular area more thoroughly.

Keep jiggling the fly over the frog till it eventually takes the bait and is hooked.

That's all there is to it. A very silent, cheap and effective method. Some times it is more recreational than fishing in the same pond.

Turtles

There are two reasons to collect turtles—to eat them or to control their population in a duck and muskrat marsh.

On a covert control project, use a quiet rifle to shoot the basking mud turtles off the logs. The rounds won't kill them instantly but the turtles will eventually die.

Also put out some barrel traps and set lines as described later in the chapter. The traps and lines will take the leathernecks and snappers plus any mud turtles that remain. Other kinds of turtles are seldom numerous enough to be a problem.

Turtles can be attracted into a concentrated area by putting chicken guts, an old dead cat or some other offal in a burlap bag along with some stones and throwing it into a deep water hole. The critters will come from hundreds of yards away to the bag, and are more easily caught as a result of their concentrated number.

The best turtle trap design I know of is a hinged board affair mounted on a large barrel. To build and set this barrel trap for turtles, sink a water tight barrel in a pond or open water area up to within 3 inches of the barrel top. Be sure there are turtles living in the vicinity of the intended set. These traps are a lot of work to build.

Use rocks, iron, or similar scrap to weight the barrel. Add water, but keep the water level inside of the barrel at least 2 feet below the outside level of the pond or swamp. It is possible to sink the barrels in the mud, but generally the water will have to be at least 2 or 3 feet deep around the trap.

The only readily available barrels that work are the big clumsy 55 gallon type, so expect some trouble getting it set up. Old wooden barrels used by farmers for buttermilk are best, but are awfully hard to find any more. Most poachers will end up using steel barrels from oil or herbicide.

I weld two hinges on the barrels and mount a light 1 x 6 inch board 4 feet long on back. The boards should be positioned so they will tip into the barrel with the slightest weight transfer. At times it is necessary to use window weights or lead puddles with holes drilled in them for counter weights.

Staple a piece of liver or other smelly meat on the end of the board over the open barrel.

Turtles, especially the small-to-medium sized snappers, will climb out of the water on to the board and work their way up till they tip into the barrel. As an added attraction, put bait around the rim of the barrel. This will bring even more turtles, and they will eventually climb on to the boards also.

In one day, I have caught as many as three snappers and dozens of mud turtles in just one barrel trap. The barrel idea also is effective for sly old leatherbacks that can't be taken any other way.

Barrel traps are also effective for muskrats. By using lots of rotten meat they can be scared off during the summer. In winter, use carrots or corn in the same set in the same location. It will catch rats when they come to the bait.

The barrel can be filled with water to hide or decommission it. Other than the fact that steel barrels rust out, the trap is good for a number of years without much maintenance.

Turtles caught by this or any other method can be stored alive in a marsh or a creek pool for months at a time. Do this by drilling a hole in the edge of their shell and tying them to a root with a piece of heavy wire or dog chain. They seem to get enough to eat, stay in good healthy condition and are instantly available.

Bank Feeling

Snapping turtles can be caught by a method known as grabbing or bank feeling. It is a damnable procedure that I am sure would lead to the early demise of any poacher who used it extensively. I have tried feeling for turtles and twice was bitten by water snakes. Next time I figure the snake will be a moccasin, so I make sure there is no next time.

Feeling consists of wading along the edge of creeks and small rivers, and reaching up under the banks for the raspy hard shell of a turtle. When one is discovered—it is an effective method and many snapping turtles are usually located—the trick is to find the tail or a rear leg and pull the turtle out. I have never been chomped by a snapper while bank feeling, but it definitely is another of the occupational hazards.

Generally the turtles are under the grassy, muddy banks in two to four feet of water. I have found them under trees and in roots, but not as many as in the mud where they can more easily dig into old muskrat dens, bank cuts and other places. The snappers are generally found facing into the hole, leaving their tail end out and making it easier to grab them.

All of the old crony friends I had who caught turtles this way are dead. Some lived to a ripe old age, but I am sure it was inspite of grabbing turtles and not as a result of it. Some of my fondest memories as a kid are of these old geezers working their way along stream banks on their hands and knees. They reached up under the bank, arms length at times, and every now and then out plopped a snapper, madder than hell.

Set Lines

Most people who have caught turtles have done it with set lines. For those who don't know, a set line for turtles consists of a 4/0 or 3/0 hook, securely fastened to a one foot piece of brass or copper wire leader. The wire must be soft and malleable, between 14 and 16 gauge. The wire leader keeps the turtle from chewing through the line and escaping once it is hooked.

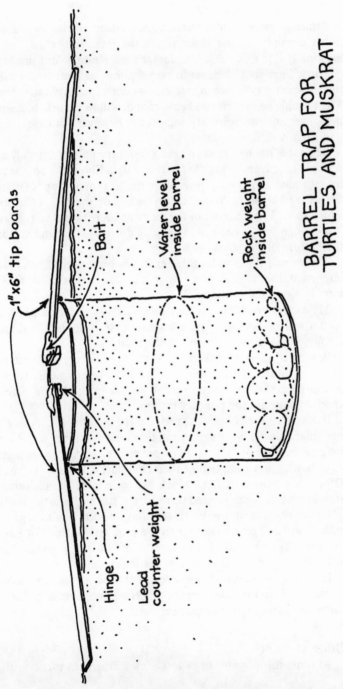

1"x6" tip boards

Bait

Hinge

Lead counter weight

Water level inside barrel

Rock weight inside barrel

BARREL TRAP FOR
TURTLES AND MUSKRAT

231

Attach a piece of 60 pound monofilament to the wire. How much depends on the place where the line will be set, but I personally don't like anything larger than a 6 to 8 foot line.

Turtle lines should be set in turgid ponds or pools. As a rule, turtles won't stay in moving water, especially the big old snappers. Most people tie the line to a heavy root or willow branch, bait with pork liver and throw in. My suggestion, however, is to use one of two slightly different plans.

Begin the first by finding an old 8 foot cane pole or a freshly cut willow branch, and tying the turtle line to it. Shove the pole as far into the mud and grass as possible in the bottom of the pool where the set is to be made. Wind the excess line on the end of the pole which should stick up out of the water no more than 4 feet. Leave just enough line so the bait is hanging down about 8 inches from the bottom of the pond.

Turtles will find the food faster if it is suspended. Even more important, the crayfish won't work it as quickly and easily as if it were lying on the bottom.

My experience indicates that significantly greater numbers of turtles will be hooked from a pole set than if the bait is simply thrown into the pond to sink in the mud.

When a turtle gets hooked, it will swim around the pole, but will pull very little. There is nothing for it to lever against to put pressure on the set, so the turtles just hang there in a placid, subdued state till the poacher returns.

If a hard or rocky bottom precludes the use of poles, try one or two quart plastic bottles. Any tough plastic container will do, as long as they are neither white or red colored. Green, brown and clear bottles, once emptied of their contents, will work very well. Other than obvious colors which are forbidden, the containers should have air tight lids and some sort of handle to tie the line to.

Fasten the line on the bottle and loop it so the bait is again 8 inches off the bottom, similar to the pole sets. Instead of being anchored as with the poles, the bottles are floated in ponds, deep holes and marshy bogs wherever turtles abound.

It is really interesting to discover all of the odd places a hooked turtle will take the floats trying to get away. Especially if it's a forty-five pound monster snapper.

Other Methods

At times it is possible to collect a few leatherneck turtles with a bow and fish arrows. Usually this happens while hunting carp. Otherwise, unless the turtles are very plentiful, it doesn't pay to use a bow.

Turtles can also be taken in steel traps. Wire the trap base plate to a floating log and bait with meat that will rot quickly. This is a poor method and the poacher will often end up with thrown traps and no game. I have never seen a place where it wasn't easier to collect turtles with other methods.

Crayfish

These little crustaceans are an ideal substitute for shrimp. They are a bit smaller and harder to clean, but if handled quickly in a sanitary manner are otherwise indistinguishable from shrimp. Where they are abundant, there are two ways to get them.

For those who want to actually stand in one place and participate in the catching process, a dip seine is ideal. I have often used one to take five gallons of crawdads per hour.

The disadvantage of the dip seine is the expense and the difficulty of transporting it without everybody and their brother asking what it is. On the other hand, most people don't care if somebody catches crayfish on their property, so it may be possible to drive right up to the target area and offload the net.

Build a dip seine as follows: Lay a 6 foot square piece of ½ inch hardware cloth or chicken wire on the ground. The wire should be the lightest gauge possible but cannot be larger than half inch mesh. Several smaller pieces can be fastened together with hog rings if need be.

Thread or sew 6 foot strands of #12 or 14 wire along each of the four edges of the wire and tie these together at the corners.

From each corner bring up a 6 foot piece of wire and tie the four together at the top, leaving a 2 inch loop.

Use a strong light pole that is as long as can be easily acquired and carried. At one time, I had a 2 inch bamboo pole from the center of a roll of carpeting 12 feet long that was ideal. Attach the pole to the four wires for use as a boom to raise and lower the net. Bait is placed in a wire pocket in the center of the seine. I like a lot of bait. Something on the order of 5 pounds of chicken guts or a large clump of hog liver works fine.

Lower the net into a quiet open pool in a creek, river, slough or marsh. Wait about five minutes and pull it up. If there are crayfish around, they will already be working the bait. Keep raising and lowering every few minutes. When the catch diminishes, it is time to move on.

The catch can be kept in a plastic bucket. If the net won't sink fast enough, use some rocks.

The other method involves building four or five small wire traps similar to miniature fish traps. They should be made from 1/2 inch mesh or less, about 16 inches long, 7 inches in diameter with double cones having a 1½ inch opening.

I put a big solid bait in these and set them one per hole along a creek or river. After about four days I check them, using a long handled rake to retrieve the trap. This is a very effective way to maintain a source of *Shrimp Louis*.

Snakes

The most profitable snake catching expedition I was ever involved with occurred the time we dumped a 55 gallon barrel of gasoline through the rocks of a small talus slope onto a den of rattlesnakes.

They were pouring out of the rocks like water even before we lit the gas. After the low grade "harrumpf" explosion, we almost couldn't catch them fast enough. At that time, rattlesnake skins were one dollar each. Four of us got almost 100 snakes in a couple of hours.

The simplest way to catch most snakes is with a copper wire snare tied to a pole.

Use the pole end to rile and hold the snake. As soon as it coils or stops, throw the snare over the head and jerk.

Along creeks, water moccasins and other aquatic snakes can be taken with a small red cloth or cotton line similar to those used for frogs. Dance the line 2 or 3 inches in front of the basking or sunning snake, and often they will take it. The bad part comes getting the damn things off the hook.

Another method of collecting snakes is to spear them. Often when frog spearing we scare up water snakes. Down south it used to be a real hazard trying to stay clear of the moccasins.

One night three of us were working a pond about 100 yards from a farmer's house. I was up on the bank and my two companions were wading the shore. One was out about 6 feet in the shallows and the other out almost waist deep, perhaps twenty feet from shore.

Suddenly the outside man stepped off into a deep hole. He kept his balance but the water was almost up to his chest. The problem was compounded by the fact that he insisted on wearing chest waders that had now filled with water.

PALAC

ENTERPRISES,

PUBLISHERS OF PALADIN PRE
POST OFFICE BOX 1307, BOULDER

S
O
L
D

T
O

HESS DEAN
3879 MODESTO ST
CASTRO VALLEY, CA 94546

YOUR ORDER NUMBER			ACCOUNT NUMBER 94546HESSD.1
	QUANTITY		
ORDERED	SHIPPED	BACK ORDERED	
1	1		(3E) SURVIVAL P
			POSTAGE AN
			TOTAL INVO
			AMOUNT PAI
			INVOICE PA
			Thank you for or

TERMS: 30 DA

A FINANCE CHARGE OF 2% PER MONTH (24% ANNUA

& SYCAMORE ISLAND BOOKS
LORADO 80306 303-443-7250

> HESS DEAN
> 3879 MODESTO ST
> CASTRO VALLEY, CA 94546

VIA MESTIC-4TH CLASS	PREPAID AMOUNT 17.95	
PTION	PRICE	AMOUNT
ING	14.95	14.95
NDLING		3.00
AMOUNT		17.95
		17.95CR
		0.00

ng PALADIN books

PLEASE PAY LAST
AMOUNT SHOWN

L BE CHARGED ON PAST DUE ACCOUNTS.

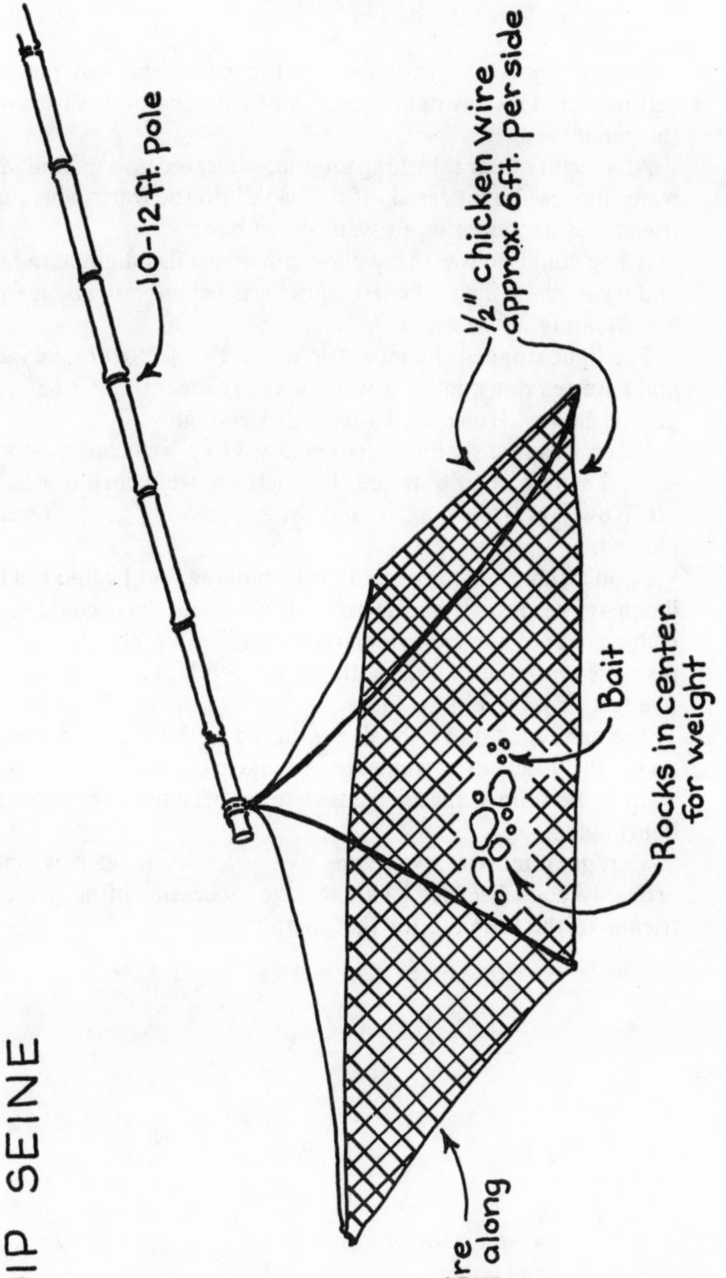

DIP SEINE

10-12 ft. pole

½" chicken wire approx. 6ft. per side

Bait

Rocks in center for weight

#9 wire laced along edge

235

Usually we wear gym shoes, cotton pants and just plan on getting wet. This guy didn't want to be cold and now was paying the penalty.

As a result of our thrashing around, we scared up a granddaddy water moccasin that raced off the bank into the water where our friend was anchored in his water-filled boots.

All he could do was throw the beam on his flashlight onto high and try to shine the snake. His spear was behind him about eight feet, floating in the water.

The light stopped the moccasin about five feet from the man, and I started down into the water with my spear to get it before it got my buddy. However, I wasn't fast enough.

When I was out in the water about ten feet, we heard car doors slam. Then an engine started. Instinctively we turned our lights off. Now it was dark again and the snake could go wherever it pleased.

I don't know what my buddy was thinking, but I could feel the damn snake, hear it and at times I even believed I could see it coming over to nab me. I stood there steady as a rock, which didn't take one-tenth the courage it did for my buddy. The moccasin was five feet or less from his face.

The car rolled down the drive, turned at the gate and was on down the road after what seemed like at least nine hours of waiting. As soon as the tail lights were out of sight we threw on our lights again.

That giant moccasin was gone. We never saw it again, which is probably good because I hate to take moccasins off a spear, or friends to the hospital, for that matter.

22

URBAN SURVIVAL

For the poor poacher stuck in the city, there is still a lot of free game available. This chapter will get him thinking about the various possibilities.

On two different occasions in my life I have had to live in large cities. Both times I was so dirt poor it was awful. But both times we made it without government help. What government assistance I did get was of the negative kind. The authorities didn't approve of what I was doing and did everything in their power to stop me. Our family got the strong impression that anybody who thought they could be self-reliant was a bad actor to be dealt with severely. The word was dependence but we didn't want to be somebody else's ward, and we weren't.

I have a strong and lasting conviction that there is an incredible amount of wild products going to waste in the average city. The suburbs and the various city neighborhoods have a lot of grass, trees, parkways, hedges, parks, ponds and similar game habitat. The potential harvest from these can be quite impressive.

I have never lived right downtown in the inner city and doubt if it would be possible to exist by poaching in that type of environment. But cities are not all core area. Most people don't live on just pavement and brick. The following are some suggestions that worked for me. The wise and prudent person might keep them in mind.

Squirrels

By far and away the best source of good meat in the cities are tree squirrels. From east coast to west coast I have only been in a few cities that didn't have sizeable populations of these animals. As an added advantage, squirrels can often be lured to the poacher rather than the other way around.

237

City squirrels are probably best taken in a box trap. They are out of sight, out of mind and easy to handle in a box trap. No one suspects the little boxes sitting around one's yard in the bushes. Under some circumstances, box traps can be set in parks.

If the yard is surrounded by brush or there is a window to shoot out of, try BB caps or other quiet rifles.

Steel traps will also work. They can be set up in a tree, along a roof line or other place that is out of sight.

Robins And Blackbirds

The British eat both, so some years ago we got a recipe for Robin Pie and tried it. Not bad, but not all that good either.

On the other hand there are a lot of these birds in many cities. They are easily taken with various methods so in an emergency situation it may be worth a try.

The best, in my estimation, is to use a bird snare. Bait with a few kernels of wheat, some flour or even cherry pits. Anything of that nature will work.

Another good method is to build a bird trap is described in Chapter 20. These are handy in the wide range of situations, and it certainly won't hurt to have one sitting around taking a few birds now and then.

Shooting robins is too destructive and slow. Better to make up a batch of bird lime and get them that way.

Pheasants And Quail

The Chicago suburb we lived in had a fair population of pheasants and quail. Over the years these creatures had become incredibly elusive. I first realized they were around when I saw their tracks in the snow.

The best plan, if these game birds are around, is to use a game bird trap or some snares. The best trap is probably a net trap or closure trap. Steel traps tear them up too much. A standard bird snare also works very well.

During the winter it is often possible to shoot pheasants and quail from a window or porch as they scratch around for food. At that time it may also be profitable to bait them in for harvest.

House Cats

Just to set the record straight before I go on, it is important to note that I never have eaten house cats. Some day, maybe, but up to now thank God I haven't had to.

All cities have a tremendous population of cats. There are two very good reasons for collecting as many as possible.

Although the price may fluctuate, the skins are almost always worth between $2.00 and $4.00. I stretch them on coonskin stretchers and sell along with the other hides.

A second reason for doing in cats is to give the natural game some relief. House cats are incredible predators that will kill a huge quantity of game in the course of a year.

The easiest method of taking cats is to use snares. They readily poke their heads in them and won't struggle when caught. Use sardines for bait, or set the snares in established runs.

Steel traps are effective but if a little old lady sees a cat in a jaw trap there is no end to the flak that can result.

Box traps are ineffective. I have never been able to get a cat to push into one.

Shooting is ineffective unless the poacher uses plenty of firepower. When I was 11, my grandpa asked me to thin out the cat population down at his farm. I took my single shot .22 and plunked one right in the head from about ten feet. Instead of running over and grabbing the cat I reloaded my rifle. The old cat came to life and ran way under the back porch next to the kitchen.

It was summer in the midwest. By the next day the 95° heat played such havoc with that dead cat that my grandpa was ready to tear the porch up—using my rifle for a pry bar. Finally it got so bad grandma moved the kitchen out front.

The smell lingered for at least two weeks and I have never unlearned my lesson about using enough gun on house cats.

Pigeons

Every city has a large number of pigeons. I have eaten hundreds of them and they all tasted fine. It's just the idea, I guess, because I won't eat any more unless things get pretty desperate.

Pigeons in cities are everywhere. For a time I disposed of pigeons for the police department in three medium sized cities. During that time I killed pigeons out of old barns, from the eaves of houses, under bridges, out of old cars, out of the attic of a school and a hundred other weird places.

Pigeons in a city are best taken in a bird trap. Bait with cracked corn and leave several in the trap at all times to call the others.

Bird snares also work well, but at three or four per trap per week the pigeons can usually breed faster than the poacher can catch them.

Bird lime works, as does shooting them.

A very good method is to blind pigeons on their roosts with a

239

powerful flashlight. Then either shoot the critters or grab them live. Most people want to get rid of the damn things, so it generally isn't hard to find a place to shine and shoot them.

Muskrats

I am constantly amazed at the number of muskrats that live in the ponds and rivers that flow through our cities. Other than one killed by a cat or dog every now and then, I don't think they have any enemies. Don't forget muskrats are vegetarians, and are not related to rats. They are very good to eat.

Keep watch in the sheltered city parks and you will probably be as surprised as I was at their numbers.

Most rats in parks have bank dens. Use a box trap or two and work on through the area till the harvest is made. People who would recoil in horror over a steel trap never give the square boxes a second thought.

Bees

People in cities are continually having problems with bees. They take up residence in the walls of their houses, in old trees, in attics, and harass passers by.

If the swarm has been there for a while, I usually agree to take it out if they will let me neatly cut into the side of the building or do what ever to get the honey and the wax.

Most of the time in cities the colony can't be saved so I use a CO_2 fire extinguisher and freeze the bees. It is the safest, easiest, non-destructive method of dispatching bees that I know of.

Possums And Coons

These are some fur-bearers that are far more abundant in many cities than anybody except the police (who get nuisance calls about them) would ever believe. They are also hard to trap since they get plenty to eat and won't come to bait well. City coons and possums are used to living around people. Even dumb old possums wise up to a certain extent, making it difficult to collect them.

If there is both an old large stand of trees and some creeks near town I can guarantee that at least raccoons live nearby. With only one or the other there is still an excellent chance that coons will be there.

About the only set that works for coons and possums is a steel trap and bait. Place the trap so it is obscured and plan to leave it for long periods without getting anything. Best bait? Probably peanut butter.

Rabbits

I probably don't have to remind readers that there are a lot of wild rabbits in most towns and cities throughout the U.S. Conditions are generally fairly good for them. There is food and cover and, other than dogs and cats, few enemies.

Best methods for rabbits are either snares or box traps. One is about the same as the other so the decision then becomes one of expedience.

Some poachers learn to set snares and become very good with them. Others like box traps. At times it is better to set a box trap than a snare or vice versa, but usually good sets can be found for either.

Shooting rabbits with a quiet .22 works in town if there is enough cover.

Mushrooms

Since this is not a text on mushrooms, I won't labor the point. But good outdoorsmen know their mushrooms and take advantage of any opportunity to collect them.

Puffballs, cauliflower mushrooms and morels grow in cities. Keep a lookout for them.

23

THE POACHER'S FAMILY

Living off the land is a cooperative venture with each member of the family expected to do his part. People who rely on poaching, either in part or wholly, for their existence, must adapt to a slightly different set of family living conditions. Two illustrations come to mind.

Folks who visit our home the first time are often puzzled and surprised to see two large 22 cubic foot freezers in our basement. No family, they reason, could possible use that much frozen storage space. That being true in our visitors' eyes, the next logical question follows quite naturally. "What," they ask, "are you folks doing with so many freezers?"

A second example involves the kids at school. Poachers' kids are no different from all the other kids their age. They enjoy telling about what happened at home and become jealous when other children tell about their daddy and brothers "getting a big elk last weekend."

Kids who are coached won't turn into blabbermouths. At times we were selective about what we told them or how much they saw when they were very young. Our family was involved. They were never a problem and often part of the solution.

After more than forty years in the business, some predictable patterns have emerged. These are all potential problem areas that the good poacher will have to adequately handle or eventually he will be forced out of the business.

Talking In School

As previously mentioned, this can be a problem, especially when no plans are made to handle the situation.

When kids are very young, most of the tales they bring to school will be dismissed as fantasies. Young children who are exposed to hunting and fishing and the catch that results from these activities will become so accustomed to this way of life that they believe everyone lives that way. Early continued exposure to outdoor activities instills a sense of the ordinary to these activities that goes a long way toward controlling a loose tongue.

By fourth grade things start to change. Everyone wants to impress everyone else and the tales will fly. At this point three things will work.

First, don't tell everything you know. If the limit is four salmon but there are six, don't broadcast the fact. Not every deer need be counted, or even the origin of the ducks in the freezer. That early sense of the mundane will have a spillover effect at this age as well. Kids who have seen bass since they can remember won't start asking how many or even how, although they may start wanting to come along and help.

Second, this is the time to start coaching the kids in earnest. Mom should impress on them the importance of not telling other people about family business. They should know about keeping personal things to themselves and not talking to outsiders. "I don't know" should be a standard answer to questions about what is happening at home.

Third, involve the kids. Start taking them out to look at fish traps, perhaps on easy deer drives or whatever. Impress them with the importance of keeping quiet about what they see, and the truism that they, indeed, are different from the anti-hunting crowd.

In high school the problems become very severe. American high schools inspire an invisible informal communications net that can be very harmful to the poacher. Involve the kids in family activities, continue to preach the privacy of family activity and be on top of any gossip that one may pick up either from the kids in high school or on the street.

Where Is Dad?

It was a beautiful August day. The sun shone down from a bright blue sky but the temperature was not oppressive. Out in the woods the maple seeds were maturing to the point that the squirrels were beginning to work them.

I figured it was a lousy day to work, so I called a neighbor who had been bugging me about doing some squirrel hunting.

His teenage son answered the phone. "Hello," I said, "is your dad there?"

"Nope," answered the lad, "dad went back to the Jessup woods with Charley Betts squirrel hunting."

It was a month before the season opened, and the kid had no idea who I was since I never gave my name. Needless to say, I was completely floored.

"How," I asked, regaining my composure, "does your dad usually do?"

"O.k.," the kid responded. "Last week he got seven or eight. Usually he brings home more like five, though."

So there it was, a complete stranger had all the information. A landowner or warden could call just as I did and get the complete program from the kids.

It may interest the reader to note that I never went hunting with that fellow. Through the years I did my best to convince him that I really had little time to hunt.

When someone calls our place, and I am not here, whoever answers always asks for a number. The response is not "he isn't here," but "give me your number and I'll have him call." If the caller is persistent, my wife or girl would always say, "Ragnar asked me to take the number. I don't know if he is here or not, but give me your number and he will call."

We did the same for the boys later on. If one of our group called, they would always know not to talk on the phone and not to expect an answer. They handled their calls the same way.

People who came to the door were handled the same way. It was always, "give us your name so Mr. Benson can get ahold of you later."

Signals

A problem related to telephone calls and occasional visitors comes up when friends drop by for a visit. Several times our pickup person has almost been embarrassed. As a result we have developed a code.

At night a light on in the porch means "don't come in." During the day, a wastepaper basket in front of the garage means the same thing.

We always have an alternate spot to meet. It isn't often that the alternate is used, but occasionally it has kept our tail out of the fire.

Visitors

If one isn't careful, visitors can get to be a problem. We are gregarious people who like to have folks over but it obviously can become a problem.

For starters, don't have a dozen of each kind of trophy strung around the house. It is tempting to recommend that no obvious display be made of game, but most hunters have big egos and want to put something up. Just keep it to one of a kind, with a set of horns or hides here and there. Be subtle.

We eat game at every meal. When visitors eat with us they have moose, deer or elk. It is our custom to always explain how special this is that we have deer or whatever for our friends. That way it doesn't look like we always eat game. Depending on the recipe, it may not be necessary to say anything at all—many times folks can't tell properly cared for deer or elk from beef.

Helping With The Harvest

My daughter used to say that she was the only girl in the state who knew how to skin a deer. Perhaps this is true, perhaps not. It does illustrate the necessity of involving the whole family in living off the land.

Three of us can put up a deer in forty-five minutes. That's from rail to bound packages in the freezer. All five of us can do two deer in one hour.

Living off the land requires total family participation. It is important that everyone have a job and that they get busy and do it when time is of the essence.

By the same token, all are involved in some phase of the actual harvest. Often the girls drive deer with me. They do a good job and have become aware of the need for knowing the territory and careful planning.

The Family Freezer

The fact that a freezer full of wild meat can be embarrassing has already been mentioned. Here are several tips to keep from being embarrassed.

Bone all the meat on big game. This saves room in the freezer and makes identification more difficult.

Wrap all the meat in the same kind of paper, using the same tape year after year.

Never date packages. A color code that changes every year is much better.

Don't ever allow the hearts or livers to accumulate. These are dead giveaways. Eat them.

Have every member of the family buy a tag every year. Keep all the tags in a bundle someplace. There should be enough going back enough years to support the contention that the season limit was never exceeded. "The problem is," says us, "that we haven't been eating the stuff fast enough. Amazing how it will accumulate. . . ."

Get rid of excess bones immediately and wisely. Wash away any blood.

Get the bloody clothes in the washer and clean up any soiled knives immediately upon completing a project.

Selling Game

I must sternly warn you that serious problems can result from selling game.

My recommendation is that whole game never be sold. The only exception occurs when it might be advisable to trade or give a few pieces of something to a friend *on a one-time only basis.*

Almost all poachers who are apprehended run aground because they either sold game or jacklighted deer.

There is good money to be made selling parts of animals. Just be dead certain to always sell **parts.** Sell them a few at a time to diverse different people, and always have a valid explanation as to where the stuff came from.

24
SELLING OUTDOOR PRODUCTS

It is indeed true that various parts of wild game are selling for astronomical figures. My first real off-the-farm income came when I was about nine selling muskrat hides, but I am not primarily referring to that kind of market. What I am referring to is the sale of odds and ends like teeth and hooves that we used to leave in the woods.

As a practical matter, I am very, very cautious about trafficking in whole wild game. More people have gotten in trouble because they sold a few rabbits or some ducks or a deer than I care to remember. Our rule is that we eat or otherwise use what we collect, without ever selling or giving any of it away.

At times we have made an exception and given a friend a few trout or a pheasant, but it is usually with the explanation that we don't like to eat whatever we are giving them. "It is fun," we say, "to hunt or fish, but we don't like to eat the stuff. This is all we got this fall and you're welcome to it."

Usually that line stops the people trying to secure game from us dead in their tracks. We never accept money but will occasionally trade for something. I have traded a landing net and another time a tank of gas for ten lousy trout, but that's about the extent of it.

Shooting a deer for someone is absolutely *verboten*. In the last forty years, literally scores of people have asked me to shoot "a really big buck" or "a nice eating doe" for them. Some have pleaded poverty and some have offered to significantly reduce my poverty, but I have turned them all down.

I am similarly careful about taking people along hunting with us. Again, lots of people ask, but I usually tell them I won't have much time to hunt this year. Sometimes we do take a visitor or two during the regular season. If so, we play it strictly straight arrow and never even violate a trespassing law. Obviously this cramps our style, so few outsiders ever get to come along.

How to become an insider in our group? Either marry into the family or be a family friend with an interest in the outdoors. Unfortunately there are no additional opportunities to marry into the family, and the friendship route takes at least ten years. I suggest similar vigilance for other poaching teams.

If the reader thinks this is a stringent program, I suggest he pick up a recent copy of *Sports Afield* or *Outdoor Life.* Almost every issue has a feature story about the undercover agent who spent three years breaking into a ring of duck poachers or deer sellers. Fish and Game departments are becoming increasingly more willing to invest that kind of time and effort into making test cases.

My advice is to be cautious, be careful, and don't do anything stupid—like trust friends to keep their mouths shut.

Tips On Selling

Selling game parts should be done with discretion. If one uses good common sense there won't be problems. Don't, for instance, go to the local taxidermist with four beautiful deer capes and try to peddle them. Stop by first and ask if he needs *one.* Don't tell him you have one. Just ask if he could use one and at what price.

Don't even try to sell all the parts of all the animals to one person. Usually that isn't possible, but nevertheless don't run over to a mountain man council with two sets of elk horns, eight elk feet, eight elk ivories and two scrotum bags and not expect someone to put two and two together.

Always have a legal explanation as to where the product came from. A few years back a friend was nailed at a fur auction with an otter skin. He hadn't thought through the process of how he could have legally acquired the skin, and it got embarrassing. As it worked out, he lost the skin but no personal hair.

One last philosophical word before getting down to basics.

I realize full well that it would be immensely helpful to give specific names and addresses of people who are anxious to purchase the items listed. Hopefully the reader will agree that to do so in many cases would be the kiss of death for the people listed. The reader will have to root around himself for discreet buyers, using the general suggestions offered.

Bears

Any kind of a scruffy old bear is worth at least $300.00 these days. Certainly a far cry from our experience twenty years ago when we often shot or trapped sheep-killing bears and left them lay. At the time they weren't even worth carrying home.

Bear claws make excellent jewelry. In the rough, cut back at the first joint and dried, they bring about $2.00 each. There are twenty on a bear, so we are up to $40.00 for starters.

The poacher can get a dollar more each by soaking the claws and pulling out the inside cartilage. Fill the hole with dark colored DuPont silicone bathtub caulk and paint the outside of the cleaned claw with good clear nail polish.

A string of ten claws mounted on a leather thong will easily bring $200.00. Should the poacher want to go that route, it is probably easier and safer to sell the necklace than it is the separate claws.

The best places to sell claws are at the mountain men's rendezvous that are becoming so popular, or to people who advertise for them in *The Trapper* magazine, *Shotgun News* or the *Buckskin Report*. One very large fur dealer will also buy them. There is a mountain man rendezous in July or August each year hear Friendship, Indiana, that is the largest of its kind. Many other smaller shows are held all over the U.S., or one can always go to a local gun show. Look in the previously mentioned magazines for leads on shows.

Necklace jewelry can be sold simply by wearing it, especially east of the Mississippi, or in large cities like L.A. or San Francisco. A year ago my daughter refused many offers when she wore her necklace on a visit to Chicago.

Bear skulls are saleable to taxidermists and at shows. They are worth about $20.00 to $50.00, depending on size. The canine teeth can be pulled and sold for $3.00 each if the skull is damaged.

Taxidermists like to get bear skulls frozen and complete. For shows it will be necessary to boil the meat off the bones in an old five gallon can. Varnish the skull lightly after it has dried.

A good long bear bacculum is saleable in taverns. Bartenders impress their guests by stirring drinks with them. These are worth what one can get, but don't take less than $10.00. Many have been sold for $50.00.

The last item on a bear is the most valuable and probably the easiest sold. If the reader hasn't heard of this before, he will be incredulous, but it is true: bear feet and bear gall bladders have much value.

Chinese people use them for aphrodisiacs.

The skinned feet, less claws, fresh or frozen, but clean, are worth about $5.00 each. The frozen gall bladder is worth no less than $30.00 to a dealer and much much more to the ultimate consumer.

In my experience, almost any Chinese running a Chinese restaurant will buy or knows someone who will buy bear feet and gall bladder. If nothing more, trade them for a meal or two for the family.

All else failing, advertise in the *Chinese Times* newspaper in San Francisco. The rates are cheap, and the paper goes to every corner of the U.S. and Canada.

The last bear part to sell is the skin. Most fur dealers will take them without claws for about $60.000 to $80.00. They are called patch bears and will bring about $100.00 from the ultimate consumer at shows. Another way to go is to sell the cape for $60.00 to $80.00 to a taxidermist and peddle the remainder as a patch bear at a show.

Squirrel Skins

Some readers may complain that they don't live near bears and that the previous information has no value. For these folks, I have some more useful information.

Squirrel tails are worth $.15 apiece to the people who make Mepps lures. Write Sheldon's, Inc., Antigo, Wisconsin 54409.

Remove the tail bone, and dry thoroughly. It doesn't make much difference if they receive ten or a thousand tails at once. They can handle it.

Deer

There are a number of parts of a deer that can be peddled. Over the years I have made the most money on their capes. Taxidermists go wild over a well caped deer head, even if the horns are mediocre. I usually ask $30.00 for the cape alone. If the critter had big horns, I hold out for $100.00 for the package. Don't get too excited about selling. See the taxidermist right after hunting season and let him know there is *one* for sale.

A deer scrotum, properly skinned and dried over a small block, is worth $5.00. Try the local taverns or the rendezvous.

Pick-up deer horns or any horns, for that matter, now sell for $3.00 per pound. Some fur buyers take them, so ask around. Fresh horns are saleable at shows and to fur dealers, or through the magazines. The price will vary from $10.00 to $50.00, depending on size. I always sell my good horns with a cape, or mount them on a board and wait for a dude to come along. Just don't display a big collection of deer horns all at once.

Chinese people eat deer feet for the same reason they eat bear feet, only the medicine isn't quite as powerful, they say. If you want to fool with them, four feet cut off at the knee and refrigerated are worth a chinese dinner.

Some taxidermists will also give a dollar or two for feet used to make gun racks.

The least valuable part of the deer is the skin. Dried and properly handled, it will bring about $4.00 from a dealer. People sometimes ask me for a deer skin which I agree to provide for the cost of tanning. As soon as possible after skinning the deer, I bundle their skins and ship them to Colorado Tanning in Denver, Colorado. When the skin gets back I charge $10.00 for all leather skins, and $25.00 for those with the hair still on. There isn't much profit after tanning charges, but there is little risk either.

Deer tails are, at times, purchased by the fly tying outfits. The price is usually about $.50 each. I sell mine to a local fur buyer for $.40 and avoid the hassle of sending them off.

Beaver Castors

These are the large glands found at the base of the tail on beaver. The price fluctuates wildly, but it probably averages about $15.00 a pound, dried. Fur dealers take them along with the beaver hides.

They smell so good around the house or in the barn I often keep them.

Raccoon And Possum

In the larger cities of some areas it is possible to build a market for the meat from these animals. They are worth about $3.00 apiece. Don't sell any that don't have the necessary credentials. It is illegal to sell the meat in many places anyway, so be sure there is a legal cover story regarding possession.

Try small variety shops, delicatessens, or ask in service stations.

Possums and coons are readily saleable in small rural communities, but the risk isn't worth the few dollars. A poacher will quickly get the reputation for being the guy with all that game.

Don't forget that raccoon bacculums are a popular item with some people. Pipe smokers use them to clean out pipe bowls. Some women wear them on a chain around their necks. Going rate is about $5.00, depending on the size and geographical area. Go to a rendezvous and sell before taking less.

251

Snapping Turtles

Snapping turtles are worth quite a lot of money dressed for human consumption and are not generally a problem to sell. Nobody seems to care about them in most places, much less the Fish and Game Commission.

I generally ask $2.50 per pound for good clean meat. Nice restaurants in big cities will pay even more.

The shell half is valuable, if it is large. Sell these at rendezvous. Price is dependent on the market at the time, but is no less than $8.00. American Indians use the shells to make portions of their regalia and often are good customers.

Elk Ivories

These are the two floating teeth that elk have. Most poachers won't have a chance to sell these but who knows? For the last few years I have lived near elk and have made a few bucks on them. Members of the Elks Lodge are the usual customers.

There aren't enough ivories in circulation to establish a market. I hold mine for a $20 bill or don't sell. It doesn't take much room to keep them, and they don't eat.

Fish

Trout are usually saleable, but I never do. The only fish I sell are carp which at times bring a fairly good price in larger cities.

Sometimes large quantities of legally netted carp can be sold to animal food processors. Inquire around. In some areas there is quite a business for someone who wants it.

Frogs

Some of the most valuable collectibles are giant American bullfrog legs. Most restaurants get their frog legs imported from India and are not interested in a domestic supply. However, we have through the years located a couple of really classy places that want the North American kind. We get $4.00 a pound for good large legs but only sell to one place once a year.

Usually we eat all the frog legs we get so there aren't many to sell.

Hides And Furs

With coyote skins worth from $40.00 to $90.00 I don't have to remind poachers that must furbearers are again valuable and worth taking. Even house cats have pretty good value.

Horns

Any horns are valuable. A good moose rack, for instance, can fetch $150.00 at a rendezvous or from a dude who wants them.

Deer horns are valuable to make buttons from, if nothing else. A big item at the shows. Rather than being left in the woods as we did for so many years, I suggest bringing them home for eventual sale.

Bird Skins

My eldest boy built a nice business for himself selling quail, pheasant, grouse and hungarian partridge skins.

Whenever he acquired a lightly shot or undamaged trapped bird, he would put it in a bag to bring it home unruffled. Carefully he would skin out the wings from the bottom and cut the bone off at the body. The bird itself was slit neatly down the belly from the beak to the tail and the skin taken off in one piece. He would pin the skin onto an old cardboard box and let it dry.

After it was dry he salted it lightly and then glued the entire skin and wings onto a piece of cardboard. The completed skin was very showy, and much easier to care for than a mounted bird.

He sold the skins as decorator pieces, at times in groups of two and three, for $4.00 each.

When he acquired a number of bird skins he would sell them to fly tyers, but the money wasn't as good. A pheasant brought about $3.50. Littler birds like huns and quail only brought $1.00, though.

Herbs And Plants

After years of languishing in the doldrums, this industry has suddenly come alive again. For twenty years ginseng, for instance, sold for $17.50 per pound. Now it is up around $150.00 and much more at times.

The two principal plants that are in demand are ginseng and Golden Seal. Both are found east of the Mississippi in hardwood forests. The range is from north of the border to the deep south.

Finding, curing and drying medicinal herbs is a field all of its own about which larger volumes can and have been written. I believe that a knowledge of wild herbs is important to the poacher to get him out in the country at a time when few people are there. In addition, the roots he collects can have significant value.

The following is a very broad brush approach to the subject. More information can be easily acquired by writing to the U.S. Government Printing Office in Washington, D.C. and asking for their publications on ginseng. The cost is less than a dollar. After this the sources of information become tenuous and uncertain. There is a book called *Ginseng and Other Medicinal Plants* published in 1936 by the A.R. Harding Co. of Columbus, Ohio. It may be possible to find an old copy of the book by writing the publisher or through a book finder.

Ginseng is a perennial plant that grows from six to twelve inches high. It has a woody, spindly stem with three large tip leaves and two small ones below. Its root looks something like a dandelion's, but is firmer and a darker yellow-brown color. Yellow flowers are produced in July and August that mature to bright red berries in late fall.

Ginseng is dug from the middle of August on. The roots are best after the plant is about five years old, so it is good economy to dig only the more mature plants. Larger roots dried over a screen make about twenty to the pound.

The root is generally found on gentle, well drained south slopes in old climax hardwood forests. Ginseng requires fairly dense shade consisting of a thick canopy of high trees and a sparse understory.

Golden Seal, the other major medicinal root, is found in about the same places as ginseng. It thrives on a little more sunlight and is usually found in open places in the woods, rather than in the shade.

Golden Seal is not as valuable as ginseng but is worth looking for. Prices for it in the $5.50 per pound range seem common.

The stem of Golden Seal is very slightly hairy and about twelve inches tall. There are several layers of yellowish scale at the base of the stem that look almost like fungus. The stem itself is light purple green. Golden Seal is very easy to distinguish by the forked stem at the top of the plant. One stem on the fork has a large crinkly green leaf shaped much like a maple. The other fork has a tiny leaf and a red berry that looks much like a raspberry.

The roots are bright yellow, generally with one big bulb and a number of stringy attachments. To me the fresh root smells terrible.

Like ginseng, Golden Seal is slowly dried in the open air on a screen or rock.

Readers who have no idea what these two herbs look like should find other information and good color pictures. The plants are not difficult to distinguish, but in places they are few. The root gatherers may get the feeling he is overlooking some plants if he isn't certain what he is looking for.

Selling roots is easy. There are literally thousands of buyers. Almost every fur dealer will take them. Other dealers who handle only herbs abound. Their ads are in every publication from *Popu-*

lar Mechanics to *Sports Afield*. And a unique plus for the poacher is that both sales and possession are completely legal.

Porcupine

This portion of the book is starting to sound like *Ripley's Believe It Or Not*, but it's true. Porcupine skins do have a significant value. At least one large dealer in the Pacific Northwest will buy all he can get his hands on (no pun intended).

The best way to realize the most money from a porky is to proceed as follows:

1. Reduce it to possession;
2. Cut the four feet off. Dried, these are worth $1.00;
3. Cut the porky from the tail to the chin and skin much the same as a beaver;
4. Before tacking the skin up to dry, carefully pull all the long guard hairs. Put these in orderly one inch bundles secured wtih a rubber band. This hair is worth $3.00 per ounce. An average porky will have one and a half ounces of guard hair;
5. Tack the skin on a board, flesh side out. When dried, the skin is worth $3.00.

Snake Skins

Rattlesnake and larger bull snake skins are worth $1.00 per foot. For some people in some places that statement is better than announcing where the gold is in them thar hills.

Cut the snake down the belly and lightly tack it to a board till dry. The rattles should be left on the skin in the case of rattlesnakes.

Almost any fur buyer will take snake skins or direct the seller to someone who does.

POSTLOGUE

It was interesting, traumatic and fun writing this book. Many of the incidents have never been told before this. For instance, it will be interesting for the old timers to learn how the dynamite really got on the river in central Illinois more than thirty-five years ago.

By now the reader is certainly aware that a few of the methods revealed in this book were sworn secrets. In some regards it was tough to bring myself to tell about these easy ways of making the harvest, but on the other hand, it was becoming more and more likely that I might not be around to pass them on. So it is a good thing that this permanent record was made, and that these methods won't pass into oblivion.

After pondering the entire philosophy of this country for too many years I have reluctantly concluded that the anti-hunters are going to win. Wardens and wildlife biologists will become guards over the vast federal and state land holdings, signaling the demise of hunting, fishing and trapping as we now know it.

Eventually it will be a game of wits dependent on safely getting into a good area, and not one of outsmarting the animals. Quick and easy poaching methods will be important, but nowhere near as important as entrance, evasion and exit techniques.

Undoubtedly many readers know some good methods of taking game that they would be willing to pass on. What is needed are more good techniques not listed in this book. Paladin Press has agreed to file any suggestions submitted by readers in anticipation of putting out a second volume on poaching. Send your suggestions to us as soon as possible. With your help, volume two is a real possibility.